Path of Souls

The Native American Death Journey: Cygnus, Orion, the Milky Way, Giant Skeletons in Mounds, & The Smithsonian

Gregory Little

Foreword & Afterword **by Andrew Collins**

Memphis, Tennessee

Path of Souls

The Native American Death Journey:
Cygnus, Orion, the Milky Way, Giant Skeletons in Mounds, & The Smithsonian

Published by ATA-Archetype Books
P. O. Box 9025
Memphis, TN 38190

ISBN 13: 978-0-9655392-5-8

About the Authors

Since 1979 Andrew Collins has been investigating the theory that an advanced civilization existed well before recorded history. In his bestselling book, *From the Ashes of Angels* (1996), Collins focused on an area in southeast Turkey where he theorized that this advanced civilization originated. In *The Cygnus Mystery* (2006) Collins was the first alternative historian to widely publicize the mysterious site of Göbekli Tepe in Turkey after he made an 2004 visit to the site. He found that many ancient megalithic structures, including the Giza pyramids, appeared to be focused on the constellation of Cygnus. A few years later he led a team to Giza where they discovered a long-forgotten cave system under the pyramid complex at Giza (*Beneath the Pyramids*, 2009). His most recent book (*Göbekli Tepe: Genesis of the Gods*, 2014) shows how hybrid humans appear to have been the origin of the development of civilization. Collins leads tours to various ancient sites and is frequently featured on documentaries.

Gregory Little began his career in neuropsychology and psychopharmacology with his first publication in 1972 appearing in the then-fledgling Society for Neuroscience's second publication. He has since published over a hundred research articles in scientific journals in psychology, addiction, and criminal justice. He has authored or coauthored over 50 books, workbooks, and textbooks. He has also published a series of books on Native American mounds and beliefs.

Note on Dating System Used

Modern archaeology journal articles typically employ a bewildering range of dating terminology that can be confusing to nonspecialized readers. These terms include BP (Before Present—1950), BCE (Before Common Era—before year 1), CE (Common Era—after year 1), and calibrated/uncalibrated radiocarbon dates. These terms are not used here as the book is primarily aimed at the general population.

In this book we chose to consistently utilize the more commonly used terminology of B.C. (Before Christ—prior to year 1) and A.D. (*anno Domini*—after year 1). All dates cited within the book are, to the best of our knowledge, based on calibrated (corrected) radiocarbon dates.

Table of Contents

Acknowledgments For Andrew Collins

I would first like to thank those who inspired my contributions to this work on a deep, intuitive level, these being Debbie Cartwright and Richard Ward. I want also to thank Greg Little, for inviting me to join him in this worthwhile literary project; Rodney Hale, for his illustration work; Catherine Hale, for her editorial suggestions, and Kim Prachniak, Stan Prachniak, Yvan Cartwright, Storm Constantine, and Paul Weston, for their help and support. It is very much appreciated.

Acknowledgments For Gregory Little

There are so many people who have contributed in one way or another to the contents of this work that it would be impossible for me to mention them all—even if I could remember all of the bits and pieces various people have contributed. For me, this work started in 1983 (but the project certainly isn't completed). Since that time I have had so many interactions with Native Americans, archaeologists, museum workers, and other interested parties that it's all a sort of blur. But thanks to all of you, it has been a very special path. As a part Native American (Seneca) my ventures into America's mound cultures have been one surprise after another. Many of us have some Native blood in us, and in some ways I think it is the best part of us. A very special thanks to my wife of nearly 35 years, Lora, for performing professional photography and spotting details that often escaped my attention. I also wish to express thanks to Brent and Joan Raynes for their continued participation and support of this long-enduring quest. I wish to express gratitude to Andrew Collins for his insights, contributions to the book, helping me to see a new path in this topic, and, most importantly, his friendship. Thanks also to Kim Prachniak who worked diligently in editing this project. Her expertise as a wordsmith is much appreciated. (As she well knows, her input was clearly needed.) Thanks also to Jim Vieira who was the person responsible for making me aware of the huge controversy involving giant skeletons. Jim was rather unfairly made the focal point of attacks from skeptics but he handled it extremely well—kudos. Finally, I wish to thank the artist Duncan Long who made the cover illustration as well as the black & white illustration depicting the three-part Native American cosmos.

FOREWORD

By Andrew Collins

Native American star myths deriving, most probably, from the rich cosmology and iconography of the Mississippian Southern Death Cult, known today as the *Southeastern Ceremonial Complex*, might well have an extremely ancient origin. What is more, they almost certainly gained their inception on another continent altogether. Indeed, there is now powerful evidence that the cosmological beliefs and practices of the native North American tribes are both universal in nature and Paleolithic in origin.

As we shall see within these pages, two asterisms in particular recur repeatedly in Native American star myths, each one playing a key role integral to the other. These are Cygnus, the celestial bird of the northern sky, envisaged on the North American continent as an eagle, falcon, turkey, or turkey vulture; and Orion, the great sky hunter of the ancient world. Among a large number

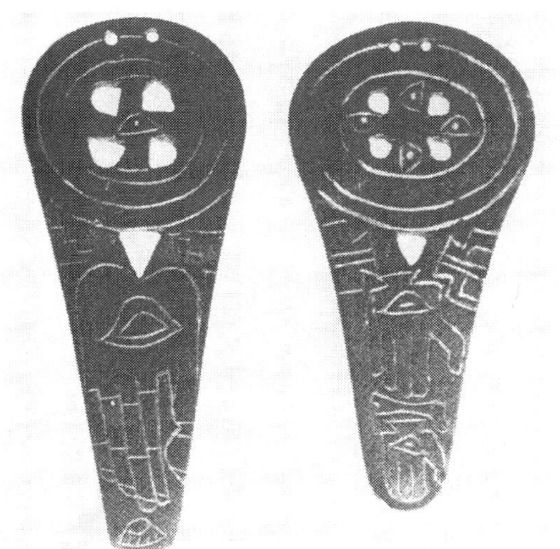

Two carved and polished stone pendants found at Moundville, Alabama. The longest one on the left is 4 inches in length. Both depict the "eye in hand" symbol, the Great Rift, and the ogee symbol inside concentric circles. From: Bureau of American Ethnology, *Bulletin 129* (1942).

of Native American tribes Orion was seen as a severed hand (the constellation's three belt stars symbolizing the severed wrist), hanging downward, with what looks like an eye symbol in its palm.

Through this eye, which is in fact an ogee (a split or opening in the fabric of physical reality), the soul of the deceased was able to gain access to the Milky Way after an initial journey that took it west to the edge of the earth's disk. Here it waited until a specific moment when the "Hand" was seen low in the western sky just before dawn. The soul then must make a leap of faith to a star portal symbolised by the ogee in the hand constellation, identified with the fuzzy nebula called Messier 42 (M42) located in the "sword" of Orion.

Once on the Milky Way, the soul uses it like a celestial highway to reach its place of destination in the afterlife. This *Path of Souls*, as it is known to many Native American tribes, swings south and then north until finally it

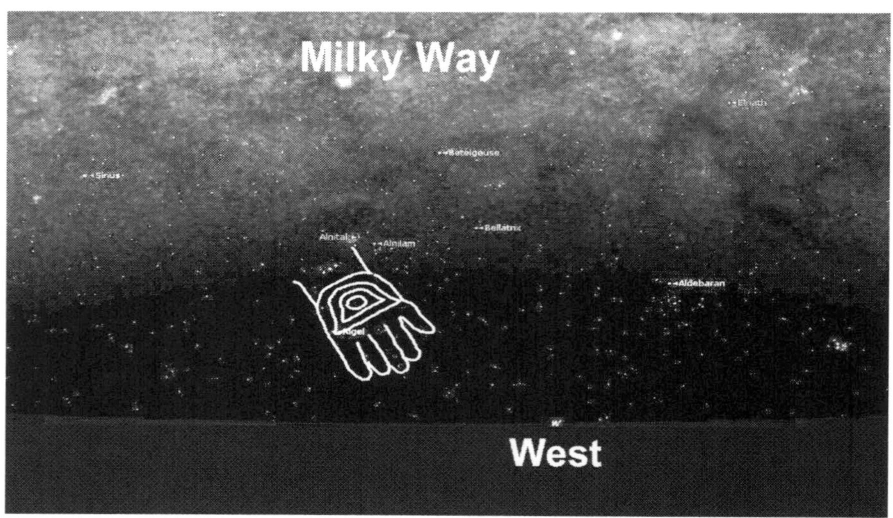

The "Hand Constellation" with the severed wrist formed by the three belt stars of Orion. During the winter months, the hand sank into the western horizon just before sunrise. Below the wrist is the "ogee"—the portal that leads to the Milky Way. Once a soul reaches the Milky Way, the trip on the Path of Souls began leading to Cygnus. The image above depicts 4:00 a.m. at Spiro, Oklahoma on December 1, A.D. 1200 and was generated from *Starry Night Pro*.

splits in two to form a fork, which astronomers call the *Great Rift* or the *Cygnus Rift*. This is where the starry stream divides into two separate branches, due to the presence of stellar dust and debris in line with the galactic plane. This noticeable division in the Milky Way begins in the vicinity of the stars of the Cygnus constellation, known also as the Northern Cross, and peters out roughly where the stars of Sagittarius and Scorpius mark one of the two places where the ecliptic (the sun's path) crosses the starry stream.

Judge of the Dead—Adversary

It is at this fork, or cleft, that the deceased in Native American star lore encounters Cygnus's bright star Deneb, personified most often as an anthropomorphic raptor bird that judges whether the soul is sinful or not (even though some Native American tribes have seen this sky being an

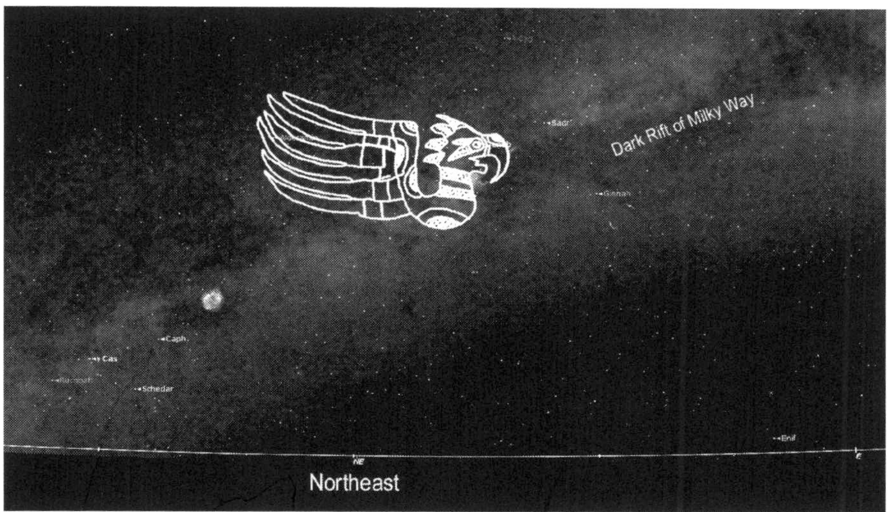

Cygnus as the Judge of the Dead depicted as a raptor bird. Once a soul begins the journey on the Path of Souls, it eventually makes its way to the Great Rift where it encounters the star Deneb, the brightest star of Cygnus. The raptor was seen as an adversary or judge who tested the soul. At dusk in the winter months, Cygnus was seen in the northwest. The image above depicts 8:00 p.m. at Spiro, Oklahoma on December 2, A.D. 1200 and was generated from *Starry Night Pro*.

adversary that tries to rob the person of consciousness). If the travelling soul is deemed sinless, it is allowed to continue its journey across a log bridge that leads to the afterlife. Here it rejoins its ancestral family and encounters the various power animals and celestial beings considered to inhabit the sky world. If the soul is deemed sinful, then it must take another route: one that leads to complete annihilation or sometimes reincarnation. These two separate paths are, quite obviously, represented by the twin streams of the Milky Way's Great Rift. The longer one, which appears to bridge the gap between the northern and southern halves of the starry stream, becomes the path to the afterlife, while the shorter one, which peters out before its reaches the stars of Scorpius, identified in Native American star lore as an underworld creature known as the Feathered Serpent or Water Panther, becomes the road to hell and oblivion.

Deneb's role as judge of the dead can also be found in the archaic sky religion of ancient Egypt (Wainwright, 1932). Under the name *Dwn-'nwy* ("he who unfolds two wings"), the star is shown on the walls of various tombs as an anthropomorphic raptor bird, a falcon or hawk, standing among

The weighing of the heart depicted on the Papyrus of Hunefer (1275 B.C.). If the sins of the heart weighed more than that of a feather, the sinner was cast into the celestial dragon's jaws. Image: *National Geographic*, Wikipedia Commons release.

a group of supernatural beings which are personifications of the stars and constellations that revolve each night around the celestial pole, the turning point of the heavens. *Dwn-'nwy* (pronounced *dun-na-wey*) is shown facing a hippo-crocodile hybrid (a personification seemingly of Draco, the constellation of the celestial dragon), into whose jaws the souls of sinners are cast if their sin is found to weigh more than that of a pure white feather, which symbolizes the concept of *maat,* cosmic "truth" or "justice."

Orion and Cygnus in Baltic Cosmology

So in both Native American myth and in the sky religion of ancient Egypt, Cygnus is personified as an anthropomorphic raptor presiding over the fate of the dead. It is a role the constellation also plays in the Baltic region of northern Europe. In Lithuania, for instance, the principal stars of Cygnus (along with key stars in neighbouring Lyra and Aquila) become

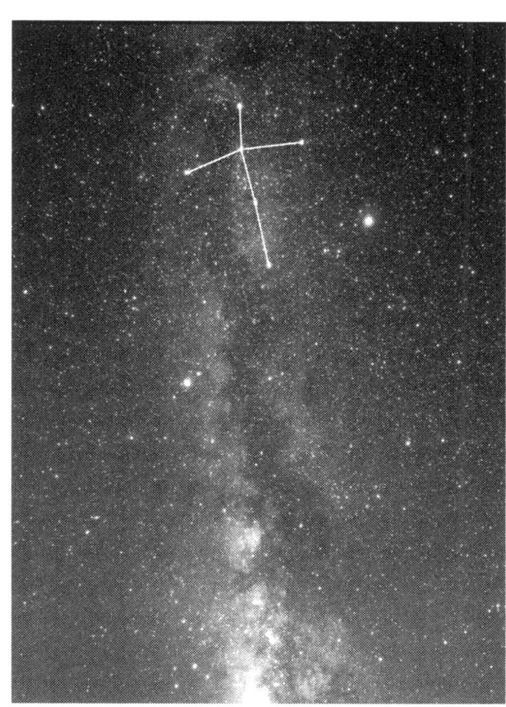

The Constellation of Cygnus shown at its location at the Great Rift forming the split of the Milky Way. Deneb, the brightest star in the cross-shaped formation, is at the top of the cross. Note that the constellation includes other stars. Image: NASA (connecting lines added).

Dangaus Svarstykles, the Heavenly Scales (Straizys & Klimka, 1997), presiding over the fate of the dead. The Milky Way is known in Lithuania variously as *Paukééiq takas,* the Way of Birds (or the Way of Geese or Cranes), and *Veliu Kelias,* the Road of Souls (or Ghost Road), echoing the Path of Souls of Native American star lore.

Also as in Native American myth, in Lithuania the soul of the deceased takes the form of a bird (usually a swan, goose, or crane) in order to gain access to the Milky Way (the Road of Souls), which leads eventually to a fork in the path (clearly the Great Rift), its whereabouts highlighted by the presence of the Cygnus star Deneb (Dunduliene, 1988: 60-61). If the soul is deemed free of sin, it takes one branch of the Milky Way, which leads to the afterlife. Yet if the soul is deemed sinful, it takes the other shorter branch of the Great Rift and falls into oblivion, exactly what was thought to happen in the star mythology of the Native American peoples.

Yet the comparisons between the sky-based funerary myths of the Baltic region and those of Native America do not end there, for in times of war, the relatives of Lithuanian soldiers fallen in battle were consoled with stories which told of the souls of the departed seen riding on a spectral horse in the middle of the heavens, upon the Road of Souls, i.e., the Milky Way. From here they departed toward eternal happiness with three stars in their hand (Dunduliene, 1988: 61), a reference most certainly to the belt stars of Orion. In Greek mythology the god Hephaestus gave Orion a horse (Fontenrose, 1991: 26-27). While in ancient British folklore Gwyn ap Nydd, the Celtic lord of the underworld, was personified in the night sky as the constellation of Orion (Leitch, 2007), leading the Wild Hunt on his horse *Du March Moro,* "Black the Steed of Moro" (Rhys, 1901, II: 438).

So in Lithuania, just as they are in North America, the belt stars of Orion are associated directly with the symbol of a hand. In this instance it is that of the departed souls of fallen soldiers who have reached the middle of the sky and are now on their way to the fork in the Milky Way, where they will encounter the path to heaven itself.

Orion and Cygnus in the Pyramid Age

Returning now to the sky religion of ancient Egypt, we find even further links with the cosmic geography of the Southeastern Ceremonial Complex and the star lore of the Native American peoples. In death, the soul of the pharaoh was transformed into the god Osiris—lord of death, resurrection, and the underworld. According to the archaic body of funerary literature known as the Pyramid Texts, inscribed on the walls of Old Kingdom pyramids ca. 2450-2300 B.C., the deceased ascends to the belt of Orion. This acts as a star portal enabling the soul access to the Milky Way, known in ancient Egypt as the Great or Winding Waterway. From here the deceased is transported on a night barque to the realm of the Imperishable Ones, the stars of the northern night sky that revolve perpetually around the celestial pole, the turning point of the heavens. Here the soul of the pharaoh ascends to the womb of his mother Nut and rejoices as an *akh,* a glorious spirit, shining as a star himself.

This return to the starry realms of the sky goddess is very significant, for the sarcophagus, coffin, tomb, and pyramid are all expressions both of the womb of Nut, which lies within the Great Waterway, and of the primeval mound of first creation. This emerged from the *Nun,* the waters of chaos, at the beginning of time in a manner likened by the pharaonic Egyptians to the way small mud islands would appear in the Nile floodplain after the waters of the annual inundation receded each year. The primeval mound was the place of emergence of the god of creation, called Atum or Re, the name of the principal sun-god of ancient Egypt.

The Cosmic Womb

The pharaoh was seen as an incarnation of the sun-god Re, who, like Osiris, was born of the womb of Nut. Ancient Egyptian funerary art shows the solar orb as the red disk of sunset being swallowed by the goddess Nut.

It is then replicated at various points on her starry body to indicate that the sun passes through her interior during the hours of darkness before being reborn each morning on the eastern horizon, a process reflected in the expression of the trials and tribulations which the soul undergoes in order to enter the afterlife.

Above: Image from the Greenfield Papyrus (950 B.C.) showing Nut stretched over the sky. Geb is shown reclining and Nut is supported by Shu. Image: British Museum, Wikipedia Commons release.

The arch formed by the Milky Way can be seen as Nut. The Milky Way was the "Winding Waterway" to the ancient Egyptians, the path that led to the "Imperishable Ones"—the stars of the north. Image: Bruno Gilli, Wikipedia Commons release.

American astronomer Ronald A. Wells interpreted this imagery, and the funerary literature behind it, as the sun symbolically "entering" the Milky Way in its form as the goddess Nut, who is generally shown naked, with her star-laden body arching over the earth-god Geb (Wells, 1993 & 1994). This occurs in astronomical terms where the ecliptic (the sun's path) crosses the Milky Way in the vicinity of the stars of Gemini and Orion. Thereafter the sun would be seen, symbolically at least, to navigate the Milky Way in its role as a waterway until it reached the Cygnus region. Here the sun god was given life before emerging from between the goddess' thighs and symbolically sliding down between her "legs," represented by the twin streams of the Great Rift. Thereafter it would be reborn as the new sun on the horizon at a point corresponding to where the ecliptic (the sun's path) crosses the Milky Way in the vicinity of the stars of Sagittarius and Scorpius. Clearly, such an event made no sense in astronomical terms, but as Wells proposes (1993 & 1994), it was meant to be seen as a cosmological expression of the rebirth of the sun based on observations of the solar disk's relationship to the Milky Way across a very long time period indeed.

So in the ancient Egyptian mindset, the Cygnus constellation was synonymous not only with the place of judgment of the soul on its journey into the afterlife, but also with the cosmic womb of Nut—represented in physical terms by the sarcophagus, coffin, tomb, and of course, the pyramid, which is itself a powerful symbol of the primeval mound.

Universal Beliefs

However symbolic and naive these ideas might seem to us today, they enabled ancient cultures to create a vivid cosmic geography relating to the passage of the soul in death and to the source of creation itself. In one form or another, they are found in the cosmology of the pre-Incan peoples of Peru (Urton, 1981; Sullivan, 1997), the Maya of Central America (Jenkins, 1998), the Vedic civilizations of the Indian sub-continent (Collins, 2006: 182-92), and also, seemingly, in the astronomical alignments of megalithic

observatories at places like Newgrange in Ireland's Boyne Valley (Murphy, 2008), Avebury in southern England (Thom, 1967; Thom, Thom, & Foord, 1976) and Callanish in northern Scotland (Collins, 2006: 121-6).

The Milky Way would also appear to have played a major role in the cosmology behind the construction of Göbekli Tepe, the 12,000-year-old megalithic complex built on a mountain ridge in southeast Turkey. Here the oldest and most sophisticated temple structures being uncovered today are aligned very specifically to the northern opening of the Great Rift, marked in this case by the setting of the Cygnus star Deneb (Collins, 2014: 77-86).

The Great Circle Alignment

The relationship between the sun, Milky Way, and the stars of Cygnus can also be seen in the construction and orientation of key mound complexes belonging to the Adena culture, who flourished between 1000 and 200 B.C., and at Hopewell culture sites, which rose to prominence around 2,200 years ago in places like Ohio and West Virginia. Almost certainly these ancient

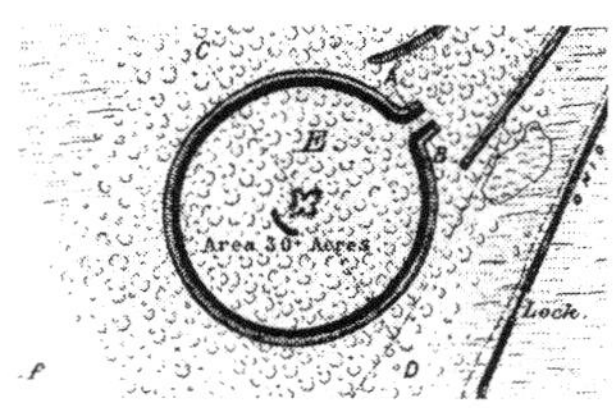

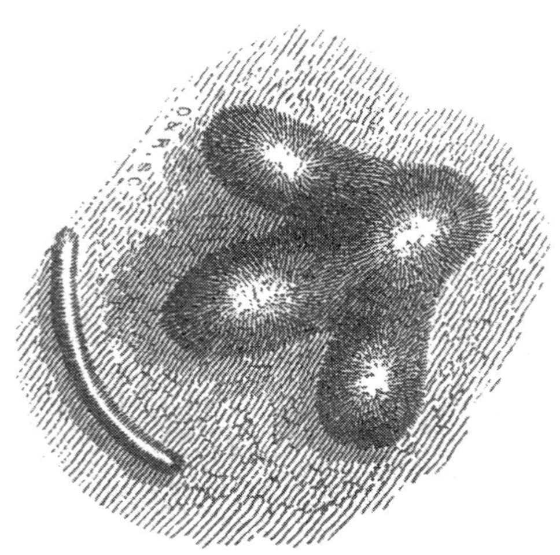

Left: Eagle Mound as depicted by Squier & Davis (1848). The mound is in the center of Newark, Ohio's Great Circle, an earthen wall with an inner moat that encloses 30 acres. Eagle Mound is oriented toward the only opening into the enclosure. Above: The Great Circle in Squier & Davis's larger survey of Newark's extensive geometric earthworks.

mound builders were the ancestors of those behind the Southeastern Ceremonial Complex, which thrived during the Mississippian period, ca. A.D. 800 to A.D. 1500.

At Great Circle in Newark, Ohio, for instance, a bird effigy mound at the center of an enormous circular plateau, nearly 1,200 feet (366 meters) in diameter, is directed east-northeast toward the earthen structure's only entrance. A person standing on the mound, known locally as Eagle Mound, in the hours of darkness immediately before the summer solstice around 2,000 years ago would have witnessed a spectacular sight. Rising vertically into the sky, framed perfectly within the entrance to Great Circle, would have been the Milky Way, looking as if it formed a natural extension of an imagined path that started at the bird mound.

Following the course of the Milky Way would have taken the eye to where the starry stream splits in two at the start of the Great Rift, almost as if the whole visual spectacle symbolized a cosmic tree, or a forked sky-pole, linking Earth to heaven. And between the "branches" or fork would have been the stars of Cygnus, the celestial bird, located almost directly above its terrestrial counterpart on the ground. Shortly afterward, as the first rays of dawn consumed the glittering light of the stars, the midsummer sun would have appeared exactly where the Milky Way (the Path of Souls) had risen into the sky just a few hours earlier.

When it was excavated, Great Circle's Eagle Mound was found to contain a number of human cremation burials. As the bones had been deposited in a disarticulated manner, their interment might well have followed what is known as a sky burial—where vultures and other carrion birds are encouraged to strip a human carcass of its flesh in a process known as excarnation. This tells us that the site's ground-sky synchronization is not without meaning. Clearly, Great Circle with its bird effigy mound acted like the sarcophagus, coffin, tomb, and pyramid in ancient Egypt, as a means of enabling the rebirth of the soul in the next world. What is more, the final destination was always

the same—a sky world perceived as existing somewhere beyond the stars of the Cygnus constellation.

Universal Beliefs

How can the same beliefs exist on two separate landmasses, separated since the submergence of the Beringia land bridge some 10,500 years ago by a narrow section of ocean known as the Bering Sea? It would be easy to

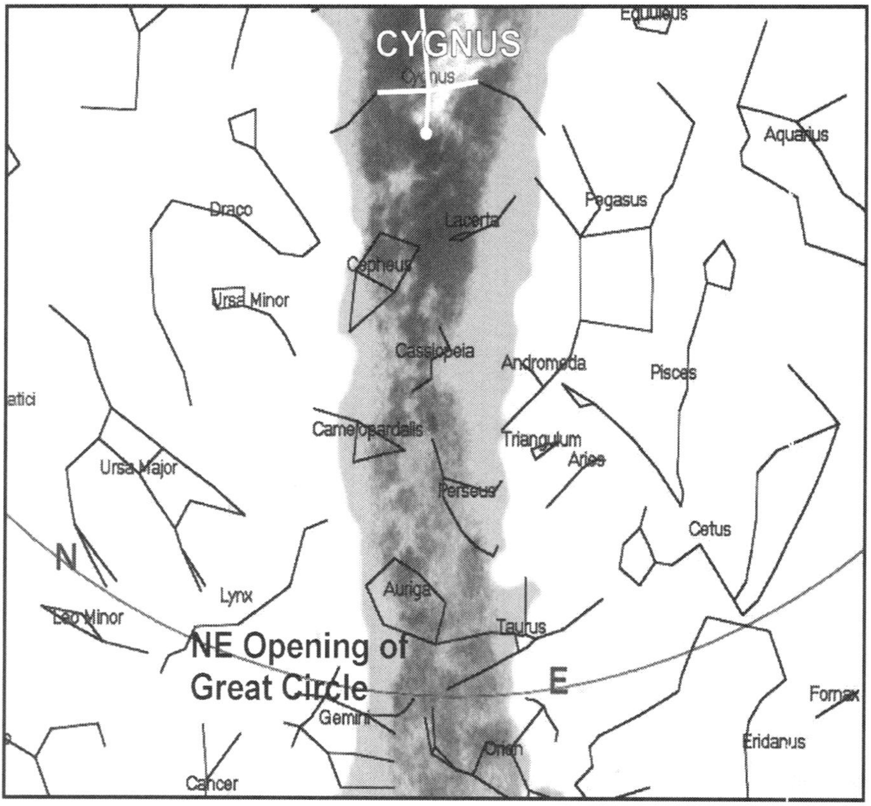

The Milky Way rising vertically from the only opening of Great Circle (as viewed from Eagle Mound) on June 21, 100 B.C. about two hours before sunrise. Cygnus would have been directly above Eagle Mound. As discussed in the text, many geometric earthworks of the Hopewell are known to have been used in rituals designed to assist dead souls in making their journey to the sky. Source: Rodney Hale/*Stellarium.*

conclude that the First Peoples of the Americas and the inhabitants of Africa and the Eurasian continent independently came to see the stars of Cygnus and the Milky Way's Great Rift as the entrance to the sky world, with Orion as a primary place of access onto the starry stream. However, there is one other possibility, one explored within the pages of this book; this being that these archaic beliefs *pre-existed* the submergence of the Beringia land bridge, and were carried from Asia to the Americas prior to its disappearance around 8500 BC.

This does indeed seem to have been the case, and what is more, there is compelling evidence to suggest that these stellar-based beliefs and practices were preserved across countless generations on the American continent by select human groups that went on to become the ruling elites of the Paleo-Indian populations, and much later those of the Adena and Hopewell cultures. More crucially, as Greg Little will make clear later in this book, these ruling elites often included individuals of exceptional height, some of them reaching in excess of seven and a half feet (2.3 meters).

The Land of Giants

Stories of the discovery of bones and/or skeletons of "giants" are something that has captured the American imagination for the past two hundred years and still dominate the ancient mysteries subject today. Many such claims, which originally appeared in otherwise reputable newspapers, such as the *New York Times* and *Washington Post,* can very often be put down to either genuine misinterpretations of the facts or else deliberate deceit on the part of those involved. Yet as this present volume ably demonstrates, there exist accounts of the discovery of giant skeletons that cannot be so easily dismissed. Found within academic journals and other scholarly works, they confirm not only that extremely tall individuals did once exist on the North American continent, but also that they might have been responsible for the spread of the earliest mound-building cultures, along with their stellar-based beliefs and practices, which went on to become the basis for the

ritualized cosmology and iconography of the Southeastern Ceremonial Complex of the Mississippian period.

In other words, the star lore held sacred today by so many Native American tribes might well have originated thousands of miles away on the Eurasian continent, having had its inception in places like the fertile steppes of Kazakhstan, the mountain valleys of Siberia, and the great basins of major inland seas such as Lake Balkhash and Lake Baikal. Here genetic evidence of the earliest ancestors of the First Peoples of the American continent is emerging today for the very first time. More importantly, we find that these Paleolithic ancestors of the Native American peoples, who almost certainly included human hybrids of exceptional height, the so-called giants of myth and legend, would appear to have possessed a profound understanding of the cosmos associated with the Milky Way and Cygnus stars in particular. How exactly they gained this cosmological knowledge, and where it might have come from, is a matter returned to (by the present writer) in the Afterword to this ground-breaking book, which is set to question everything we thought we knew about the origins and beliefs of America's earliest inhabitants.

Chapter 1

America's Ancient Mounds: Giant Skeletons, The Smithsonian, & The Southern Death Cult

I vividly recall when my interest in America's "Indian" mounds started. It was in early 1983 and what I knew about mounds back then could have been written on a postage stamp. I took a couple of anthropology classes in undergraduate years, but there was nothing in the classes about mounds or ancient America's history. When I started visiting the mounds and earthworks scattered everywhere across the eastern half of America, what I found was a continual surprise. It remains a shame that the American educational system all but ignores this important part of history.

In 1983 I was in the middle of a drawn-out process waiting for my first book to be released. I then worked in a prison-based mental health unit and had routinely been publishing research articles in psychology and criminal justice journals beginning in 1972. Suddenly, seemingly out of nowhere, I started experiencing a colorful, recurring dream. For about 10 straight nights I had the same dream. In the dream I was standing on an "Indian" mound and photographing it. Then I was on another mound, and another one, and so on. This went on until I felt compelled to visit my first mound site—Chucalissa in Memphis. At that time many museum sites displayed actual skeletal remains, and at Chucalissa, an excavated and exposed burial mound was enclosed in a large building. In the building, visitors could walk paths running through the many burials and see about a hundred skeletons with

Above: Dickson Mounds in Illinois was one of many mound sites that used to display excavated skeletons *in situ*. From: Throop (1928).

Above: Display of skeletons *in situ* at Wickliffe, Kentucky mounds a they used to be shown to visitors. Photo: Greg Little (1986).

the artifacts found with each one—*in situ*. It was eerie and was a place where Memphis area schools took students to gawk at the exposed skeletal remains. Walking "inside" a burial mound and seeing real skeletons leaves a deep impression on people. But it also ignores the feelings of the descendants of the dead who are on "display." My wife Lora and I eventually visited about 20 museums that displayed excavated Native American burials in that manner. You won't find any such displays in America now, with the exception of a few "private" museums. Private museums are ones that accept no government funds at all.

By 1994 I had visited all the major sites in America and most of the smaller ones—around 1000 mounds—and had amassed a couple thousand photos. By 2014 I had seen virtually all of the larger mound complexes more than once and visited countless smaller sites. I also had spent enormous amounts of time in university libraries reading archaeology textbooks and journals and carefully perusing all of the old books I could find on the topic. The more I read and the more mound sites I visited, the more entangled I became in the depths of the mystery. It was like getting trapped in a spider web—and the spider is a key symbol in Native American mythology. So I called my first book on mounds *People of the Web* (Little, 1990). My second book on mounds was entitled *Grand Illusions* (Little, 1994). Both books covered other "mystery" topics that various writers had linked to mounds including UFOs, rituals, and apparitional phenomena. To me it was a topic related to my professional interests, but I have never pretended to be an archaeologist—neither professional nor amateur. Over the years I faced no ridicule whatsoever from my professional peers. In fact, other psychologists, psychiatrists, and a vast array of government officials often expressed support and even admiration. The only genuine ridicule I have received came from a few archaeologists and a couple geologists.

My attempt to visit as many mounds as possible and gather background information on them was an overwhelming task for a couple reasons. There are probably 100,000 mounds and earthworks in existence. Over half of the mounds that survived are small burial mounds in remote, private locations.

Another reason is that there are tens of thousands of articles, field reports, site surveys, surface collection reports, theses, dissertations, and texts on the topic. A lot of these reports contain a wealth of information but are hidden away on dusty shelves. Most of them will never see the light of day again because the internet has become the primary "research" tool for most people. Not too long ago a *History Channel* producer told us, "As far as we are concerned, if you're not on the internet, you don't exist." A related statement might be "if it is on the internet, it does exist." That statement relates to a Native American mound topic that has become a huge issue—giant skeletons.

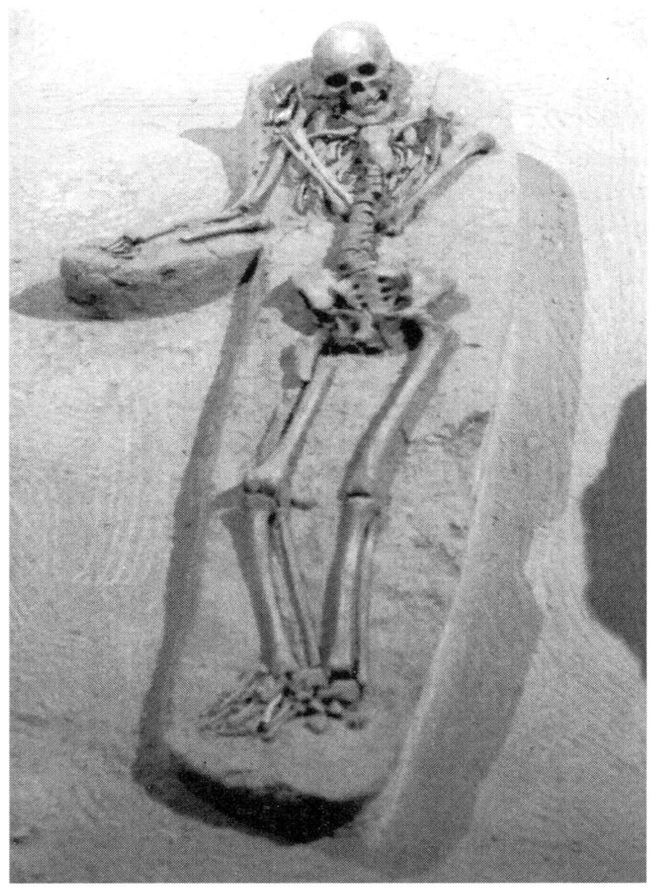

In situ skeleton displayed at Moundville, Alabama *circa* 1986. Photo: Greg Little.

Giants in the Mounds

Until about a decade ago, the fact that quite a few very large skeletons were excavated from Native American mounds in the 1800s and early 1900s was not widely known. At the time the "giant" skeletons were found, they did make headlines, but from around the 1940s, other than an occasional mention in obscure articles and books the issue faded away. Sometime in the 2000s, the topic suddenly reemerged. By 2014 over 1,000 old newspaper articles on excavations of the giant skeletons had been posted on internet sites and about a dozen books on the topic had come out. Most of the books reprinted the newspaper articles and occasionally tried to find the original source. Some of the authors were actually quite thoughtful and reasoned. Others assumed that with so many newspaper articles reporting "giants," that it had to be true—and their speculations about the "giants" ran wild. In essence, a few writers argued that ancient America had been ruled by a race of giants who were probably descendents of the Nephilim. Another assertion was that the Smithsonian Institution was—and still is—actively involved in a cover-up about the giant rulers of the ancient world. It was part of a murky conspiracy. Many authors asked, "Where are the skeletons?" and "Why can't they be displayed?"

The answers to those two questions are simple but require a bit of explanation. First, many of the "giant" skeletons supposedly disintegrated or crumbled a few minutes after they were exposed as explained in the archaeological reports and newspaper accounts. In some other cases, the skeletons were not the focus of the digs. For example, in their 1800's mound survey, the Smithsonian specifically asked its excavators for skulls and artifacts that could be displayed. Many other mound excavators of that era, such as the exceedingly prolific C. B. Moore, were not primarily interested in skeletal remains. Moore will be discussed later; his personal obliteration of a couple thousand mounds was essentially a quest for artifacts. However, he did mention the giant skeleton reports and investigated some of them.

The skeletons, including those of the so-called "giants," that were excavated and shipped to the vast majority of government-supported institutions *other than the Smithsonian* were returned to recognized Native American tribes and reburied after the Federal NAGPRA law (Native American Graves Protection and Repatriation Act) was passed in 1990. Oddly, few people know that NAGPRA *did not apply* to the Smithsonian. A different law applying to the Smithsonian's cultural remains was passed in 1989 and was amended in 1996. It is called the "National Museum of the American Indian Act." Since the 1989 law was passed, the Smithsonian has actively been sending skeletal remains to tribes that submit valid claims. Once the tribes received the remains, they subsequently reburied them. This process of repatriation/reburial is essentially completed. The Smithsonian's National Museum of the American Indian (NMAI) website on repatriation relates, "The Repatriation Office places a high priority on determining the cultural origins and affiliations of the human remains in its possession and on returning them to their descendants and places of origin. At present, the NMAI retains fewer than 300 catalogued human remains, the majority of which originate from Latin America." It is explained that all of the 300 human remains and burial objects are stored at a "separate" facility until they get reburied. Access to them is highly restricted. Only specific staff members and recognized officials from Native American tribes can view them [http://nmai.si.edu/explore/collections/repatriation/].

If any Native American giant skeletal remains do exist in Smithsonian warehouses (which is not at all likely), they won't be displayed and will never be scientifically examined. But this, of course, isn't the entire story. In fact, the real story of the Smithsonian's involvement in the 1800's excavations is far more interesting than commonly known. And a lot of large human skeletons were found by the Smithsonian, much to the dismay of modern archaeologists and skeptics.

My interest in this issue stems from the long personal involvement I have had with mounds. In 2008 I completed a 25-year-long project leading to the publication of a book describing the major mound and earthwork sites in America entitled *The Illustrated Encyclopedia of Native American Mounds & Earthworks* (Little, 2009). As a result, I am frequently asked questions about mounds. One consistent question is about the "giant" skeletons. Another question people often ask is about the meaning of certain symbols and Native American beliefs about death.

Many of the artifacts that were dug out of mounds over the past 250 or so years are incredibly intricate and carefully shaped. The artifacts often have the same stylized, enigmatic symbols etched, painted, or engraved on them. These symbols have turned up at mound sites located over vast distances, so whatever the messages are that the symbols are conveying, it is certain that the beliefs associated with them were widespread. There were marble statues, massive stone effigy pipes, copper artifacts of all sizes and shapes, and countless types and styles of pottery found in mounds. But most intriguing to me were the symbols of what was once called the *Southern Death Cult*.

The Southern Death Cult, Southern Cult, Southeastern Ceremonial Complex, and Mississippian Ideological Interaction Sphere: Changing Terminology Referring to a Shared Belief System

Most of the artifacts depicting curious death-related imagery were excavated from mound sites that were constructed during the Mississippian era. The timeframe when the Mississippian sites were constructed is roughly from A.D. 800 to 1500. But it is accepted that the imagery made its way through the earlier Hopewell Period, which extended back to approximately 500 B.C. or earlier. No one knows the origin of the beliefs attached to the symbols, but that is a relevant question.

The death symbols found on artifacts at these Mississippian sites included a severed hand with what appears to be an eye in the palm, skulls showing "fire" coming out of the mouths, a cross or plus sign in a circle, a feathered serpent, raptor birds, a forked eye, birdmen, and bones. The artifacts with

the symbolic images were initially excavated from mounds, but they have also been found on numerous pottery vessels dug up from village sites associated with mounds located in the South. To archaeologists, these images immediately seemed to be symbols of death (after all, they *were* found with burials). Thus archaeologists termed the cultures that made the symbols the *Southern Death Cult*, later shortening it to the *Southern Cult*, and because of the connotations associated with the term "cult," they started using the term *Southeastern Ceremonial Complex*. Recently archaeologists have suggested

Above: Drawing of the images on the Willoughby Disk found at Moundville in the late 1800s. From: Moore (1905).

Below: Drawing from Moore (1905) depicting lifeless skulls and the "eye in hand" images found on pottery at Moundville, Alabama.

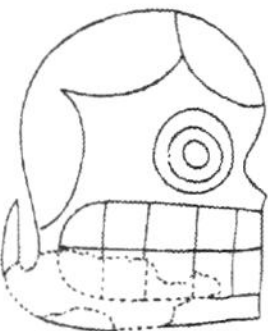

changing the accepted name of this "culture" to the *Mississippian Ideological Interaction Sphere* (Reilly & Garber, 2007). There is consensus among archaeologists that the symbols evolved over a vast time period and had regional variations. Yet, no matter what the region or the variation, they retained the same essential meaning. "The symbols describe the location of the 'realm of the dead' and the journey of dead souls to that otherworldly location" (Reilly & Garber, 2007: 5).

Like almost everyone who has seen them, when I first saw the symbols associated with the Southern Death Cult, I was intrigued by the possible meanings. I surmised that we would probably never know exactly what these symbolic images really meant. I never would have guessed what the meanings of the symbols actually are. Even more surprising to me is that an ongoing controversy about pyramids in Egypt may well be solved by the Native American symbols.

Cygnus *versus* Orion in Egypt

In 2004 England's Andrew Collins visited America and we escorted him to numerous mound sites. Andrew noticed that some Ohio mounds and geometric earthworks aligned with the Constellation of Cygnus and suggested that the complexes were used in death rituals. By that time Andrew had also discovered that the three pyramids of Giza were perfectly aligned to Cygnus—essentially mimicking the three central stars of the cross-shaped constellation. However, almost everyone—except the most prominent Egyptologists—had already accepted the idea that the pyramids were built to mimic Orion's Belt.

Andrew's book, *The Cygnus Mystery* (Collins, 2006), ignited a massive controversy that rages on today. Were the pyramids built to mimic Cygnus or Orion? Andrew has continued to research how ancient sites targeted Cygnus, but we also know that the Constellation of Orion was very important to the ancients. What did Orion and Cygnus really mean to the ancients?

Now, oddly, emerging in America is the most likely answer. We probably now know the truth about what the ancients believed. It is a stunning revelation, and the solution surprisingly comes from mainstream American archaeology. Excavations at American mounds recovering pots, copper sheets, incised tablets, and shell carvings made by ancient Native American artisans have perhaps answered one of the greatest mysteries of all time. The background stories of the symbols on these artifacts and their meanings revolve around the 1800's quest to discover the origin of the mound builders. The 1800's quest also looked for "giants," but ultimately, it was undertaken to discover the true origin of what these ancient people believed and from where they came. The "giant" skeletons excavated from America's mounds in the 1800s may help answer these questions.

We begin by describing what archaeologists currently accept as "facts" about America's mound-building cultures and eras, the timeframes involved, why Native Americans all but forgot about their mound-building ancestors, and the excavations that took place.

Chapter 2

Overview of Ancient America's Mound Builders

The term *Mound Builder* is not meant to imply anything other than what should be obvious. Mound Builders are people who build mounds. Mounds are found in nearly every country in the world. People often ask me what is America's first or oldest mound? The "oldest" mound site in America changes from time to time. New discoveries are frequently made. In addition, archaeologists have changed their terminology several times. At one time, terms such as *Mound Builder I* and *Mound Builder II* were commonly used. The term *Woodland Period* is a sort of all-embracing description that covers the time from 1200 B.C. to A.D. 1000 and it refers to pottery-making people in the southeast. But it also embraces the mound-building cultures of that timeframe (Anderson & Mainfort, 2002). To make it a bit more confusing, the Woodland Period is subdivided into different timeframes.

While the focus of this book is on American mounds, it clear that mounds were built in South America well before they appeared in North America. In fact, if you visit South and Central American museums, you will see map displays that show the first people coming to the Americas from the Pacific and arriving at least 30,000 years ago—in South America. Of course, mainstream United States' archaeologists scoff at the idea and claim, "*We were first*." Archaeologists south of the border consider this cultural professional bias or outright racism (Dillehay, 2000; Little, Van Auken, & Little, 2002). The current mainstream archaeology belief about the first migrations to America is that Siberian hunter-gatherers arrived around 25,000

years ago (Reich, et al., 2012). But the oldest mounds in the Americas are in South America.

At the site where the Tapajos River flows into the Amazon in Brazil is a massive shell mound dated to at least 8000 B.C. In 2013 a team of international archaeologists reported on several shell mounds located in the Amazon wetlands of Bolivia. These were dated to 8400 B.C. (*Popular Archaeology*, 2013). However, it is also clear that many shell mounds in that region have not been dated. More mounds will be found there, and it is likely that older shell mounds will eventually be found along the shallow coastal waters of both North and South America. For our purposes, the American mound-building cultures will be briefly summarized using more traditional and common terms.

Mound Building in America

If you read journal articles and archaeology textbooks on America's mounds, it is easy to become confused. Many mound-building cultures are named by the types of pottery they produced. Archaeologists have come up with over 2,000 different terms for pottery, and they will often use the pottery term for the mound site where that type of pottery was recovered. Pottery was first made in America starting roughly around 3000 B.C.

In addition, you will find some large differences in the timeframes various archaeologists cite for different mound cultures and specific sites. It all depends on what you read and when it was written. For example, if you look up "Poverty Point" on the internet, you will find the National Park Service citing that Poverty Point reached its *pinnacle* in 2000 B.C.; however, the online encyclopedia Wikipedia (which anyone can edit) gives a date of 1600 B.C., and the Louisiana Office of State Parks relates that it was constructed between 1700 B.C. and 1100 B.C. If you visit the site and ask the site staff when it was built, you will probably be told that some earthwork or mound construction started there well before 2500 B.C. As will be described later, the same "dating" problem is seen at *Serpent Mound* in Ohio.

Finally, it is important to understand that the different cultures which erected distinctive mounds and earthworks often overlapped each other by hundreds and even thousands of years. Thus, there is no definitive point when one culture vanished and another took its place.

The Table below presents a basic temporal outline of the mound cultures in America using the most commonly utilized terms followed by a brief description of the culture's characteristics. A thorough description of major mound sites is well beyond the scope of this book and those interested are referred to *The Illustrated Encyclopedia of Native American Mounds & Earthworks* (Little, 2009), which was the primary source for the descriptions that follow.

Mound Culture	Dates	Regional Area
Archaic	4000 B.C. — 1000 B.C.	Southeast & coastal states
Poverty Point	2500 B.C. — 1000 B.C.	Louisiana, Mississippi
Adena	1000 B.C. — 200 B.C.	Ohio Valley, NY, PA
Hopewell	500 B.C. — A.D. 1200	States from Texas to the East
Mississippian	A.D. 800 — A.D. 1700	States from Texas to the East

Archaic Mounds (4000 B.C. — 1000 B.C.)

About 6,000 years ago in the lower Mississippi Valley, relatively small mounds were erected on coastlines and rivers. There are approximately 100 known Archaic-era mound sites with many of them in Louisiana. These mounds do not appear to have been used for burials, but at the oldest mound currently known called *Monte Sano*, cremation remains were found. Monte Sano, in Louisiana, dates to 4000 B.C. (Cordell, et al., 2009). A mound adjacent to the famous *Poverty Point* site in Louisiana, known as the *Lower Jackson Mound*, was dated to approximately 3800 B.C. in the early 2000s. It is an 8-foot-tall conical mound with a diameter of 130 feet. Another Louisiana mound site near Monroe is known as *Watson Brake*. It consists of

an egg-shaped earthen embankment enclosing 22 acres. Located at intervals on the oval embankment are 11 mounds, the largest of which is 26 feet in height. Starting in 1993, a series of core samples were taken leading to over 100 carbon-dating tests. The results showed that the site was constructed around 3200 B.C., and for several years Watson Brake was the oldest American mound site known.

Around 3000 B.C. massive shell mounds, also called *midden* mounds, were being erected along the coasts of South Carolina, Georgia, Florida, and Mississippi. Many of these are huge elevated rings made from mollusk, clam, and other shells. Some of these mounds are horseshoe-shaped while others are massive heaps up to 60 feet in height. The diameter of some of the rings exceeds 800 feet. The U. S. Park Service has identified and studied over 50 coastal shell mounds and rings. However, shell mounds are also found along many rivers throughout the southeast. The Archaic mound culture was clearly active until the Poverty Point and Adena cultures developed. It is not clear whether the people responsible for Archaic mounds gradually became more sophisticated in mound construction or if there was an incursion of a different culture that simply absorbed the Archaic peoples.

Watson Brake reconstruction by Dee Turman. From: *The Illustrated Encyclopedia of Native American Mounds & Earthworks* (Little, 2009).

Erosion of the archaic Spanish Mount shell mound on the South Carolina coast shows how mollusk and other shells were densely packed together to form these large mounds. This mound has been dated to about 2000 B.C. Photo: Lora Little.

Poverty Point (2500 B.C. — 1000 B.C.)

Poverty Point is a unique and distinctive culture that simply seemed to "appear" in the center of the region where earlier Archaic mounds were built. The main Poverty Point site is located in northeastern Louisiana. The *Lower Jackson Mound*, located nearby, was long considered part of the main complex. When that mound was dated to 3800 B.C., archaeologists concluded that it was not a part of the Poverty Point Culture but was an earlier Archaic site. However, starting perhaps as early as 2500 B.C., some additional earthen construction began in the area. Sometime around 2000 B.C. to 1500 B.C., the 400-acre complex was completed. It consists of a series of raised semicircular terraced rings of earth that were piled 6 feet high. The rings are a uniform 80 feet in width and spaced 150 feet apart. The combined length of the raised terraces is almost 8 miles. There are four straight flat walkways cutting through the rings of earth. These were used for making solar

Reconstruction of Poverty Point, Louisiana site by Jon L. Gibson.
From: *Poverty Point* (1983) Louisiana Archaeological Survey.

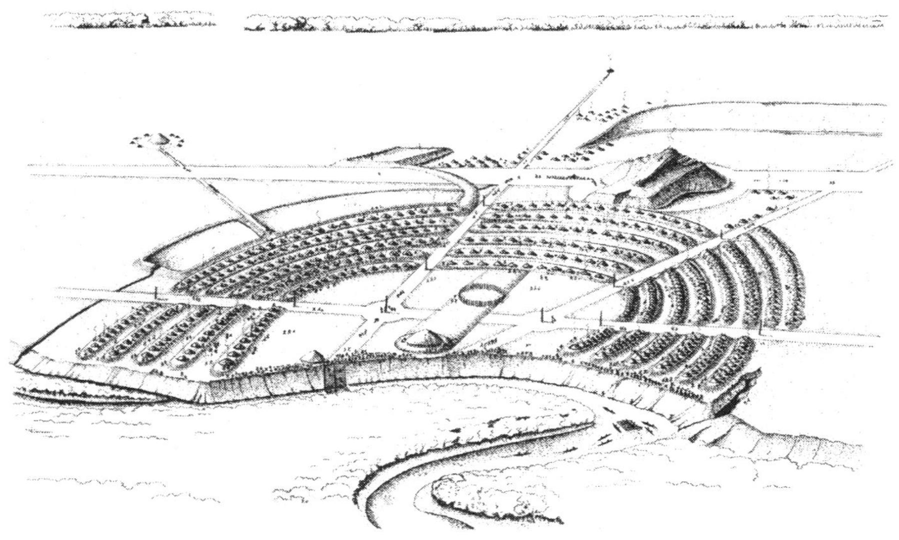

alignments. There were several woodhenges erected at key points on the walkways to allow for solar or stellar alignments. A woodhenge is a circle of vertical logs embedded into the ground, which was used to make straight-line sightings from post to post.

On the western side of the terraces, a massive mound was erected. The mound is thought to be a bird effigy depicting an eagle with outspread wings. It is 72 feet in height, and it measures 640 feet from wing-tip to wing-tip and 710 feet from the head to tail. Small dome-shaped houses were constructed atop the rings of earth, and archaeologists believe that 4,000 or more people lived at the site. Literally millions of artifacts have been recovered from the complex including distinctive decorated cube-shaped and rounded clay balls. It is also known that huge trading networks were active when Poverty Point was utilized. Artifacts and materials from the Great Lakes area and North Carolina have been found there.

Poverty Point however is not a single site. It is a culture extending to smaller village and mound sites located in Louisiana and parts of Mississippi.

At least 30 other sites have been identified that are believed to be associated with this culture. It was once asserted by a few archaeologists that the Olmec culture of Mexico influenced the development of Poverty Point, but today the notion is largely dismissed.

Adena Culture (1000 B.C. — 200 B.C.)

The Adena Culture is named for the site where it was first identified—the Adena Mansion grounds in Ohio. Adena mounds are found in many states but are most numerous in Ohio, West Virginia, Indiana, Pennsylvania, Kentucky, Maryland, and New York. Adena-era mounds are typically large, steep conical mounds, some of which reached massive sizes. These were usually burial mounds with a large log or stone-lined tomb at the base of the mound or in chambers dug below the base before the mound was formed. Some of the larger mounds had several chambers built on top of each other. Many Adena mounds had raised earthworks and a moat encircling the mound.

The Wilmington Tablet (found in an Ohio mound in 1879) is a good example of Adena Tablets. Most are 4 or 5 inches in length. They are thought to have been used as stamps to paint tatoos on clothing or skin. Photo: (replica) by Greg Little.

One unique artifact associated with Adena burials was a polished stone tablet engraved with complex zoomorphic designs. A total of 14 Adena tablets have been found but only one was found during an archaeological excavation. The others were found by amateurs.

There may have once been thousands of Adena mounds, but today only a few hundred survive. Thousands of skeletal remains have been excavated from Adena mounds. Many of the old reports of giant skeletons found in mounds come from excavations of Adena sites. These will be discussed in detail in a later chapter.

The largest Adena mound is the *Grave Creek* site in West Virginia. It is 69 feet tall and has a diameter just under 300 feet. It was encircled with a moat. In 1838 two tunnels and a shaft were dug into the mound, and a museum was set up in a large tomb found at the base. The museum failed and the mound was refilled. Almost as large is the *Miamisburg Mound* in Ohio. It stands 65 feet in height with a diameter of 300 feet. It is known that this mound once had a stone facing, but the mound was enlarged at a later time. The stones are still present and are located inside the mound about 25 feet below the surface.

Grave Creek, West Virginia Adena mound. Photo: Lora Little.

The tallest Adena era mound may be located in Pinson, Tennessee. The Pinson site is a 400-acre complex with (maybe) 17 mounds, 5 of which are platform mounds. (A later chapter discusses Pinson's mounds.) There is at least one circular earthwork at the site, but standing in the center of the complex is a steep conical mound named *Saul's Mound*. It is 72 feet in height with a diameter of 120 feet. It is believed that the mound was once a truncated pyramid, which has eroded to the conical shape seen today. The top of the mound has a large depression at its center. An interview which I conducted with the site's Director (State Archaeologist Robert Mainfort) in the mid-1980s revealed that a collapsed tomb in the base of the mound could be the probable cause of the indentation. This was a trait of Adena mounds. The Pinson mounds are unique in that some platform mounds have been dated to 200 B.C., which is thought to be too early for platform mounds. Saul's Mound has never been dated or excavated. Mainfort, however, believes that the Pinson site is a Hopewell era construction. Pinson is a good example of how many mound sites show characteristics of several overlapping mound-building cultures.

Saul's Mound stands in the center of a large mound and earthwork complex in Pinson, Tennessee. Photo: Greg Little.

Rock Eagle Effigy Mound near Eatonton, Georgia is made from milky quartz stone piled 10 feet high. The wingspan is 120 feet. Photo: Lora Little.

In addition to the hundreds of burial mounds and circular earthworks built during the Adena period, there are a few stone effigy mounds typically attributed to the same people. *Rock Eagle Effigy Mound* and *Rock Hawk Effigy Mound* in Georgia—only 13 miles from each other—are the two main sites. These are large bird mound effigies formed by piles of large, milky-quartz rocks.

Hopewell Tradition (500 B.C. — A.D. 1200)

The construction of mounds and geometric earthworks reached its design pinnacle during the Hopewell period—now called by archaeologists the *Hopewell Tradition*. It is thought that the Hopewell culture was a natural development from the earlier Adena culture. The name *Hopewell* comes from the Ohio site where the Hopewell Tradition was first identified. Hopewell sites are characterized as having large complexes of mounds and associated geometric earthworks. It was a widespread culture extending throughout most of the eastern half of America. Hopewell burials were

extremely elaborate, and tens of thousands of artifacts have been excavated from Hopewell mounds. The Hopewell people traveled widely with their trading network extending throughout Canada and virtually all of the United States. The most elaborate sites are located in Ohio, but many other states have large Hopewell earthworks and mounds.

In later chapters we will discuss the Newark earthworks, the largest set of ancient geometric earthworks in the world. One important formation at Newark is called *Great Circle*, a near perfect circular *henge* that encloses 30 acres. The henge is a circular earthen wall of earth and is 10 feet in height. Inside the henge is a 7-foot deep moat. There is only one opening leading into the circle, which is located on the northeast side. The size and formation of the outer wall and inside moat is essentially identical to England's famous site of Avebury. In the center of the Great Circle is an effigy mound believed to represent an eagle.

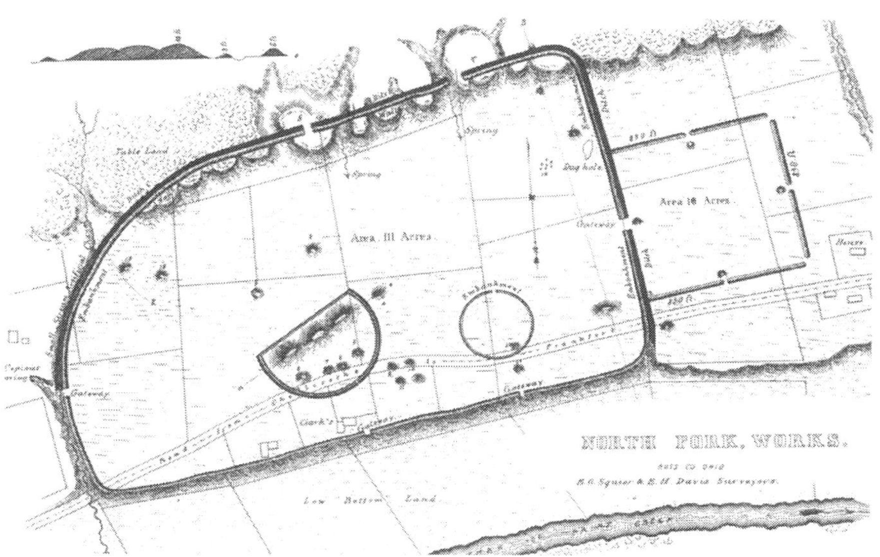

Squier & Davis' (1848) survey of the Hopewell Mound Group near Chillicothe, Ohio. The large, D-shaped outer earthwork enclosed 111 acres. There were 25 mounds at the site.

Near the Great Circle in Newark is a massive circle and octagon formation. The circle encloses 20 acres and is formed from a wall of earth from 8 to 14 feet in height. The circle connects to an earth-formed octagon that encloses 50 acres. At the 8 points inside the octagon stand rectangular, truncated mounds. It is accepted by archaeologists that the formation was used to chart the 18.61-year cycle of the moon's movements, which allowed for eclipse predictions. There once was a 56-mile-long road or pathway outlined by a set of parallel linear earthworks extending south from the circle and octagon in Newark to a nearly identical formation at Chillicothe, Ohio where dozens of other mounds and geometric earthworks are found. There are several other similar formations located in Ohio and in adjacent states including numerous square formations, fully enclosed circles of earth, horseshoe-shaped embankments, and long, curving linear earthworks. An

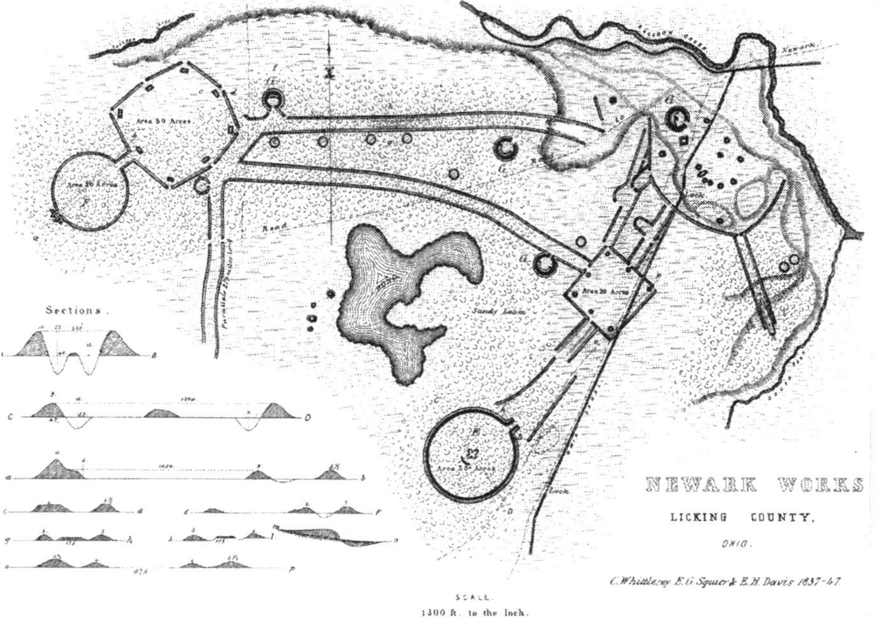

Squier & Davis' (1848) survey of the Newark, Ohio earthworks, the largest and most complex set of ancient earthworks in the world. There are several distinct but connected earthworks in the formation. They include the Circle and Octagon (upper left side) and the Great Circle (bottom center).

extensive complex at Portsmouth, Ohio—which runs across the Ohio River into Kentucky in two different directions—is one of the most elaborate earthwork formations ever made by the Hopewell. It was during the Hopewell timeframe that several other types of mounds and earthworks were also constructed. These include effigy mounds and what are often called *Hilltop Forts*.

There are thousands of effigy mounds located in northern states with fewer of them in the South. Wisconsin has numerous bird effigy mounds and also effigies of bears, turtles, a lizard, and even one depicting a man with an unusual double-peaked head. *Effigy Mounds National Monument* in Iowa has 200 remaining mounds and 31 animal effigies. A series of studies in the 1970s found 54 groupings of effigy mounds along the upper Mississippi River with 1,438 different effigy mounds. It has been estimated by archaeologists that 10,000 effigy mounds once existed in Iowa alone (Little,

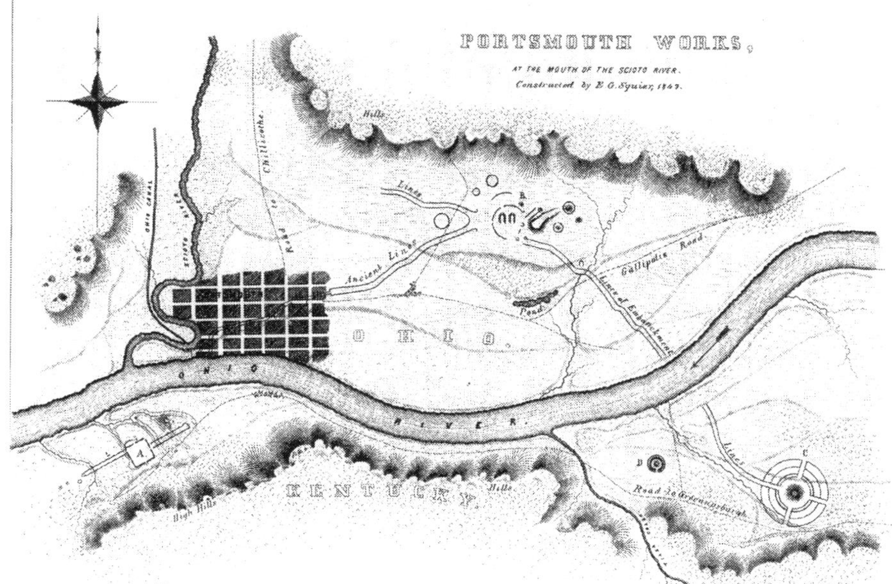

Squier & Davis' (1848) survey of the Portsmouth, Ohio earthworks. The site connects to several unusual earthwork and mound complexes on the other side of the Ohio River in Kentucky. Connecting the various sites were approximately 15 miles of 160-foot-wide walkways enclosed by parallel earthen walls.

2009). Most have been destroyed by farming and construction. The most famous effigy mound is, of course, *Serpent Mound* in Ohio. Some archaeologists believe it was built by a later Hopewell Tradition culture referred to as the *Fort Ancient* culture, and today most archaeologists think that it was constructed around 1070 A.D. However, archaeologist William Romain presented evidence at a 2013 conference that it might have been built between 600 B.C. and 100 A.D. (Romain, et al., 2013). To my knowledge, the number of Hopewell mounds and earthworks has never been calculated, but they probably numbered more than 50,000.

Artifacts from excavated Hopewell sites have shown a sophistication and complexity in design. Stone pipes, engraved copper, carved mica sheets, and countless pottery pieces have been found. The symbolic images associated with the ideas of the death journey—which are related to the Milky Way, Cygnus, Scorpius, and Orion— began appearing during the Hopewell era. Archaeologist William Romain has linked some Hopewell sites to alignments with the Milky Way and the constellations of Cygnus and Scorpius (Romain, 2005).

Hilltop Forts or *Hilltop Enclosures* are massive enclosures located on steep hills and mountaintops that had usually first been graded level. Some of these have mounds within or incorporated into the outer walls. These were initially called "Hilltop Forts" because, to the people who first reported them, they were *obviously* defensive structures. Then archaeologists pointed out that some of the earthworks and stonewalls around the forts were not high enough to be effective defenses. Besides, these same archaeologists reasoned, there were gaps in most of the walls of these alleged forts. They concluded that most, if not all of them, were actually "sacred enclosures" used for rituals. More recently it has been found that many of the Hilltop Forts had palisade walls constructed around them and embedded into the outer earthen or stonewalls. The wooden fort walls had been burned, leaving nothing behind but the embankments piled on the sides (Mainfort and Sullivan, 1998). The gaps in the walls could have been wooden gates or bastions. Archaeologists continue to debate the uses of these structures, but

the argument has boiled down to two possibilities. Some were definitely defensive fortresses while others were sacred enclosures used for unknown "ceremonies."

Many of the hilltop enclosures are attributed to the *Fort Ancient* culture centered in Ohio. The Fort Ancient culture is a subset of the Hopewell Tradition. Most of these enclosures date from 500 B.C. to A.D. 600. The Fort Ancient site itself consists of an 100-acre enclosure built on a steep bluff. The earthen walls surrounding the site are up to 68 feet in width and vary in height from 4 to 23 feet. There are more than 60 gaps in the outer walls, and several stone-covered mounds are inside the walls. It is now accepted that various astronomical alignments were made from mounds looking through the gaps to the horizon.

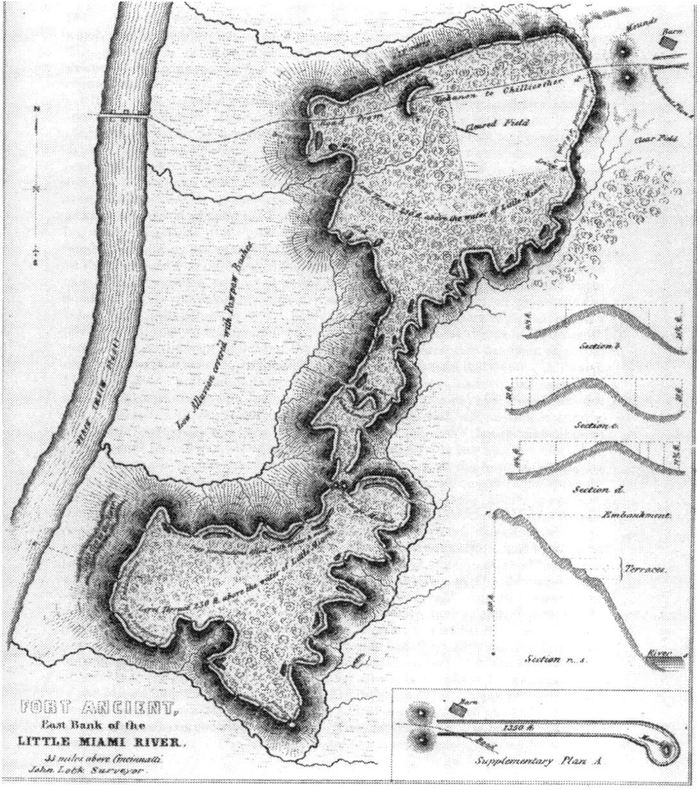

Squier & Davis' (1848) survey of Fort Ancient, Ohio.

Another similar structure is called *Fort Hill*, also in Ohio. It is a large enclosure of 40 acres and is located at the top of a very steep hill. The walls around the hill were made from earth and stone and are about 40 feet wide and 6 to15 feet in height. There are 33 gaps in the walls, but it clearly was used as a defensive fort at some point in time. Hilltop Forts have been found in several other Ohio locations as well as in New York, Pennsylvania, Tennessee, Georgia and other states. Exactly what happened when these structures were made is a mystery. So too are the reasons why such immense structures were necessary for defense.

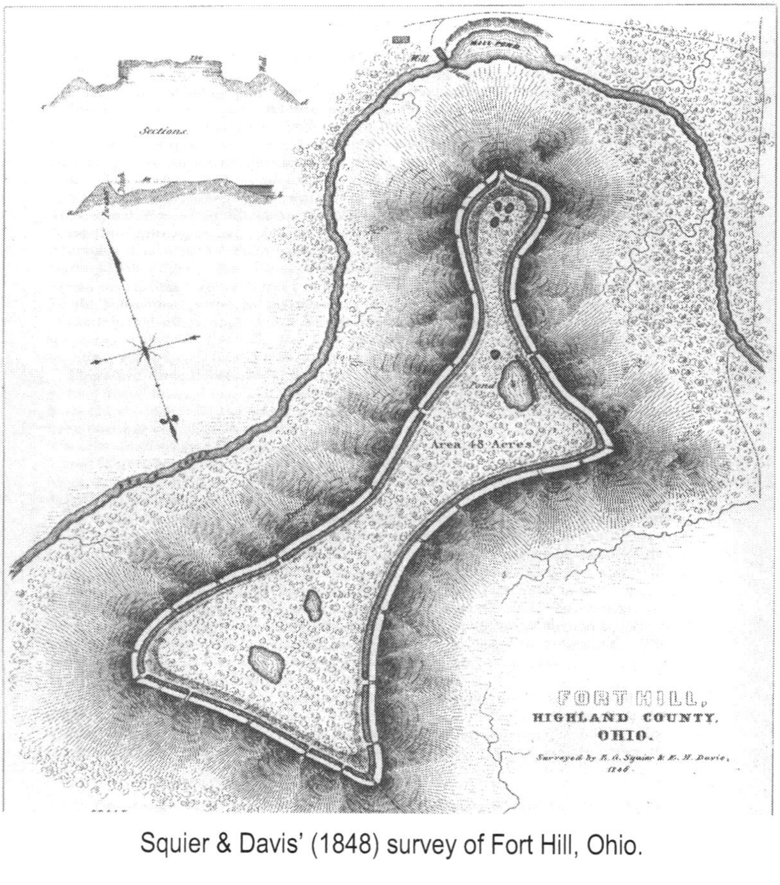

Squier & Davis' (1848) survey of Fort Hill, Ohio.

Mississippian Culture (A.D. 800 — A.D. 1700)

Mound building reached its pinnacle in the *Mississippian* era. The culture was partly a natural development from the Hopewell Tradition, and it emerged around the year A.D. 800. The culture extended across the entire eastern half of America with the largest sites located near the Mississippi River valley and along the many rivers located there. Most of the artifacts displaying the death journey symbols that are the major focus of this book were excavated from Mississippian sites.

Cahokia in Illinois is the largest Mississippian site. It is a complex that once had 120 mounds. About 20 of them were completely destroyed, and only 68 are within the modern archaeological park. Mound construction at

Illustration of Cahokia's Mound 72 ritual sacrifice (by strangulation) of 53 young women who were killed to join the burial of an important person. The male burial is known as the "Birdman" because beads were arranged in a falcon shape around the body. Archaeologist Tim Pauketat's *Cahokia* (2010) explains that the actual number of human remains discovered at Mound 72 was 260. The women were all in their 20s, and some were buried alive after drinking poison or being strangled. Illustration by Hironymous Rowe, Wikipedia Commons.

Cahokia began around A.D. 700, and the complex was inhabited until A.D. 1400. The site reached its peak around the year A.D. 1100, and at least 20,000 people lived in its vast residential areas covering 6 square miles. There are many smaller mound sites found to the north and south of Cahokia that are now known to have been in the Cahokia chiefdom.

The largest mound at Cahokia (and in America) is called *Monk's Mound,* named after a French monk who lived there in historic times. The mound has four terraces and was built in stages from A.D. 900—1200. It is 100 feet tall and has a base that covers 13.1 acres, slightly larger than the base of the Great Pyramid at Giza. On the flat summit of the mound, a huge temple once stood. Archaeologists assert that the temple was 105 feet long, 48 feet wide, and had walls 50 feet in height. Surrounding the central mound and plaza area was a tall wooden stockade that had a total length of 2 miles. Excavations have shown that the walls were rebuilt four times and that bastions were located at regular intervals. It is apparent from arrowheads and burned posts excavated along the palisade wall that Cahokia was attacked several times.

Standing as tall as a 10-story building, Monk's Mound is the largest mound in America. Photo: Lora Little.

Literally hundreds of burials have been excavated from Cahokia with thousands of artifacts removed. One burial was a male with 20,000 shell beads forming a bed for his corpse. Many artifacts from Cahokia depicted the death journey symbols. The death-related symbols are the focal point of the *Southeastern Ceremonial Complex*—or the *Southern Death Cult*. This Mississippian "cult" extended from Spiro in Oklahoma, north to Aztalan in Wisconsin, south to the Gulf and Atlantic Ocean, and throughout the North. Florida, Georgia, Alabama, Tennessee, Arkansas, Louisiana, Mississippi, Missouri, North Carolina, Illinois, Indiana, Ohio, and many other states had large Mississippian mound complexes. Archaeologists have developed a variety of terms to describe subgroups of the Mississippian culture partly based on pottery styles, region, and timeframes.

Almost all Mississippian culture sites included large, truncated pyramid-shaped mounds. These are also known as platform mounds as they typically were used as the base for temples or dwelling structures for the elite—the rulers and religious leaders. The mounds are usually arranged around a central plaza—a flat gathering area used for celebrations, public and political events, and religious ceremonies.

Moundville, Alabama is the second largest Mississippian site and has seen some of the most impressive death journey artifacts ever found. It is a 326-acre complex with 20 large, truncated earthen pyramids arranged around a wide central plaza. A palisade wall surrounded the mound complex where 1,000 people lived. Village areas just outside the walls had at least another 10,000 inhabitants. It is clear that the culture had a ruling class of elite who saw themselves as descended from gods. It is also clear that they had centralized political and religious control that encompassed vast regional areas with smaller mound sites. They were an agricultural society, growing extensive areas of maize (corn), beans, squash, and other crops. Their trading networks extended across all of North America. Because of the exquisite artifacts that have been recovered, it is also apparent that these cultures had a class of highly-skilled artisans devoted to the production of materials incorporating religious iconography.

A few other Mississippian sites will be described later, and it was the Mississippians who had contact with early explorers and settlers. They are often described as "sun worshipers," however, that is not an accurate depiction of their beliefs. It is the same as calling Christians who gather for Easter sunrise "sun worshippers" or people who go to the beach, the same. The religious beliefs of the Mississippians were complex and detailed.

At perhaps several thousand sites scattered across all of eastern America, the Mississippians built palisade forts encircling their main mounds, villages, and cities. Many of these were massive fortresses with walls 8 to 16 feet in height. The walls were then plastered with clay or mud to keep them somewhat fireproof. As will be detailed in the next chapter, Hernando de

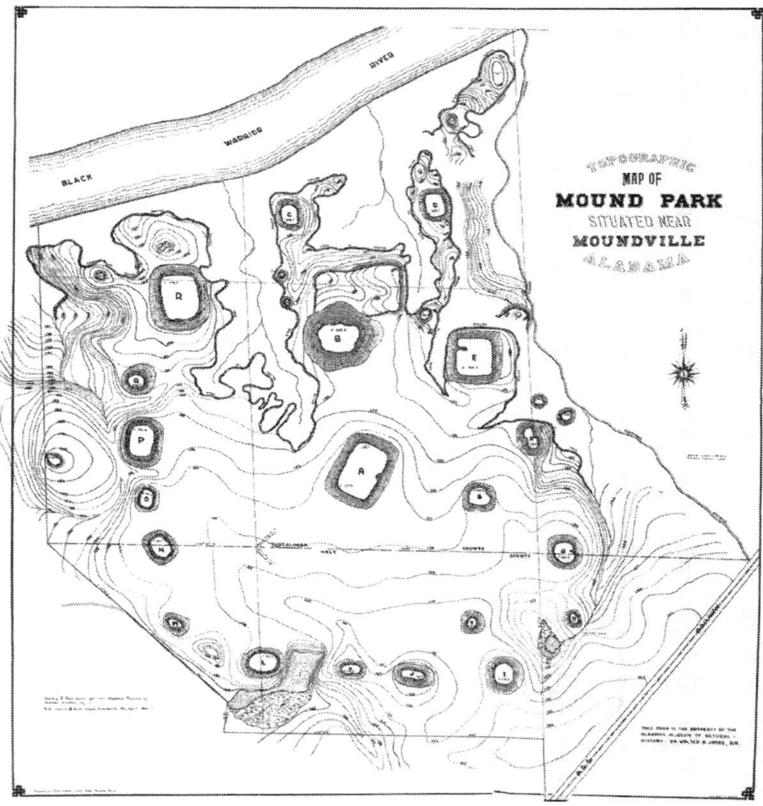

Survey of Moundville, Alabama site from 1930.
Source: Alabama Museum of Natural History.

Aerial photograph of the Moundville, Alabama site taken by U.S. Air Force in 1980.

Below: One of the platform mounds at Moundville, Alabama arranged around the plaza area. Photo: Lora Little.

Soto "visited" many active mound sites and several walled fortresses. His chroniclers have given us a first-hand picture of these people and their way of life. They were very religious people who conducted prolonged ceremonies for the dead. While de Soto and his army were completely disinterested in their rituals and ideas of death, their descriptions of the mound culture and its people are useful.

Archaeological reconstruction of Winterville, Mississippi mound complex, located near Greenville. It was once called the *Blum Mounds* and is a good example of a typical Mississippian site. The central mound was 55-feet high, and 23 mounds were at the site. Illustration by Dee Turman. From: *The Illustrated Encyclopedia of Native American Mounds & Earthworks* (Little, 2009).

Chapter 3

Early Explorers in North America and the "Virtual Amnesia" that Resulted

It was October 12, 1492 when Christopher Columbus first arrived in the Americas landing in the Bahamas. He made four trips to the Americas but never touched North America. His "discovery" of the "West Indies" and the "Indians" who lived there excited Europeans who were completely unaware that the Norse had made visits to and even made a settlement in North America some 500 years earlier or so. It was left to John Cabot to "discover" North America, when he briefly landed in Newfoundland in 1497.

One of the volunteers who accompanied Columbus on his second voyage in 1493 was a 19-year-old named Juan Ponce de León. He soon became Governor of Hispaniola and then was made Governor of Puerto Rico. In 1513 Ponce de León set sail in search of gold that had been rumored to be found in uncharted lands to the north. (As a side note, it is known that Spanish slave traders had briefly visited Florida around this time leading to the rumors of gold.) After visiting several small Bahamas islands on his journey, it was on April 2, 1513 when de León landed in what he called *La Florida* (flowers). The exact site is not clear but it appears to have been around St. Augustine or further to the south. Strong currents from the Gulf Stream caused his boats to drift north, so he hugged the coastline and sailed south until he reached what is today Key Biscayne. Here they found a mound village that had been hastily abandoned just before their landing. Ponce de León

continued to sail around the Keys and then went up the Florida Gulf Coast where his ships were attacked by canoes filled with hostile natives who shot waves of arrows at them. Further north, he anchored his ships to make repairs and gather food and water. At that point, a series of minor battles ensued between the Spanish and the Calusa Indians. Several Spanish were killed, but they took eight natives hostage. Disheartened, Ponce de León returned to Puerto Rico after 8 months of exploring. The truth behind the "Fountain of Youth" search attributed to Ponce de León's journey is not entirely clear, but the main goal of the expedition was to find gold (Hudson, 1976).

In 1521 the Spanish explorer Lucas Vasquez de Ayllon mounted a brief expedition landing at Winyaw Bay in what is today South Carolina. After inviting friendly natives to his ships, Ayllon immediately shackled them as slaves. He made another "visit" in 1524 in the Chesapeake Bay, and in 1526 he took 600 colonists to an area near Sapello Bay in Georgia where they established the first colony. They enslaved more natives as workers but the venture came to a sudden end from disease and constant battles with the native tribes. Ayllon died in 1526 and the surviving 150 colonists abandoned the settlement and went to Hispaniola. Not too long after the early visits of the Spanish to North America, the diseases carried by the Europeans began to make their way through the Native American tribes who had no resistance to them. Smallpox, measles, mumps, and tuberculosis ravaged natives in the Caribbean in 1518 (Hudson, 1976).

In 1528, 300 Spaniards led by Pánfilo de Narváez landed at Tampa Bay in Florida. Moving north in response to reports of gold, Narváez had a series of battles with the Apalachee Indians. The Spanish ran out of foodand soon fled to Mexico. But several men in the Narváez expedition ended up stranded near Galveston, Texas where they were taken in by tribes that made them into "medicine men." These men later wrote about their ordeal. There was at least one other survivor from the Narváez expedition, a man named Juan Ortiz, who lived with the tribes near Tampa Bay for 11 years until he was found by the de Soto expedition in 1539 (Hudson, 1976).

Hernando de Soto's March Through the Southeast

Hernando de Soto arrived in Panama at the age of 14, and he spent 20 years in Central and South America. In 1532 de Soto joined Pizarro's conquistadores (conquerors) and soon became a Captain during the campaign to conquer Peru and the Inca Empire with its 16 million inhabitants.

Pizarro did not trust de Soto. After de Soto befriended the Inca Chief (named *Atahualpa*) and swore an oath to protect him, Pizarro had the chief murdered. Pizarro then ordered de Soto to attack Cuzco, the capital city, with only 40 men. De Soto followed the orders and managed to win a prolonged, massive battle. He was awarded a huge share of the plundered gold and silver. In 1539 de Soto returned to Spain a hero and exceedingly wealthy. Some accounts relate that he was the second wealthiest man in Spain. But de Soto wanted to return to the "New World" and was made the Governor of Cuba with orders to colonize North America within four years. De Soto was delighted with the appointment and saw it as his opportunity to search for more gold and claim land.

De Soto gathered 620 volunteers and about 100 African slaves for his expedition to *la Florida*. They took 237 horses, 200 pigs, mules, large amounts of armor and weapons, and large Irish dogs trained to hunt and kill. The ships from Spain arrived in Havana in mid-May 1539. Almost immediately they set out for Florida and landed south of Tampa Bay on May

Illustration of de Soto arriving near Tampa Bay in 1539. From: Schoolcraft (1854).

25, 1539. In an astonishing turn of events, they were met by Juan Ortiz, the survivor of the 1528 Narváez expedition. Ortiz had become fluent in native languages and subsequently served as de Soto's interpreter (Hudson, 1976).

The Spanish immediately encountered Timucuan natives and started moving north where they were periodically attacked. By October they reached the Apalachee tribe areas of North Florida where they remained for the winter. They were attacked frequently and in response, the Spaniards either enslaved or killed every native they encountered.

In March 1540 the group broke their winter camp and started moving north. There was no way that de Soto's army could have carried sufficient food and supplies for the expedition, but de Soto had learned in South America that food, women, slaves, and whatever else was needed could simply be taken from the natives. They began raiding one village after another as they moved north. By this time de Soto had developed a systematic method of subduing the tribes—essentially the same methods that worked in the Inca conquest. He typically sent an emissary to make peace with the tribal leaders

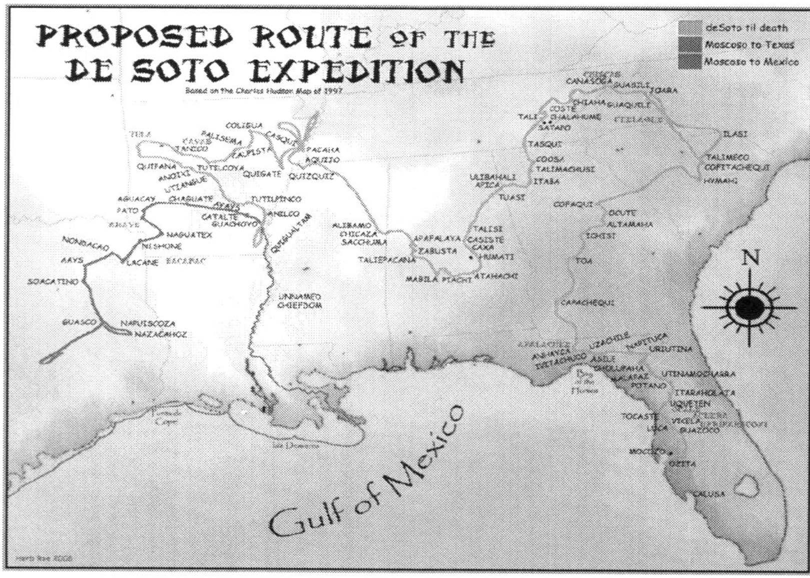

Map showing the proposed route taken in the de Soto expedition based on Hudson's map (1997). Credit: Heironymous Rowe, Wikipedia Commons.

and request a peaceful meeting with them. At the meeting de Soto would take the chief, tribal leaders, and their families hostage. The Spanish used leg irons to shackle 30 natives together at a time. With the captives in tow, his group would enter the towns and villages. Because these Mississippian sites were under so much social control by the chiefs, when the chiefs and their families were taken hostage, the people simply didn't know how to respond. After plundering the villages and towns of food and anything else of value, de Soto usually executed the hostages and enslaved any other natives they could find to carry materials. Gradually they would kill all of the captured Indians or let them die of hunger (Clayton, Knight, & Moore, 1993).

The purpose of relating these details is to explain some of the consequences of the Spanish incursions. Only a few key encounters will be detailed here, but it's important to know that by the time de Soto's expedition ended in 1542, they had marched through what is now Florida, Georgia, North and South Carolina, Tennessee, Alabama, Mississippi, Arkansas, Oklahoma, Louisiana, and Texas. They went through hundreds of towns and villages, plundered numerous major mound sites, and found dozens of fortresses. They also found vast fields of corn and other crops. Most people think of ancient 1500s America as a sort of unexplored, largely uninhabited wilderness. But populations in some areas were so thick, it was difficult to tell where one village ended and another began. In some places, the army moved through 12 villages a day as they plodded along (Clayton, Knight, & Moore, 1993).

As they moved from town to town, de Soto's interpreters were consistently told that a city filled with gold was not too far in the distance. This resulted in the army making a meandering path. In Georgia the army experienced at least one peaceful encounter. They came to the present-day mound complex at Lamar, near Macon. At the time de Soto visited, it was called *Ichisi*. They were met by colorfully clothed women and given baskets of corn and green onions at the mounds. In response, de Soto's priests erected a large wooden cross on top of the largest mound. They may have also visited nearby Ocmulgee and then Etowah, a major Mississippian site with massive

mounds and hundreds of houses inside the fortress walls. In a town called *Ocute*, the chief Patofa asked to join de Soto's army and offered to lead them north to *Cofitachequi* where, according to the chief, considerable gold could be found. After wandering through dense swamps, they eventually reached a small mound village that was in the Cofitachequi chiefdom. Patofa and his 700 warriors who accompanied him immediately attacked the village and killed everyone there—and then scalped them. They immediately looted the temple and encouraged de Soto to keep moving deeper into the region. They moved on to several more mound villages with Patofa and his warriors repeating the same carnage. Suddenly, Patofa and his men turned around and quickly left, presumably returning to their town of Ocute. Archaeologists believe that Ocute had a long-running war with Cofitachequi (Hudson, 1976).

Lady of Cofitachequi & the Temple Mound

In April of 1540, de Soto's army reached the banks of a swift river thought to be the Savannah River. Cofitachequi was located on a high bluff just on the other side of the river, in present-day South Carolina. It is thought to be

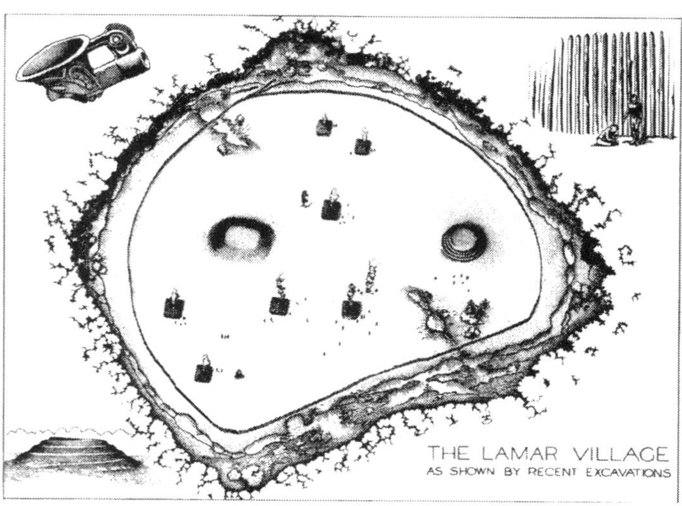

Reconstruction of the Lamar site near Macon, Georgia. It was one of the few places where de Soto did not fight. Credit: Charles Fairbanks, National Park Service.

the mound complex known today as Mulberry. By now, all the towns and cities in the path of this army knew they were coming. As the main body of the expedition force was preparing for the crossing, they were met with a sight they had never before seen. A single huge canoe with a large ornate cloth draped across an overhead roof slowly approached them. A group of unarmed natives dressed in brightly colored adornments methodically paddled the craft, and in the middle, sitting on a white cloth atop an elevated pedestal, was a beautiful, young female native. She was called the "Lady of Cofitachequi" by de Soto's chroniclers. When the canoe pulled up on the shore, the young girl was carefully carried off the canoe by her helpers and she was seated on her white cloth-covered stool by the river's edge. She graciously and respectfully spoke to de Soto through an interpreter and presented him with a massive string of pearls. She explained that her town had been decimated by a plague some years earlier and there was little food available, but her offer to take de Soto to the other side was accepted. At the same time, the main force of 600 soldiers crossed on their makeshift barges they had been constructing the past few days (Hudson, 1976).

On the other side of the river, the natives bowed and presented de Soto and his army of invaders with blankets, skins, food of various sorts, and salt. The natives were described as extremely clean and polite, wearing colorful animal skins and unusual ornate leggings. The town, which had over 500 building structures, was largely deserted. Inspecting the empty buildings revealed that most of them had been abandoned and unused for years. It was again explained to de Soto that a plague had killed most of the residents. It is likely that the earlier Spanish expeditions had spread diseases that had already taken a major toll on the population (Hudson, 1976).

In the center of the town was a grouping of large flat-topped mounds, shaped into pyramids. The largest was several hundred feet in diameter and about 65 feet high. On its top stood a large temple constructed from vertical wooden logs and adorned with colorful decorations, pearls, and conch shells.

The expedition's chroniclers wrote that the building was 100 feet long and 40 feet wide with a high roof covered with matted cane. Shells were

arranged on the roof. The Spanish quickly moved up a ramp leading to the temple on the summit. The entrance to the temple was formed by two massive wooden doors that pivoted open. When the doors opened, a long hallway was encountered. On the two sides of the hall were six pairs of life-sized wooden statues with each pair depicting identical warriors using different weapons and posed in a different menacing stance. The first pair showed the warriors with diamond-shaped heads carrying maces. The second pair of warriors brandished broadswords. The third pair carried hinged clubs. The next pair wielded battleaxes. Bows and arrows were carried by the next pair, and the sixth and final statues were adorned with pikes and copper spear points. One of de Soto's chroniclers wrote, "...if they had been found in the most famous temples of Rome in the most flourishing period of its power and empire, [the statues] would have been esteemed and valued for their grandeur and perfection" (Clayton, Knight, & Moore, 1993, Vol. 2: 299).

The interior of the temple was highly decorated and ornate. Full-size statues of both men and women were found everywhere in the temple. They were adorned by strings of pearls. But catching the attention of the intruders were numerous highly-stylized, wooden chests located all around the interior walls and stacked into rows running across the entire floor. Opening the chests was the first order of business.

Inside the largest chests were pearls. So many pearls were found that the Spanish wrote that the entire force and all the horses could not possibly carry them away. They also found hundreds of finely detailed animal skins, ornate shields, and copper ornaments. Inside many of the smaller chests, they found only human bones carefully placed in bundles. The bones were the remains of previous chiefs. The chroniclers mentioned that the natives took great care with their dead, and they described the use of charnel houses atop some mounds.

The room was quickly plundered of the copper breastplates, furs, the best pearls, and anything else of value. Six small outer rooms were then discovered, which were attached to the temple. All of the rooms were packed with decorated weapons and shields. De Soto's men spent two weeks in the

Right: The famous Etowah, Georgia statues, which are made from polished marble and were excavated from a mound. They probably depict the type of carved statues found by de Soto in temples. Photo: Heironymous Rowe, Wikipedia Commons.

Middle: The largest mound at Etowah standing 61 feet tall. Photo: Lora Little.

Below: One of the smaller mounds at Etowah. Photo: Lora Little.

village and packed everything that had value, but they found no gold. Having taken everything else of value, the young girl who had greeted de Soto with so much respect was then kidnapped by the Spanish. Some days later the young girl bravely escaped along with a small chest of the finest pearls that had been plundered from her temple. She was one of the lucky ones. At least it seemed so at the time. With gold being the focus of the expedition, de Soto decided not to send his men after the young girl.

Less than two months later, the expedition had moved deeper into the interior entering the land of the Coosa (modern-day Georgia) where they found huge fortresses and dense populations. One by one, large, fortified towns and mound complexes were looted as the Spanish now moved southwest, led by tales of gold in the next city—or the one after that one. The leaders of each town were nearly always kidnapped and then collared and chained in iron—to become slaves to carry supplies. Nearly all of them were eventually put to the sword or used as training bait for the attack dogs. Some of the captured died of starvation, and others committed suicide. The expedition moved through North Carolina, Tennessee, and back into Georgia where they were told about a city called *Mabila* in Alabama. Four of de Soto's chroniclers detailed the events surrounding what is referred to now as *The Battle of Mabila*. It is an incredible story that marked the point where the Native American tribes essentially became doomed. Ironically, it also marked the point where the will of the Spanish expedition began to crumble (Hudson, 1976).

The Battle of Mabila & the "Giant" Chief Tuscaloosa

Plundering the town of Mabila or Mavilla (in Alabama), which supposedly had vast stores of gold within it, became the major goal of de Soto when he left Georgia and entered Alabama. While staying at a small village called *Talisi* in Alabama, de Soto was visited by an envoy group representing the great Chief Tuscaloosa (spelled in various ways) who ruled Mabila and the region. Tuscaloosa means *Black Warrior*.

The envoy group was led by Tuscaloosa's son, who was consistently described as about 7.5 feet in height and 18 years of age. Both Tuscaloosa and his son were called "giants" several times in the chronicles (Clayton, Knight, & Moore, 1993, Vol 2: 327). De Soto was invited to follow the envoy to meet Tuscaloosa himself. The march took five days and they passed through five different large towns. On October 11, 1540, de Soto met Tuscaloosa at the village of *Atahachi*. Atahachi was a palisade-walled mound complex. Inside the walls, de Soto approached the largest mound where Tuscaloosa was seated on the top and surrounded by 100 "nobles, richly dressed in fine mantles of various kinds of furs with long plumes on their heads..." (Clayton, Knight, & Moore, 1993, Vol. 2: 328). Above Tuscaloosa was a banner with a cross painted on it. De Soto's chroniclers likened it to a Templar or military symbol (328). Tuscaloosa stood as de Soto approached and walked to the top step of the mound where he stretched out his arms to welcome the Spanish. The four chroniclers related that the giant chief stood well over 7 feet tall and had huge proportions—the tallest Indian they encountered (328). However, quite oddly, one of the chronicles describes Tuscaloosa's hands and feet as very delicate and small.

Three days later, de Soto left for Mabila with Tuscaloosa taken along as a somewhat cooperative prisoner. De Soto ordered that Tuscaloosa be allowed to ride a horse to Mabila, and the Spanish had problems finding a horse big enough and strong enough. They finally settled on the largest packhorse they had, but Tuscaloosa's legs almost dragged on the ground as they moved. The trip took three days, and they passed through densely populated areas.

The cross enclosed in concentric circles or a sunburst was a common symbol among south-eastern tribes. It has long been incorrectly interpreted as a sun symbol. From: Dover (1975).

Village after village was encountered, some densely populated and others hastily abandoned. When they reached the outskirts of Mabila, two Spanish soldiers disappeared and the Spanish suspected that they had been captured and killed by the natives. Tuscaloosa had become increasingly hostile to the Spanish during the journey, but when they got to Mabila, Tuscaloosa encouraged de Soto to go into the city with him.

Mabila was a large, fortified town with 16-foot-high, wooden palisade walls plastered on the exterior with hardened clay. At 50-foot intervals, there were towers (bastions) erected on the walls, each one large enough to enclose 8 warriors. De Soto saw that the bastions were being manned. Two large wooden gates led through the walls. Inside the protective walls was a huge plaza area with 80 large houses. The houses were described as barracks, able to house 500 or more warriors in each. It is asserted by archaeologists that this is probably an exaggeration (Hudson, 1976).

The gates to the walled fortress swung open and de Soto and Tuscaloosa entered. About 100 Spanish soldiers and slaves leading pack animals carrying all of the Spanish supplies and looted goods accompanied them. They were

Photo of actual Spanish conquistadors' armor displayed in Cuernavaca, Mexico museum. Their faces and bodies were completely encased. Credit—Tim Davis (www.downtheroad.org).

immediately swarmed by warriors who, happily it seemed, greeted them with cheering and singing. De Soto noticed that armed warriors were in the towers and on the walls, and he also saw through the open doors into the houses that there were many armed warriors milling around. Tuscaloosa immediately disappeared into a nearby house with a group of warriors. One of de Soto's soldiers ordered Tuscaloosa to come back out but then a warrior drew his bow and arrow. In response, a Spaniard pulled his sword and cut the arm off of the Indian who instantly fell dead. Suddenly the Spanish were attacked by a barrage of arrows and ax-wielding warriors who ran from the houses. One chronicler estimated the number of warriors at Mabila at 10,000, while another related 7,500. Archaeologists assert this too was an exaggeration with their "guess" more like 2,000 to 3,000 (Hudson, 1976).

De Soto managed to reach his horse and escape, but he was wounded. There are several descriptions in the chronicles of armor-covered Spanish cavalry being hit by 7 to 8 arrows at a time. The arrows simply bounced off their armor. Two important Spanish soldiers who were killed inside the

Illustration from Theodor de Bry's (1591) *Grand Voyages* depicting Spanish conquistadores fighting Indians in Florida. Note the tall Chief exhorting his warriors shown in the upper right side.

fortress were shot through an eyehole and in the neck—areas where there were gaps in the armor. Before the Spanish escaped, several horses were killed and all of their supplies, food, and plundered loot were left behind. None of it was recovered. A total of 14 individuals of the Spanish group were left inside—all presumably killed. When de Soto's men raced out of the fort, they were pursued by hundreds of screaming warriors shooting arrows and throwing spears (Hudson, 1976).

Outside the fort de Soto ordered his cavalry to attack the warriors who were chasing them. Several major skirmishes took place when waves of warriors attacked. They were repelled each time by the Spanish-mounted cavalry. The cavalry soldiers were fully armor-clad and their horses also were covered with armor. Eventually the warriors retreated inside the fortress and they closed and locked the gates. At that point the other 500 Spanish soldiers arrived having served as a rear guard. They surrounded the fort.

The infuriated de Soto ordered attack after attack on the fort—to no avail. His men were not hurt by these attacks, but they couldn't scale the walls or push open the gates. He then ordered his armor-suited ax wielders to break the gates open. With arrow after arrow bouncing off their armor, they managed to cut one gate open. With his rage growing, de Soto then ordered his mounted cavalry to go into the fort and burn the town to the ground. The horsemen started numerous fires in houses and the interior walls. Soon the entire town was ablaze with the screams of the inhabitants actually disturbing de Soto's men. Any natives who tried to escape were killed by the Spanish who had surrounded the fortress (Hudson, 1976).

When the Spanish entered the fort and took over the still-burning town, some warriors were barricaded inside large structures where the fires had not yet reached. De Soto had these buildings sealed from the outside and burned. Soldiers stood guard outside each burning building. When natives ran out, they were either shot at close range with the Spanish guns or hacked to death with swords. In this battle, the entire town of Mabila was wiped out, and the horrible devastation greatly saddened even de Soto's chroniclers. Although no one knows how many natives died in this one battle, the Spanish

chroniclers wrote that 2,500 to 3,000 natives were killed outside the fort, including Tuscaloosa's son. Virtually everyone else inside the walls was burned to death or killed trying to escape the fires. Tuscaloosa's body was not found. There may have been as many as 10,000 natives who died. De Soto lost 120 soldiers and another 80 "helpers" in the battle. Another 250 soldiers were seriously wounded. The expedition force remained in the area for a month trying to heal. The loss of all their supplies and all of their looted goods greatly disheartened the force, and many wanted to turn back. In response, de Soto ordered the force to move away from the Gulf of Mexico and they subsequently went into Mississippi (Hudson, 1976). The site of Mabila has never been found, but archaeologists believe they have narrowed it down to just a few possible locations.

In the spring of 1541, the Spanish force met the Chickasaw in Mississippi, and de Soto ordered the tribe to give him 200 men who would carry his supplies. That night the Chickasaw attacked the Spanish, killing 40 of them and taking all the supplies that the group had managed to gather. For unknown

ASSAULT ON INDIAN FORTRESS OF MAUVILA.

Illustration of de Soto's axmen breaking down the gates to Mabila. From: Cady (1894).

reasons, the Chickasaw did not attack again and de Soto quickly moved north to escape (Hudson, 1976).

On May 8, 1541, de Soto "discovered" the Mississippi River, although it's likely the tribes knew that it was there. When he reached the river somewhere near Memphis, Tennessee, de Soto was opposed by thousands of brightly dressed warriors who had gathered in canoes on the Arkansas side. After building barges for his force that now numbered 400 men, the Spanish crossed the river some 2 miles away from the hostile warriors. From there they went through Arkansas, Oklahoma, Texas, and Louisiana. In the winter of 1541, the "interpreter" Juan Ortiz died (Hudson, 1976).

On May 21, 1542, de Soto died of a disease on the west side of the Mississippi River. In fear that news of his death would embolden the natives, his men weighted his body and sank it in the river. The remaining Spanish built barges and for two weeks made their way down the Mississippi under constant attack by natives in canoes. When they reached the Gulf coast, they followed the coast to the southwest for some 50 days. It is believed that 311 of his men eventually made their way to Spanish-controlled Mexico bringing with them only a few remaining swords and the rough skins they were wearing (Hudson, 1976).

The Nodena site reconstructed by Hironymous Rowe, Wikipedia Commons.
Nodena was the site of Pacaha visited by de Soto.

The back of the female statue excavated at Etowah. The Etowah statues are perhaps the best examples of the statues remaining from the Native American mound cultures. Photo: Lora Little.

The "Virtual Amnesia" of Native American Tribes & Hernando de Soto

The cultures that built and used the mounds were far more advanced and skilled than most people realize. The temple site de Soto looted at Cofitachequi shows us how sophisticated their buildings and artifacts were. But many of their finest achievements were carved into wood—such as the numerous full-sized statues found in the temple. None of these have survived, but marble statues found at the Etowah, Georgia mound complex show the craftsmanship of their work. The details of de Soto's encounters were largely unknown to the general public when the mounds were being "discovered" by settlers and looted by pothunters. And even after de Soto's horrible march through the southeast, there were more incursions that continued to spread disease and destruction. By the 1600s, nearly all of the mound sites had been abandoned. When asked about the mounds in the 1700s and 1800s, some tribal leaders told early historians that they "didn't know" who built

them. At the same time, the "Indians" who survived were being forced further and further west by the settlers who came into America in ever-increasing numbers. A mythology about an advanced race of mound builders who were exterminated by the "savage Indians" developed and became the dominant idea in the public. It provided a murky justification for displacing the Indians and taking their land. When so many "giant skeletons" were found and widely reported, the most popular idea about the mound builders was that they were a race of advanced giants. And the Native American tribes did, in fact, have legends of powerful giants who had been exterminated by their ancestors.

When Columbus arrived in 1492, it is conservatively estimated that there were over 57 million indigenous people in the Americas. North America's population at that time has been conservatively estimated to have been 4.5 to 7 million, but many others believe it could have approached 20 million (Folsom & Folsom, 1994; Little, 2009). By the time settlers arrived, the populations of "natives" had fallen by at least 90%.

A couple of facts asserted by archaeologists illustrate the devastation the diseases inflicted. At the time de Soto went through the Mississippi Valley around Memphis, there were at least 80 large towns and villages by the Mississippi River between Memphis and mid-Louisiana. De Soto's expedition spent about 5 months in the area during a winter. The next visit to the region by a European was in 1682 when La Salle explored the river. La Salle found only 5 villages in that same area. By the time European settlers entered the mound areas, the remaining tribes had what archaeologist Charles Hudson has called "a virtual amnesia" caused by the catastrophic disaster that befell them (Hudson, 1976: 3). Nearly all of their storytellers and older knowledge keepers had died. Few of the surviving natives recalled the past history of their people. Thomas (Powell, 1894: 293) quotes an 1818 article wherein a Rev. Cornelius asked a chief and several natives who were visiting Etowah Mounds about their legends and traditions of mounds. The chief replied, "They were never put up by our people."

In retrospect, it is obvious that even if de Soto and various other explorers had not made their way into the heartland of America, the diseases would

have probably come anyway, sooner or later. It is useful to know the details and descriptions of the tribes encountered by the Spanish. That being said, it is also obvious that the destruction of the tribes through diseases created the virtual amnesia of the natives who were present when the colonists came to America. It is the most important factor involved with the development of the myth of a lost race of mound builders that dominated 1800's America. And it was that myth that ultimately led to the Smithsonian's efforts to solve the question of "who built the mounds?"

The story behind the Smithsonian's mound survey is truly incredible, and it reveals the underlying truth of several controversies. The Smithsonian's story, along with a couple others that reveal the early days of archaeology, are in the next chapters. But we don't pretend that they explain everything. There is a quote that aptly sums up what many books on mysteries do, and it

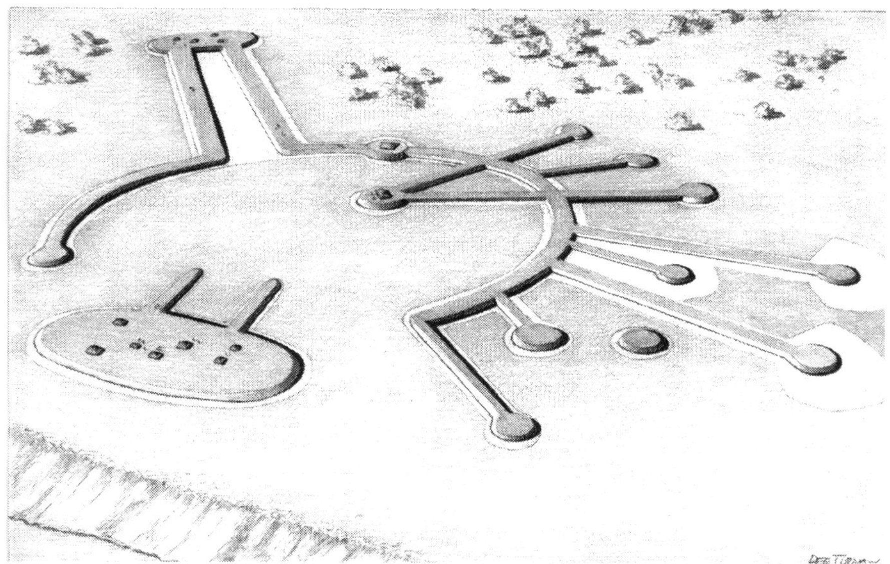

Big (Tony's) Circle Mounds near Clewiston, Florida. Reconstruction: by Dee Turman. Dated between 450 B.C. to A.D. 200, the complex had 14 mounds with linear earthworks incorporated into a large curving earthwork. Hernando de Soto did not venture into the Okeechobee area where several similar unusual mound formations are found. Some of the sites in Florida also had canals. From: *The Illustrated Encyclopedia of Native American Mounds & Earthworks* (Little, 2009).

is probably applicable here too. It is a quote from a book by Tony Hillerman made into a Native American movie titled *Coyote Waits* (2003). Near the end of the movie, Native American actor Wes Studi states, "Sometimes we don't solve anything, we just rearrange the mystery."

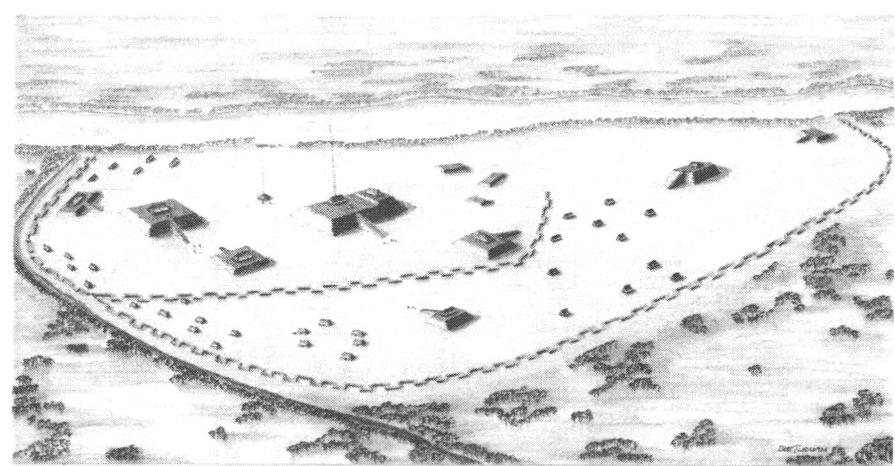

Angel Mounds near Evansville, Indiana is a good example of a fortified, Mississippian mound complex. Nearly 3 million artifacts have been excavated from the site. The complex had 11 platform mounds and a high, palisade wall that extended over a mile in length. Reconstruction: by Dee Turman. From: *The Illustrated Encyclopedia of Native American Mounds & Earthworks* (Little, 2009).

Great Bear effigy mound in Effigy Mounds National Monument (Iowa). Reconstruction: by Dee Turman. From: *The Illustrated Encyclopedia of Native American Mounds & Earthworks* (Little, 2009).

Chapter 4

The Smithsonian, Schoolcraft, & Giant Skeletons:

Who Built the Mounds?

The founding of the Smithsonian is a strange tale that many readers will be familiar with while others will not. James L. Macie was born in Paris in 1765. He was the illegitimate son of Hugh Smithson, the First Duke of Northumberland. Macie attended college in England and became a chemist, and at the age of 22 he changed his last name to Smithson. He traveled extensively and accumulated wealth mainly from inheritances. Because Smithson never married he created an unusual will that left his fortune to a nephew or the nephew's family—provided that the nephew had children. If the nephew died without children the money was to go to the United States to establish an organization in Washington, D.C. that would be called the *Smithsonian Institution*. Its stated purpose was to increase and spread knowledge.

James Smithson died in 1829, and his nephew died without a family in 1835 thus ceding the inheritance to America. In 1836 Congress accepted the gift and in 1838 President Jackson sent a diplomat to England to retrieve the money. He returned with 104,960 gold coins valued then at a half million dollars ($13+ million today). Congress, in its wisdom, invested the money in treasury bonds issued by the state of Arkansas. The bonds defaulted and became worthless. In 1846 President Polk signed into law a bill that funded and established the Smithsonian Institution as a governmental trust to be

run by a Board and Secretary. It is neither governmental nor private (Smithsonian, 2010; Wikipedia: Smithsonian).

The Smithsonian's first publication was *Ancient Monuments of the Mississippi Valley* in 1848. It was a monumental and famous work written by Edwin Davis and Ephraim Squier. The wildly popular volume gave descriptions and site surveys of Native American mounds, earthworks, and artifacts. The book tried to avoid speculation but essentially supported the popular view that a mythical race of mound builders, who were superior to the Native American tribes, erected the mounds. However, well before the Smithsonian became involved in Native American ethnology and mound archaeology, many others published large books combining ethnological and archaeological research.

Henry R. Schoolcraft & Giants

In 1822 the already famous geologist/explorer Henry R. Schoolcraft was appointed a U.S. Indian Agent in Michigan. Schoolcraft and his first wife (part Ojibwa) were fascinated by tribal myths, beliefs, and lore and began gathering information from tribes and evaluating archaeological sites. Schoolcraft had a long and distinguished career in politics, university appointments, and in various Indian Affairs positions giving him ample opportunity to research. He suffered a stroke in 1848 and died in 1864—some years before the Smithsonian's Bureau of Ethnology was created. He married several times, and his last wife Mary Howard assisted him in finishing and publishing his massive works. Schoolcraft's many books contain a wealth of information and are nearly forgotten today, but most university libraries still have copies. In addition, most of his works have been made available online. Schoolcraft went against the common belief in his time that the mounds and earthworks were built by a "lost race of mound builders." He asserted that the ancestors of the Indian tribes had erected the mounds and he was well acquainted with the de Soto expedition (*Encyclopedia Britannica*).

Schoolcraft documented several tribal stories about giants. In his 1856 work, *The Indian Fairy Book*, the story of "White Feather and the Six Giants" is told. The tale is about a child whose entire family had been killed by a race of giants. The tale related that only six giants remained from their tribe and they lived on a "high lodge." In the story the young child grows up and manages to kill the remaining giants. Oddly, in a part of the story, one remaining giant was able to enter a lodge where a council meeting was being held indicating that the giant was a big man and very tall, but not what one might consider to be a giant (147-158).

In Schoolcraft's *Notes on the Iroquois* (1847: 267) he documented a story told by the Shawnee. They related that a powerful tribe of tall "giants" once invaded their land and subjugated the Shawnee. They were described as "tall, fierce, and hostile cannibals" (267). It was explained that the tribe was under the rule of the giants until another "giant from heaven" came and destroyed the invaders (267).

In another book (Schoolcraft & Drake, 1884), the general mythology of giants is explained. The giants are called "Windegoes" and were the most formidable and dreaded beings of all. Again they are described as cannibals. In another section of the book (275), the Alleghan Tribe is described. They were, according to Schoolcraft, the oldest tribe remaining in America and had lived in the Ohio River valley—the heart of the Adena and Hopewell Tradition. The Lenape described the Alleghans as a "strong and mighty people" who had giants among them. They built palisade forts, mounds, and earthworks. Schoolcraft concluded, "It is not improbable that the Alleghans were the Mound-Builders" (276).

Still another myth about giants was reported in the Bureau of Ethnology's 19th Annual Report (Powell, 1900). The large volume was devoted to a paper entitled "Myths of the Cherokee" and was written by James Mooney. Mooney wrote, "James Wafford, of the western Cherokee, who was born in Georgia in 1806, says that his grandmother, who must have been born about the middle of the last century, told him that she had heard from the old people that long before her time, a party of giants had come once to visit the

Cherokee. They were nearly twice as tall as common men, and had their eyes slanting in their heads, so that the Cherokee called them... 'The Slant Eyed People'" (391).

A related Cherokee tale is the "Killing of Stone Coat," a giant perhaps related to the Slant Eyed People (Lankford, 2008). He was part of a group of giants inhabiting Cherokee and Iroquois' territory in ancient times. They were twice as tall as normal men and wore suits of rock-hard "scales" on their bodies that repelled normal weapons.

The Flatheads (one of the Salishan Tribes of the north) spoke of a past time when there were "giants" roaming their lands. "Fully half of Flathead stories deal with these giants" (Clark, 1966: 64, attributed to Turney-High, 1933). They were described as "terrible men who would kill everyone they met" (64). They dwindled in number until they were finally gone. Still other tales come from the Kutenais Tribe that once existed near the Rocky Mountains where their stories and legends were collected in 1812-1817. They had many tales of the once-existing giants who were cannibals (Clark, 1966). There are numerous other giant myths existing in nearly all Native American tribes. Whether they are simply "children's stories" or myths with some basis in fact is debatable. But it is clear from the ethnographer's reports that the stories were told to them as if they had a basis in reality.

The Smithsonian's Bureau of American Ethnology

In 1879 Congress established the Bureau of Ethnology as a branch of the Smithsonian to be the storehouse of various records and materials related to Native Americans that were then kept in the Department of the Interior. Most of these "materials" were collections of ethnology reports and site surveys with some artifacts collected from tribes and sites. (In 1897 the name of the bureau was changed to The Bureau of American Ethnology.) They were given an annual budget of $25,000. John Wesley Powell was appointed as the Bureau's Director where he stayed until his death in 1902.

Powell was a Union veteran who lost an arm during the Civil War. After the war, he made numerous well-publicized expeditions to the Rocky Mountains and the Grand Canyon. A geologist intensely interested in Native American history and archaeology, Powell expanded the Bureau of Ethnology's vision and saw them as the nation's agency that would organize all "anthropological research in America." Archaeologist Marvin Jeter (1990: 13) wrote, "It is probably futile, if not ludicrous, to try to sum up the human torrent that was John Wesley Powell in a few words, or a few thousand." Powell was a dynamo who drove his staff relentlessly. The Bureau issued its first Annual Report in 1882.

John Wesley Powell in the Grand Canyon (1871) with a Paiute named Tau-gu. Source: Wikipedia Commons.

The Bureau's Division of Mound Exploration is Created

In February 1881, the U.S. House of Representatives was about to pass its annual $25,000 appropriation for the Bureau of Ethnology, which had just finished only its second year of existence. After the bill was read, Congressman Warren Keifer stood up and offered an amendment reading, "five thousand dollars of which shall be expended in continual archaeological investigations relating to mound-builders and prehistoric mounds" (Rhees, 1901: 863). Keifer (R-Ohio) had been a Union Brig. General in the Civil War and had also served as Speaker of the House. The amendment passed by a large margin and the Smithsonian's "Division of Mound Exploration" came into being.

Powell, who fervently believed that the mounds were built by the ancestors of the Native American tribes, actually opposed the Bureau's involvement in mound excavations. The prior year Powell had resisted efforts being made by various people to engage in excavations. He felt that the focus should be on ethnological research of existing tribes and creating a historical record of them. But after the bill passed establishing the mound exploration division, he wrote to Congress that he would comply with the bill. He immediately appointed Wills de Hass as Director of the new Division of Mound Exploration.

De Hass was actually a harsh critic of Powell's and the appointment was an effective and shrewd method for Powell to stop the criticism coming his way. De Hass was an antiquarian and medical doctor who had been involved in the Grave Creek excavation that opened a museum in the mound's tomb. But the monumental project that was about to begin was more than the 65-year-old de Hass wanted. De Hass resigned in the first year and Powell then appointed Cyrus Thomas as the Division's Director in 1882 (Jeter, 1990).

Cyrus Thomas & The Mound Exploration Project

Cyrus Thomas became a lawyer in 1851 at the age of 26. He then became a school superintendent and later entered the ministry. At the age of 44 he decided to join an expedition to explore the Rocky Mountains. He went on to become an entomologist for a branch of the U. S. Geological Survey and was appointed to the faculty of Southern Illinois University. In 1882 he was appointed head of the Smithsonian's Division of Mound Exploration.

Thomas was not a field archaeologist and spent the majority of his time in Washington. A little-known fact is that Thomas was an ardent believer in the "mythical race of mound-builders." He was on the side of the head of the Chicago Academy of Sciences, the highly acclaimed geologist J. W. Foster. Foster had been impressed with Squier & Davis's 1848 volume on mounds and agreed with Squier that the mounds showed a superior knowledge than the Native Americans supposedly had. In 1873 Forster wrote that the idea that the "Indians" built the mounds was "preposterous" (Jeter, 1990).

Thomas saw his role of the Division's Director as one of organizing and managing his field staff to excavate sites, check surveys for accuracy, document everything, and ensure that his field staff would carefully pack and ship artifacts back to headquarters. Thomas stayed in constant contact with his field agents through weekly mail and telegraphs.

Cyrus Thomas during the 1870 survey of the Yellowstone National Park. Photo: US Geological Service.

Working with an annual budget of $5,000, Thomas hired three field agents starting in July of 1882. The field agents were paid $125 a month. The letter from Cyrus Thomas that employed Edward Palmer as a Field Agent read,

> "You are hereby appointed a temporary Assistant to the Bureau of Ethnology at a monthly compensation of One hundred and twenty-five ($125) dollars, to date from June 1, 1882. This amount is to include your salary, expenses for traveling, cost of excavations and all incidental expenses..."

In outlining the goals of the mound excavations Thomas wrote,

> "1. To make a collection of skeletons, especially crania found entombed in the mounds or graves.
>
> 2. To make a collection of all works of art in stone, copper, clay, or other material.
>
> 3. To give a description of the mounds including size, form, and topographic position.
>
> 4. As fast as collections are made they should be carefully packed in boxes accompanied by labels giving a description of each find, and the boxes should be forwarded by freight..." (Jeter, 1990: 86).

Thomas also ordered that monthly progress reports be submitted to him.

The agents typically traveled by train to mound sites. At the location, they usually hired local labor workers as excavators. Typical manual labor pay at that time was less than $1 a day. The agents' trips to sites often drew newspaper reporters and locals who watched with anticipation. The reporters interviewed the Smithsonian Field Agents when they could but also interviewed many of the local workers who assisted in excavations. Some of the newspaper articles with exaggerated claims came from the local laborers who assisted with the digs and from spectators. In addition, it is clear that the local workers sometimes confused the names and locations of the actual mound sites where large skeletons were found. The reports by the agents detailed quite a few large skeletons without ever using the term "giant."

The first major report on the mound exploration project came in the *Fifth Annual Report of the Bureau of Ethnology* (Powell, 1887). Powell explained in the "Introduction" that three regular Field Agents had been utilized with three others occasionally serving as temporary assistants. The main paper in the volume was written by Cyrus Thomas, which was a compilation of the field notes sent to him by the agents. It is known that Thomas often used their notes verbatim in his reports (Jeter, 1990).

The title of Thomas' paper, 100 pages in length, was "Burial Mounds of the Northern Sections of the United States." Thomas, a former believer in the "lost race of mound-builders" idea, wrote in the conclusion of his report, "That there is nothing found in the mode of constructing these mounds, nor in the vestiges of art they contained, to indicate that their builders had reached a higher culture-status than that attained by some of the Indian tribes found occupying the country at the time of the first arrival by Europeans" (p. 108). He then concluded, "That all the mounds which have been examined and carefully studied are to be attributed to the indigenous tribes found inhabiting this region and their ancestors" (p. 109). Whether or not Thomas' conclusions were influenced by Powell isn't known, but it is likely that Powell's notions about the mound builders played some role. Despite this initial attempt to dispel the "lost race" idea as a myth, the Division's mound excavations continued.

Correspondence between Thomas and his agents shows that he was continually pushing them to move quickly from site to site. He was also increasingly interested in obtaining good specimens for display—primarily skulls and artifacts. His letters often threatened that obtaining the next month's pay was dependent on them performing adequately. He complained about incomplete and inaccurate reports and wanted "more and better artifacts" as well as "covering more territory in a shorter period of time" (Jeter, 1990:

Smithsonian Field Agent Edward Palmer shown in 1865. Source: National Anthropological Archives, Jeter (1990).

33). He hired and fired and rehired some of them because of various issues. Thomas also hired a cousin, John Rogan, as a Field Agent. Rogan resigned just before the project ended but was not thought to be a good excavator. Many letters sent by Thomas indicated that he was repeatedly unhappy with Rogan's artifacts and progress. Another agent, John Emmert, was considered to be an excellent worker who recovered many specimens to Thomas' liking. But Emmert was also fired for drunkenness and complaints about his behavior from the places where he stayed. Emmert was also rehired by Thomas and described as an uneducated man who had a good work ethic. One temporary agent who became a regular Field Agent was Gerard Fowke. Fowke was hired under various names including Charles Smith and Kentucky Q. Smith.

In their return correspondence to Thomas, the agents complained of poor weather, severe travel difficulties, and lack of payments owed to them. Sometimes they pleaded for another chance when they received letters that threatened to fire them. But it is clear that they moved quickly—very quickly. Over a 12-month period, Field Agent Edward Palmer excavated in 8 states while another agent, Col. P. Norris, excavated in 11 different states. The main mound exploration project was begun in July 1882 and ended June of 1890 (Jeter, 1990).

In an interesting side note, one agent, Edward Palmer, utilized an African American named H. J. Lewis to make drawings of sites in Arkansas. Lewis is widely cited as "the first Black political cartoonist," and he published drawings in several magazines and newspapers. Palmer met Lewis in Memphis in 1882 and hired him for several months. Cyrus Thomas sent a letter and even a follow-up telegram to Palmer ordering him to fire Lewis, allegedly because Thomas thought the drawings that Lewis made were inaccurate. In response, Palmer wrote to Thomas that he had discharged Lewis, but he secretly kept him on for a time afterward. One of Lewis' drawings is shown below (Jeter, 1990).

H. J. Lewis' (1883) drawing of excavation of Adams Mound in Arkansas. Edward Palmer wrote that he made a 6-foot cut into the side of the mound and a smaller cut on the top. He found nothing. Source: Smithsonian—National Anthropological Archives; Jeter (1990).

Below: Gerard Fowke, one of the Smithsonian Field Agents. Fowke continued to perform archaeological excavations until the 1930s. Credit: St. Louis branch of the Archaeological Institute of America.

Below: Rev. W. M. Beauchamp of Baldwinsville, NY. Beauchamp served as an assistant for the Smithsonian's Division of Mound Exploration during excavations in New York and nearby states. Photo: Find A Grave.com.

The "Final" Smithsonian Report on the Identity of the Mound Builders

In 1894 the Smithsonian released its *Twelfth Annual Report of the Bureau of Ethnology* (Powell, 1894). The thrust of the report was on the results and conclusions of the Bureau's mound explorations conducted from 1882 to 1891. The report was organized and written by Cyrus Thomas. The Preface was penned by Powell who explained that in 1882 "the Director organized a small division in the Bureau to which he assigned the work of investigating the mounds and other ancient monuments in the United States east of the Rocky Mountains" (19). Powell summarized the purpose succinctly, "The most important question to be settled is, 'Were the mounds built by the Indians?'" (21).

Stone vaults in Brenner Mounds (Missouri) excavated by the Smithsonian in 1906. Note the passageway in the top photo. Many people have seen the Smithsonian drawings depicting stone chambers and stone tombs inside mounds, but few people have seen photos of the actual design and layout of them. The top photo shows what was under a 4-foot-high, 38-foot-diameter earthen mound. The stone-lined vault was well designed and had an entranceway. The bottom photo was the stone chamber found under a 5-foot-high, 45-foot-diameter earthen mound. From: Fowke (1910).

BUREAU OF AMERICAN ETHNOLOGY

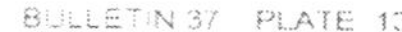

BULLETIN 37 PLATE 13

EAST WALL, DOORWAY, AND PASSAGE IN MOUND NO. 1

In the 1894 report, the Bureau revealed that it had obtained more than "40,000 specimens" and that "over 2,000 mounds" had been excavated (22-23). After detailing the results of the mound excavations in about 600 pages, Thomas gave the answer to the question about who built the mounds: "the author believes that the theory which attributes these works to the Indians ... to be the correct one" (610). That represented the official position of the Smithsonian and it remains the same today. To amplify this point, the 1986 book *The Smithsonian Book of North American Indians* (Kopper, 1986: 78) states this about Thomas' 1894 conclusion that Native American ancestors built the mounds: "This compendium settled the issue so far as science was concerned." Jeter (1990) wrote that the results of the Mound Survey "demolished the theory that a lost race of non-Indian Mound Builders" had existed and that "the myth was shattered; the mounds had been built by the ancestors of the historic eastern North American Indians" (3). American archaeology texts simply relate that the mounds (dating back to about 4000 B.C.) were built by the ancestors of modern Native Americans. As far as mainstream archaeology is concerned, the Smithsonian's 1894 answer is the final answer.

Giants? Tall People? Conspiracy?

The term "giant" isn't used in the 1894 Bureau of Ethnology report, nor was it used in the earlier 1887 report. The 1894 report did mention and summarily dismiss all the other theories that had been proposed to explain who built the mounds. It was a wide-ranging list of hypothetical places and people who were alleged to be the mound builders. The list included virtually every lost continent, every lost race, every seafaring culture, and every ancient culture that ever existed. All of these ideas were simply dismissed as totally and utterly wrong. But in their reports, Powell and Thomas didn't mention the alleged discovery of giant skeletons in mounds. That omission has become a controversial point today, at least within the non-professional archaeological community.

As previously mentioned, the 1894 and 1887 reports did detail the excavation and discovery of numerous "large" skeletons at many sites. The large skeletons that were listed in the earlier 1887 Bureau report were cited again in 1894. Sometimes the measurements of these were given, and sometimes not. It is clear that some of the old newspaper accounts issued on the discovery of "giants" in the mounds were generated through interviews of the local workers. But oddly, the Smithsonian remained silent on the reports of "giants" that had been swirling in the newspapers. Mainstream archaeologists scoff at the idea of a conspiracy to cover up the giants.

There Were Some Tall People Back Then Just As There Are Some Tall People Now

A couple years ago I asked an experienced, former excavation archaeologist who was visiting my home about the old reports of giant skeletons. He only laughed a bit. In response I pulled a book from my shelf written by archaeologist Don Dragoo (Dragoo, 1963). Dragoo excavated (obliterated) the Cresap Mound in West Virginia in 1958 for the Carnegie Museum. The excavation took place over 13 weeks and was done before a coal company built a factory by the site. Dragoo found 54 burials in the mound. One skeleton was measured at 7 feet 1 inch. In his book, Dragoo included both a drawing and photo of it and I showed them to my friend. Without a pause, the visiting archaeologist said, "there were some tall people back then just as there are some tall people now." Dragoo's tall skeleton is indeed impressive-looking but if you look at it statistically, out of the 54 burials he recovered, just one, or 1.8%, was 7 feet tall. So how many large skeletons, we might ask, were in the Smithsonian reports? We decided to determine that number because of an unusual report of giant skeletons found in Arkansas.

Stone vault in Keller Mound (Missouri) excavated by the Smithsonian in 1906. There were 18 mounds at the site and three were excavated. The walls of the chambers were described as "well laid up" (69), but previous looters had disturbed the graves found inside the tombs. Nothing was found except for scattered bones and some cremated remains. No large skeletons were reported by Fowke (1910) in his Missouri excavations.

b NORTH WALL, AND CLOSED DOORWAY IN SOUTH WALL, IN MOUND NO. 3

Chapter 5

Giants, Chickasawba Mound, Hoaxes, & the Smithsonian Skeletons

It is unrealistic to call a person measuring 7 feet tall a "giant" in the true sense of the word. Seven feet tall *is* unusually tall but certainly not a giant. On the other hand, in the 1,000+ old newspaper articles about giants, there were reports detailing skeletal remains 9 feet, 12 feet, and even taller.

In his 2014 book, *The Ancient Giants Who Ruled America*, journalist Richard Dewhurst wrote, "Typically, the height of Americans today ranges between five feet, four inches, and five feet, ten inches" (14). His reference for the statement comes from the published U.S. government National Health Statistics. It is true in a very limited way, but it does not give a good method by which to judge a "giant." It implies that anyone taller than 5' 10" is, well, rather tall, andmaybe even a giant. Andrew Collins and I are sadly both just under 5' 10".

Digging a bit deeper into the National Health Statistics shows that it is more accurate to say that about 67 percent (66.667% to be precise) of the American *male* population ranges from 5' 7' to 6' 1". Fully 95% of American males are between 5' 4" and 6' 4". Only 0.5% of men are taller than 6' 7". For those interested in the real statistics, the relevant and important number is what is termed the *standard deviation*. (With respect to the height of American men, the standard deviation is 3 inches.) Applying the standard deviation to men's mean (the arithmetic average) height only, what results is

that about 0.1% (one-tenth of one percent) of men are 6' 10" tall or more. A much, much smaller percentage of all people are 7 feet in height or more. The actual percentage is roughly 0.000007. If you multiply the current population of all humans (just over 7.3 billion) by 0.000007 you'll find that about 50,000 people are 7 feet tall or more. That is a lot of people, but it is just a small percentage of the entire population. In essence, for about every 146,000 people, there will be one person that is 7 feet tall or more. As my archaeologist friend related, there are tall people today, but the truth is that they are in a minutely small percentage.

The disorder *gigantism* is typically cited as a simple explanation of excessive height. It is often a genetic disorder that causes the pituitary to secrete too much growth hormone. A tumor in the pituitary is often the cause. But very, very few "tall" people have the disorder. In fact, genuine gigantism that results in excessive height is so rare that the National Institutes of Health have no incidence statistics for it. Remember that only one in 146,000 people is 7 feet tall or more, and very few of them actually have gigantism. In fact, in the entire medical history of the United States, about 100 cases in total have been documented (Skull Base Institute, 2013). However, it is notable that in 2014 a disorder related to gigantism was found in a large skeleton removed from an American mound (Bartelink, Willits, & Chelotti, 2014). A skeleton of a male (about 30 years in age) originally excavated in 1947 from the Blossom Mound in California was examined by a group of paleopathologists. The skull was enlarged and thick with excessive growth giving him the appearance of having a beaklike face. He also had an unusual growth of teeth in his middle, lower jaw area. He was 5' 10" in height, but the researchers related that the disease they found, acromegaly, usually results in a growth spurt around ages 30-40, an age the male never reached. Acromegaly is exceedingly rare (6 of every 100,000 people) and is caused by a pituitary tumor. This was the first and only report verifying a gigantism-like disease in a skeleton taken from an American mound.

Much more relevant to the discussion is the known height of Native Americans. Hudson (1976) remarked that tribes varied quite a bit in height and mentioned that many Southeast tribes were renown for having males well over 6 feet in height. Romain (2006) cited two studies of skeletons removed from mounds in Hopewell areas. He related that 5' 6" was the height of the typical Hopewell male (94). However, for our purposes, we should certainly accept that ancient skeletons from 6.5 feet and up were certainly tall people, especially for an era when it is known that humans were actually shorter than today.

From Chickasawba Mound to the Smithsonian Reports

In February 2014, Andrew Collins came to America for three weeks. Our main intention was to review material about the symbols of the death journey found on Mississippian artifacts—especially those that related to Orion and Cygnus. The symbols of the death journey will be discussed in detail later, but as we evaluated the research on them, we became sidetracked by the "giant" skeletons controversy.

Part of the research we were doing was carefully going through the Bureau of Ethnology reports and the reports of C. B. Moore because virtually all of the relevant symbols were detailed in those publications. As we began to investigate the symbols, time and time again, the reports of giant skeletons popped up. The giant skeletons and the artifacts with the symbols were found in mounds, sometimes in the same mound. One of those places was at a famous mound in Blytheville, Arkansas. The entire set of the symbolic images depicting the death journey to the Path of Souls was found on artifacts recovered from the Blytheville site. But a lot of "giant skeletons" were reportedly found at that same site.

We decided to do some site investigations, so we visited mounds in Tennessee, Alabama, Mississippi, Arkansas, and Oklahoma, including a few

mentioned in the "giant skeletons" newspaper accounts. We spoke at length with several state archaeologists. We subsequently decided to do a thorough investigation of the Bureau of Ethnology reports by carefully reading the entire volumes and noting all the large skeletons reported. Years ago I had started acquiring the massive books—not reprints but the originally published books. Included in the ones I have are both of the volumes reporting the Smithsonian's mound investigations. This made our task easier, but the books are now unfortunately falling apart. The reason we decided to complete this task is explained in the next section.

The Chickasawba Giants

Several years ago I read one newspaper account relating that in Blytheville, Arkansas, numerous "giant skeletons" had been excavated from and near the Chickasawba Mound. I was initially highly skeptical of the newspaper story, but because the mound had also yielded so many artifacts

Chickasawba Mound at Blytheville, Arkansas. Photo—Lora Little.

with the death journey symbols, the story about the giant skeletons also being found there became of interest. The most widely-reported article came from the *Idaho Daily Statesman* and was issued June 12, 1899. The article explained that the mound was named after Chief Chickasawba who died and was then buried at the foot of the ancient mound in 1865. At some point after the Chief's death, a group of people began digging in the mound and also in the associated village area around it. They supposedly recovered a skeleton 8 to 9 feet in length. The article reported that several similar skeletons were also found and that they were being kept in a local doctor's office. They were shown to an Editor of the Memphis newspaper, the *Daily Appeal*. The Idaho article related that it had been reprinted from the *Daily Appeal*. (I actually worked full-time at the same newspaper, now called the *Commercial Appeal*, for 9 years while I was an undergraduate and graduate student at what was then Memphis State University.)

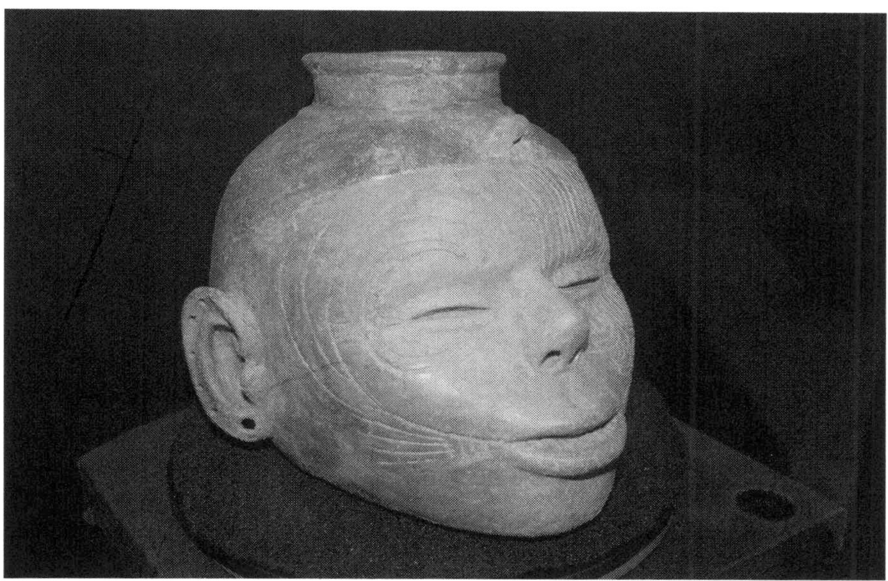

One of many "head effigy pots" from the Nodena site in Arkansas, not too far from Chickasawba. (Effigy shown is at the Hampson Museum in Wilson, Arkansas.) Descriptions of the pots essentially "looted" from Chickasawba reveal that many of the vessels recovered there were similar to Nodena-style pottery. Photo—Lora Little.

We decided that before going to the actual mound we would run down the "giant skeletons" story, so we started by perusing the microfiche of the *Memphis Daily Appeal* at the library. Initially we could not find the article but eventually Andrew found it. Andrew also found another version of the report in Philadelphia's *Daily Evening Telegraph* (September 15, 1870). Like the Idaho article reported, the Philadelphia article stated that one complete skeleton measuring 8 to 9 feet in height was found and that a local doctor showed the Memphis paper's Editor another thigh and shinbone that had also been found. The doctor "correctly joined the two bones together" and measured them at just over 5 feet. The doctor estimated that the individual had to stand somewhere between 9 and 10 feet tall. The articles led us to references to the City Editor of the *Memphis Daily Appeal*, Dr. Frank Lowber James, who left the newspaper in 1871 when he moved to Shawnee Village near Blytheville. There he practiced medicine and became quite well-known for his compounded medicines. Lowber moved to Osceola, Arkansas a couple years later and became the County Surveyor. Memphis State University Press published a book about him in 1977. James became intrigued with the Blytheville mound when he wrote the first newspaper article.

As County Surveyor, James produced a map of the northeast Arkansas area and watched the ongoing "looting" of the Chickasawba Mound area carefully. Thousands of exquisite pots were dug from the site and nearly all of them have long since disappeared into private collections. In addition, James supposedly kept the skeletons and huge skulls that had been pulled from the mound in his medical office. These details then led us to finding a copy of a long article about the Chickasawba site published in *The Arkansas Archaeologist* in 2009. The article was written by archaeologists Terry Childs and Charles McNutt. I was now even more intrigued, because Charles McNutt had been the Professor for two anthropology classes I took at Memphis State in 1969-70.

The article (McNutt & Childs, 2009) detailed Dr. James' involvement with the site and reprinted James' November 22, 1877 letter to the Smithsonian. In the letter, James wrote that "a spade can scarcely be thrust without turning up human remains, and those too of a most interesting and valuable character. Not only are these scattered bones in great quantity, but entire skeletons of gigantic size are frequently found. I have seen several over 7ft, 6in, in height" [*sic*] (33).

In a much-delayed response to James' letter, in the fall of 1881 Edward Palmer, one of the Smithsonian Field Agents previously mentioned, came to Chickasawba for one day. His notes about the visit are both brief and contradictory. He wrote that the owner of the site would not let him dig and added that nothing of importance had been found at the mound (Jeter, 1990: 129-130). But he also wrote that digging into the mound would essentially be too much work and cost too much (129). Palmer measured the mound and found it littered with potholes. He refused to pay locals to do any digging and subsequently went into the adjacent field alone and found a couple large sherds on the surface. The pottery pieces were striped red and white. Palmer then left. His report to the Smithsonian explained that he believed there was probably nothing of significance remaining at the site except for "hundreds of graves" (McNutt & Childs, 2009: 33). He was wrong.

For years, extending far into the late 1990s, people removed thousands of complete, decorated pottery pieces from the large site. In 1972 for example, the owner of the mound and field around it created a two-month "open season" allowing anyone to dig for pots. Up to 80 people were present every day digging (36). "Hundreds of pots were removed" and the "site resembled a bombed battlefield" (36). Adjacent to the mound was a large Indian cemetery that eroded into a nearby river. Many more skeletons were exposed until the river was altered and a road built on top of the cemetery area (Childs & McNutt, 2009). In their article, Childs & McNutt also mention that a 7-foot-tall skeleton was found in an area next to the site in 1976 (36). There wasn't a hint of skepticism in the article with respect to the large skeletons reportedly found there. The article simply provided these details as part of the history of the site.

After finding all these surprising details, in February 2014 we went to Chickasawba mound, mainly to get photos. We intended to move on to

Cahokia, Illinois after obtaining the pictures. As fate would have it, during that entire day a major ice storm hit, but we still hoped to make the trip to Cahokia. After we visited the mound in Blytheville, we drove north into Missouri, but traffic was slowing to a crawl as the ice storm intensified. So we turned back.

Andrew had seen a small bookstore in downtown Blytheville named, "That Bookstore in Blytheville," and he wanted to stop there and inquire about a museum. We entered the store and asked about the local museum and found out that it was closed for the day. The owner of the store, Chris Crawley, told us that he was on the Museum's Board and that he also knew the state archaeologists who were—at that moment—working in the nearby Arkansas Archaeological Survey Field Station not far from the mound. After a long discussion, he called them and arranged for us to visit. We followed Crawley through ice-covered streets until we came to the state building located by the old Eaker Air Force Base in Blytheville. Inside we met two state archaeologists. They were busily copying a long article to give us, which they told us explained everything that was known about the site. They were extremely informative and cordial. We were shown many shelves stuffed with boxes of artifacts and various photos from the area. In some areas pottery was being pieced together.

When we were handed the article, I saw that it was the report coauthored by McNutt, the one we had found a few days earlier. I asked one of the archaeologists, Michelle Rathgaber, if she knew about the old reports of "large" or "giant" skeletons recovered from the site. She looked a bit befuddled by the question and simply replied that she had never heard any such stories. So I took the paper they had just handed to us and mentioned that McNutt, one of its authors, had taught two of the classes I took at Memphis State. I then opened it to the section where the report discussed the large skeletons and showed it to her. She looked at it for a moment and said that she hadn't noticed that part of the article and had never heard about Dr. Frank Lauber James and the earlier work at the site.

When we returned to Memphis that night, Andrew and I decided that we had to look further into the mystery of the many old newspaper accounts about giants. We both had accepted that the Chickasawba report certainly had some validity. But we also suspected that some of the old newspaper reports might have been hoaxes. We found a hoax immediately.

The Tampa, Florida Giant Hoax

The first newspaper report we examined when we returned to Memphis was dated August 25, 1927 from the *Lawrence World Journal*. It was entitled simply "Giant Skeletons" with the location given as "Tampa, Fla." It had been sent out on the wires by the *Associated Press* (without a date) and was reprinted in many other newspapers. The article stated that on an island near Tampa, unusually large skeletons and skulls had been found, and they were described as "veritable giants." It concluded by relating that the bones were sent to the Smithsonian. We found an identical article about the same "giant skeletons" that had been published some four years *earlier* in 1922 in the St. Petersburg, Florida *Evening Independent*. The 1927 article simply reprinted the 1922 article as if it was current news.

A 1923 St. Petersburg newspaper article reported that the Smithsonian had followed up on the skeletons sent to them from Tampa and was currently excavating the site. Ultimately, we found that all of the articles were based on events that took place in 1922-24. The 1927 reprints were essentially fodder for newspapers needing a story that drew readers.

Oddly, an August 14, 1948 article in the St. Petersburg *Evening Independent* was entitled, "Safety Harbor 'First Settlers' Were Not Giants." It concerned an excavation in 1948 by Florida Park Service archaeologist John Griffin at the site where the alleged giants had been found. Griffin stated that the reports of giants in the Tampa Bay area mounds had "no basis in scientific fact."

The actual island referred to in the "veritable giants" newspaper articles is in Tampa Bay and is known today as Weedon Island. Until 1922 it was

inaccessible except by boat. In 1922 a wooden toll bridge was constructed from the mainland to the island. The island is dotted with shell mounds. In 1923 a land speculator named Eugene Elliott obtained the rights to the island from the Weedon family by promising them profits from the sale of the land to people who would want to build homes there. The Weedons never received anything from Elliott for their land. Elliott also managed the toll bridge and was paid in accordance with how many people crossed the bridge.

Elliott was initially unable to get any attention for the venture, and his land company began to fail. In 1923 Elliott concocted a scheme to garner headlines by claiming that giants were in the mounds. He managed to get local newspapers to write that giant skeletons were being found in the mounds on Weedon Island. He then sent the articles to the Smithsonian. The Smithsonian didn't respond. Then Elliott obtained various bones and artifacts and carefully buried them in one of the mounds. He called the reporters back and dug the artifacts out in front of them. The bones, subsequent

Above: Eugene Elliott.
Photo: www.tampapix.com

Above: Jesse W. Fewkes in 1919, Director of the American Bureau of Ethnology who investigated the Tampa mounds. Source: www.archive.org.

newspaper articles, and photographs were sent to the Smithsonian. It is also relevant to point out that Elliott took out a series of full-page ads in the same newspapers when they reported his discovery of giants.

Jesse W. Fewkes was then the Director of the Bureau of Ethnology. According to archaeological reports referenced below, Fewkes immediately recognized that the artifacts were fakes, but realized that many mounds there had not been previously investigated. In 1923 Fewkes went to Weedon Island and conducted excavations into several different mounds. He eventually pulled out 400 skeletons and thousands of pieces of pottery. Oddly, it isn't clear exactly when Fewkes became aware of the hoax. The 1924 Report of the Secretary of the Smithsonian was still touting Fewkes' work on the island in cooporation with Eugene Elliott. There was no mention of the hoax in the section about the Weedon Island excavations. In fact, it appears that the Smithsonian was quite pleased with the publicity and attention their work was receiving from the public.

1923 photo of the Smithsonian excavating at Weedon Island.
Their excavations often drew large crowds of spectators.
Source: Central Gulf Coast Archaeological Society.

According to Fewkes' subsequent report, not one of the 400 skeletons was a giant or was even large. As Fewkes was excavating on the island, the local newspapers ran articles as well as more full-page advertisements by Elliott's land company. The advertisements enticed people to "cross the bridge" to watch the Smithsonian excavate. Hundreds of people came to watch the famous "Smithsonian Excavations." *The Weedon Island Story*, published by Pinellas County (2005), relates that Elliott arranged to have some prospective buyers taken close to see the excavations as part of his sales pitch. He also offered his buyers an opportunity to dig for their own pottery. In 1925 Elliott began giving away pottery to his prospective buyers if they would just visit (University of South Florida, 2011). Fewkes left in 1924.

Elliott was unsuccessful in getting people to buy land, especially after his hoax was publically revealed. But it was the Prohibition Era, so Elliott converted Dr. Weedon's house into a speakeasy so that his prospects could drink and dance. It burned down. He rebuilt another speakeasy and opened it in 1926. But the Tampa area housing market suddenly collapsed and a never-solved murder occurred on the island at the same time—scaring away anyone who had any interest in building on the island. Then, in June 1926, Elliott was arrested for the murder of his wife, who had just filed for a divorce demanding 2 million dollars from him. The state dropped the charges when the only witness to the crime simply disappeared. Elliott left Tampa and died of cancer in 1945. Tampa historian Ray Arsenault wrote, "Elliott's crude hoax had led to the discovery of a major untapped archaeological site" (Hartzell, 2000). In truth, it was an easy task finding all these details; however, one of the big complications is that a lot of the old newspaper articles reprint stories that often happened years or sometimes decades earlier—issued as current news. It is important to note, though, that many of the actual newspaper accounts of large skeletons have credibility.

Stone vault excavated from Dawson Mounds located near Hartsburg, MO in 1906 by the Smithsonian. The site had 15 mounds, all of which were totally excavated. Inside virtually all of them were well-formed, large stone vaults with burials—but no large skeletons. From: Fowke (1910).

Below photo shows the chamber found inside Mound 9 at the Dawson Mounds. The slightly oblong stone chamber had outer measurements of 11.5 feet and 14 feet on the long sides. The ends were 6.5 feet and 7.5 feet. The walls were about 3 feet high with a top formed from carefully fitted stone slabs. The jumbled remains of 12 people were found inside. From: Fowke (1910).

Bureau of Ethnology's 12th and 5th Annual Reports: The Large Skeletons

It took me some time to carefully read the 742-page, oversized 12th volume, which was organized by mound excavations in different states. The 5th report has only 100 pages. It is impossible to calculate the total number of *all* skeletons that were actually removed in these operations because of several factors. One reason is that very often the Field Agents found huge masses of jumbled bones. In other cases they simply related that "many" or "numerous" skeletons were found or removed. Occasionally skeletons were measured but more often they were not. Sometimes they were said to be male, female, adolescent, a child, or an infant. When they found skeletons that were extraordinarily large, they cited them as "large" or "extremely large." In some cases they gave the measurements, but apparently only if they were impressed. They also related that many times the skeletons "crumbled" when exposed to air or handling. The crumbling of skeletal remains in mounds was also noted by Squier & Davis (1848: 288): "... the skeletons are almost invariably found at the base of the mounds, and in such

Example of a stone box grave excavated by Moore at Shallow Bluff Island, Tennessee. From Moore (1915).

a state of decay as to render all attempts to restore the skull, or indeed, any part of the skeleton, entirely hopeless. The crania, when not so much decomposed as to crumble to powder beneath the touch, are crushed ..."

Large Skeletons in the Smithsonian Bureau's 5th Annual Report (1887)

Wisconsin. A large mound in Sheboygan County yielded a "large" skeleton (19).

Illinois. At the Dunleath site near East Dubuque, a skeleton longer than 7 feet was found (35).

West Virginia. At the Smith farm in the Kanawha Valley, a "large skeleton" was recovered (52). At a lower level in the same mound, another skeleton, 7.5 feet in length, was found (52). Another mound (#7) in the same area yielded a 7-foot skeleton (56). Two "very large skeletons" were found in the Poor House or Institute Mound (57).

North Carolina. The Nelson Mound yielded a 7-foot-long skeleton (62). The Jones Mound, not too far from the Nelson, also yielded a "very large" skeleton (67).

Georgia. At the famous Etowah site, a 7-foot skeleton was excavated (98).

Large Skeletons in the Smithsonian Bureau's 12th Annual Report (1894)

Illinois. At Dunleith Mounds near East Dubuque, they reported "One of the largest skeletons found by the Bureau agents." It was measured at between 7 and 8 feet in length (113). The Welch Mounds in Pike County revealed two. One was "more than 7 feet long." Another was of "extraordinary size" (117).

Mississippi. In Union County at the Ingomar Mounds, a "large skeleton" was found (273).The femur measured 18.5 inches. My calculations based on anthropological tables showed that the individual was about 5' 10" in height (Bass, 1995).

Georgia. At Etowah, the 7-foot skeleton described in the earlier Bureau report was again cited (302).

North Carolina. At the Nelson Mound (as previously mentioned), an "unusually large size skeleton" over 7 feet in height was excavated (335). In the nearby Nelson Triangle, two skeletons of "large stature" were found (336). The "very large" skeleton found in the Jones Mound was again reported (340).

Tennessee. On Long Island in Roane County, a skeleton "7 feet 3 inches in length" was found (362).

Ohio. Stone graves near Ripley, Ohio yielded two "extremely large skulls" and "long femur bones" but no complete skeletons (453).The femurs were 22.5 inches in length. My calculations based on anthropological tables showed that the individuals were about 6' 5" in height (Bass, 1995). In Coshocton County, a stone box grave with a 7-foot-long skeleton was found (458).

Pennsylvania. The remains of one "large size adult" were found in McKees Rocks Mound (495).

West Virginia. By far the greatest concentration of large skeletons was in West Virginia, with most of them found in the Kanawha Valley near Charleston. A mound in the Spring Hill enclosure (numbered 11) yielded a 7-foot skeleton (419). In the Great Smith Mound at nearby Dunbar, a 7.5-foot skeleton was found buried below another "large skeleton" (426). "Two very large skeletons" were found in Mound 31 (Institute or Poor House Mound) in the same grouping as above (432). "Many large skeletons" (the actual number was not given) were found in rock mounds nearby (436). In the nearby McCulloch Mound was another "very large skeleton" (437). Another "very large skeleton" was excavated from Barboursville (440).

The Criel Mound in South Charleston, West Virginia. It is 33 feet high and has a diameter of 173 feet. A total of 13 skeletal remains were found by the Smithsonian. Its size and shape was nearly identical to the nearby Great Smith Mound. Photo—Lora Little.

Below: The Poor House or Institute Mound in Dunbar near South Charleston, West Virginia. It is 25 feet high. The Smithsonian found two "very large skeletons" in their 1884 excavation into the mound (numbered 31 on their map). Photo—Lora Little.

Illustration from Smithsonian (Thomas, 1887) showing the skeletons in excavated T. F. Nelson Mound In North Carolina. Number 16 on the right bottom side was at least 7 feet tall.

McKees Rocks Mound in 1896. One "large size adult" skeleton was found here by the Smithsonian. From Dragoo (1958).

Summary of Large Skeletons in Both Reports

Not double-counting the large skeletons excavated and discussed in both Annual Reports, 17 skeletons or portions of skeletons were reported by the Smithsonian that were probably approaching 7 feet or more in length. Then there is the one vague report in the Kanawha Valley of finding "many" large skeletons. For the sake of the record, it is possible that a few large skeletons were missed when I went through the books.

I also went through just the West Virginia section in the 12th Report and counted the total number of skeletons that were detailed there. The total number of skeletons excavated in West Virginia was 105, but I did not include the ones that gave no actual numbers. The 12th Bureau Report on West Virginia related that 7 of these were large skeletons (of the 105 total excavated), meaning that 6.7 percent of the remains were 7 feet tall or approaching it. That's actually quite impressive, especially since a lot of the other skeletal remains that were reported were children. Recall that only a tiny fraction of the present population of adult males are 7 feet tall. When women and children are added to the statistic, the percentage is exceedingly small. The actual percentage is about 0.000007—or one person in every 146,000. In total, the mounds in the Kanawha Valley alone yielded at least 6, seven-foot skeletons plus the "many" that were found in another mound there. It appears that at least in the case of Kanawha, there were quite a few tall people.

Even if all of the recovered "large" skeletons were only 6' 7", you would statistically expect only 0.5 percent of only males to be that large. That is, you would expect to find just one male skeleton 6' 7" tall out of every 200 male skeletons examined.

Did the Smithsonian's Number of Seven-Foot Skeletons Exceed What Might Be Expected?

The 17 seven-foot-tall (or extremely large) skeletons recovered by the Smithsonian's mound project may or may not seem impressive depending on whether you are a "skeptic"—using the more recent meaning of the term. A skeptic is traditionally thought of as a person who logically questions and doubts certain claims. But today, skeptics are more like true disbelievers. They tend to immediately dismiss and ridicule any claim that opposes what they consider to be their accepted beliefs.

In Chapter 4, Dragoo's excavations at the Cresap Mound were described. He found *only* one seven foot skeleton among the 54 total burials in the mound (which is 1.8% of the total). Skeptics would immediately say that it was "only one" and add of course, "there were some tall people back then just like there are tall people today." However, in the section just before this one, it was revealed that in the Kanawha Valley of West Virginia, 6.7 percent of the reported skeletons were 7-footers or close to it. In truth, both of these figures, the 1.8% and the 6.7%, are well beyond what would be expected. If modern data about height is applied to the Smithsonian's 17 reported 7-foot-tall skeletons, they would have had to excavate a total of 2.5 million

skeletons to find those 17. Remember that today only one of every 146,000 people reach that height.

While it is obvious to anyone who knows statistical procedures that the number of tall skeletons found by the Smithsonian in the Kanawha Valley mounds far exceeds what would be expected by chance, I ran a statistical evaluation called *Fisher's Exact Probability Test.* The test compared the actual findings from the Kanawha mounds (7 of 105 skeletons were 7 feet or approaching it) to what would be expected by chance (1 of 146,000). The not-surprising results showed that there is a statistically significant difference between the two and the probability that the results are due to chance variations is as close to zero as it gets. An additional statistical test (*Chi-Square* with correction for continuity) was also run with the same results: zero probability that the results are due to chance. What these results mean is that the simplistic statement, "there were some tall people then just as there are some tall people today," does not explain away the unexpected number of large skeletons found by the Smithsonian at Kanawha. There is something unknown and unexplained at work.

The implications of these many tall skeletons might—or might not—be profound. The fact that these tall skeletons were often found in prominent tombs within mounds implies that they were members of the elite. They may have been chiefs, great warriors, or priests of some kind. Clearly they were important people. While it is known that members of the elite were given special status burials—and these are the types of burials we would expect to find in important tombs—the high numbers of tall people in an ancient population is something that should not be expected. However, as we shall discuss, these exceedingly tall people seem to have been concentrated in only a few areas. For example, Clarence B. Moore, who will be discussed shortly, excavated several thousand mounds and detailed literally thousands of skeletons found in them. He did not find a single large skeleton—and he actually looked for them. But Moore did not excavate in West Virginia, Ohio, or in most of the other states where the Smithsonian found the 17 large skeletons they reported.

Chapter 6

Large American Skeletons: Measuring Errors, Mastodons, Hoaxes, or a Real Mystery?

I've been told by one archaeologist that, "back then they didn't know how to measure a skeleton." This is the most common argument made against the validity of so many reports of large skeletons. This assertion is probably a valid one in some cases. Clarence B. Moore found that lack of knowledge about skeletal anatomy frequently led to overestimations in height, especially with uneducated people. Even today, height is one of the most exaggerated physical attributes. For example, it's known that at least three-quarters of all college basketball players have their heights exaggerated (Rogner, 2012). In high schools, the exaggerations are even more prevalent. In the National Basketball Association, it's accepted that at least half of the players who have been billed as 7 feet tall are not actually that tall (Diamond, 2012). However, it is likely that the Smithsonian's field agents and Dragoo neither measured incorrectly nor exaggerated. But some of the most vocal skeptics insist that *all* of the old newspaper reports about large skeletons are false.

In a sweeping dismissal of all the old newspaper accounts about large and "giant" skeletons, skeptic Jason Colavito wrote, "These reports have several sources, ranging from misidentified mastodon and mammoth bones to outright hoaxes" (2013a). Despite making the claim, Colavito fails to provide a single example where a mastodon bone was the source of an American "giant skeleton" newspaper article. And he fails to provide any examples of relevant hoaxes. He then accuses the proponents of using what

he calls "backward logic" in assuming that the old newspaper reports are true. Oddly, his logic that *all* of the reports are untrue is essentially the same type of reasoning. But if even *one* of the reports is true, then Colavito's sweeping assertion is wrong. Of course, there are many of the old newspaper reports that were accurately written. The following paragraph mentions just a few:

One of the "old" accurate newspaper accounts was published by the *Banner* (Athens, Georgia) on May 6, 1884. It detailed the removal of a 7' 2" skeleton from a mound at Etowah, which was excavated by the Smithsonian and cited later in their Annual Reports. Another newspaper article (*Charleston Daily Mail*, April 5, 1952) reprinted an earlier published account of one of the laborers who assisted in the Smithsonian excavations in West Virginia where several large skeletons over 7 feet tall were excavated. A *New York Times* article published on November 20, 1883 recounted the discovery of a 7-foot-long skeleton dug from a West Virginia mound by Col. Norris of the Smithsonian. In addition, let's not forget the several newspaper articles on the Chickasawba skeletons. There are other newspaper accounts that are true, of course, but the point is that the sweeping dismissal of *all* these reports is false and misleading.

Colavito is one of the most active online skeptics who consistently supports mainstream archaeology beliefs. He has no advanced degrees in

A GIANT'S REMAINS IN A MOUND

From the Charleston (West Va.) Call.

Prof. Norris, the ethnologist, who has been examining the mounds in this section of West Virginia for several months, the other day opened a big mound on Col. B. H. Smith's farm, six or eight miles below here. This is the largest mound in the valley and proved a rich store-house. The mound is 50 feet high and they dug down to the bottom. It was evidently the burial place of a noted chief, who had been interred with unusual honors. At the bottom they found the bones of a human being measuring 7 feet in length and 19 inches across the shoulders. He was lying flat, and at either side, lying at an angle of about 45 degrees, with their feet pointed toward the chief, were other men, on the one side two and on the other three. At the head of the chief lay another man, with his hands extended before him, and bearing two bracelets of copper. On each side of the chief's wrists were six copper bracelets, while a looking-glass of mica lay at his shoulder and a gorget of copper rested on his breast. Four copper bracelets were under his head, with an arrow in the centre. A house 12 feet in diameter and 10 feet high, with a ridge pole 1 foot in diameter, had been erected over them, and the whole covered by dirt that formed the mound. Each of the men buried there had been enclosed in a bark coffin.

Accurate *New York Times* article from November 20, 1883.

archaeology and says he has a "day job." He claims that he is an editor. He is a self-published author who has recently written a book about *Cthulhu*—a bizarre octopus-like creature invented by H. P. Lovecraft. In his actual description of the book on his website, Colavito makes the preposterous and utterly absurd claim that, "Ancient myths, once dismissed as fantasies, can now be seen in their true light—as a record of the coming of Cthulhu and his reign on the early Earth" (Colavito, 2014).

The above paragraph is accurate—in a very biased way—but it is highly misleading. Colavito has a bachelor's degree and "one" of his majors, he says, was anthropology. The statement relating that he has no advanced degrees is an *ad hominem* attack. It seeks to reduce his credibility. In reality, the presence or absence of a degree in something does not make a person's beliefs true or untrue. So too is the mention of his "day job," which apparently is unrelated to archaeology. It is mentioned here because skeptics often describe those they intend to ridicule by their "day-job." The implication is that the person is unqualified. The statement that he is a "self-published author" is also an *ad hominem* attack designed to denigrate him as a writer. He has several books that have been issued by other publishers, but the business of publishing has dramatically changed. Not too many years ago, calling someone a "self-published author" was a tactic employed to ridicule the person and dismiss the individual's ideas. But again, it has no bearing on the truth of the ideas proposed. Finally, the sentence related to his book on Cthulhu applied the words "preposterous and utterly absurd" to what he presents. It is an appeal to ridicule, intended to give the impression that not only are his ideas about Cthulhu absurd, but it implies that many of his other ideas might be just as absurd. The book is partly a satire on the Ancient Aliens phenomenon. I'll add that I often agree with a great deal of what he says on his blogs. However, the major point being made here is that many skeptics utilize these same ploys.

One common strategy used by skeptics is to dismiss the actual reports by somehow ridiculing and belittling the people involved. In a dismissal of the giant reports from the 1800s, Colavito (2013b) wrote, "The Victorians,

for example, were not aware of modern paleopathology, which has studied how bones change in various environments."

I'm clueless as to why the term "Victorians" was important to use. The term typically describes people living during the era in British history covering the time from 1837-1901. Is Colavito asserting that in 1902 anthropologists suddenly became aware of modern paleopathology? Or is it an *ad hominem* attack implying that the people involved were "old fashioned" or ignorant?

With respect to skeletal remains buried in mounds, Colavito explains how modern paleopathology can explain the giant bone reports: "Standard texts on pathology state that the repeated freezing and thawing of the water 'will produce expansion by ice crystal formation.' This can make the bones appear larger..." (Colavito, 2013b). He continues by adding that the increase in bone size would be "enough to turn a slightly above average body into a gigantic one."

That is an astonishing assertion: a slightly above average body can turn into a gigantic one through freezing and thawing! Is it true?

Colavito links to a book on Google for this rather intriguing bit of information (Aufderheide & Rodriguez-Martin, 1998: 16). However, the actual text he links to relates that water accumulating in a bone followed by "subsequent freezing will produce expansion by ice crystal formation to a degree that will fragment the bone structure." The text continues, "Freeze-thaw conditions may shatter a buried bone" (16).

The assertion that the bones will "appear larger" as Colavito states, simply isn't in the book he cites as his proof. Instead of just becoming bigger and bigger and bigger as they freeze, as Colavito appears to be asserting, they actually shatter. How he concluded that buried bones can become "gigantic" is mystifying. Even more relevant to this dismissal of skeletons supposedly becoming larger over time is an interesting piece in the May/June 2014 issue of *Archaeology* (Sharpe, 2014). The article begins with, "Just like the bones of living people with osteoporosis, human remains in the archaeological record can lose bone mass over time" (12). In brief, the argument that bones get "bigger" over time simply isn't the case. Based on the reference he cited, it seems that it is really Colavito who is not aware of modern paleopathology.

One of the main proponents of the "giant skeleton" reports is Jim Vieira. Vieira became interested in the topic while researching stone chambers in New England. He gave many public presentations on the subject and began a Facebook page where he posted an old newspaper article each day. I became aware of many of the old reports from Vieira's postings. In a Facebook reply to attacks from skeptics, Vieira wrote, "My goal in all of this was to simply make the case that there is enough evidence to warrant further investigation of this controversial topic... There is nothing wrong with asking questions, simple as that." Vieira has never asserted that *all* of the old reports were true. He simply presented the reports on his popular Facebook page, one by one.

Colavito also claims that when the old newspaper articles came out, some people had actually found mastodon and mammoth bones and thought they were human (Colavito, 2013a). He might be right in a few cases, but as mentioned previously, he doesn't cite a single example from the American newspaper articles—he just says it is so. And my review of these old reports didn't turn up a single case of mastodon bones. Paradoxically, he cites books written during the Victorian era claiming that many of the classical stories from Europe about giants could have been the result of people finding mastodon or mammoth bones and thinking they were human (Colavito, 2012). So he seems to be saying something completely contradictory: that the Victorians knew about mastodon bones—but they often mistook mastodon bones for human bones!

Mastodon remains were first reported in America in 1705 in New York's Hudson River Valley, and they were indeed thought by the discoverers to be remains from giants. By the 1760s it was shown that they were from animals thought to be extinct. Well before the Victorian era even began, the huge mastodon and mammoth bones were widely accepted to be from animals. In 1803 Thomas Jefferson instructed Lewis and Clark to look for the animals on their famed expedition, because Jefferson hoped that a few of them might

have survived. In 1807 Jefferson financed a hunt for mastodon and mammoth bones at the Big Bone Lick Site in Kentucky (National Park Service; Oregon History Project). In the 1800s, basic knowledge about mastodon and mammoth bones became almost common in America. Murray (1908: 17-19) cites examples of mammoth bone discoveries in 1782, 1788, 1799, 1843, 1855, and 1872 along the Susquehanna River, none of which were initially touted as giants.

It is a certainty that mastodon bones do not account for the large human skeletons found by the Smithsonian's Field Agents, Dragoo at the Cresap Mound,or at the Chickaswaba Mound, as well as some others. Nor is it likely that medical doctors involved with a few other reported cases would make that mistake. Ridicule and simplistic, misleading explanations made by skeptics to dismiss *all* the claims of very tall people is just that—misleading.

It is quite likely that most, if not all, of the large skeletons reported by the Smithsonian Field Agents were measured accurately. But measuring errors most certainly did occur when people unfamiliar with anatomy accidentally found skeletal remains—or when scattered bones were encountered. We will probably never be able to make a final conclusion on most of the old newspaper reports of giant bones. However mainstream archaeology does come down on Colavito's side. A recent article about the reported "giants" quoted a Smithsonian physical anthropologist, who related that people

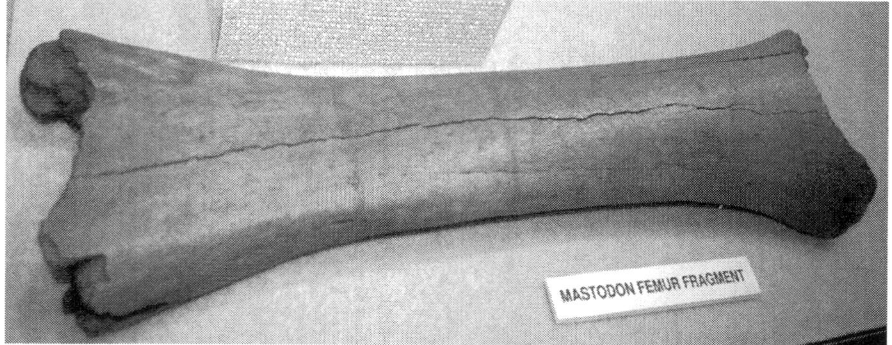

In the 1800s, many Americans, and almost all educated people, were aware of mastodon and mammoth bones. A mastodon femur found near the Nodena Site at Wilson, Arkansas is displayed in the Hampson Museum. Photo—Lora Little.

unfamiliar with human anatomy don't understand how bones connect, leading to overestimated sizes. The article simply concluded that, "there was no prehistoric race of giants" (*Science News*, 2012). I would agree with that—to a point—but it is another sweeping dismissal. In ancient America, there isn't any solid evidence of actual giants, but there were a lot of tall people—far more than should be expected. But many of the actual "giant" newspaper reports—skeletons 10 feet and up—do seem to evaporate when they are scrutinized.

Evaluating a Few Giant Reports From Newspapers & The Internet

With respect to a lot of the other old reports of what we might call real giants, skeletons 10 feet tall and higher, I have run down many of them. A lot of the reports, like the "Ten Foot Giant" of Winona County, Minnesota do exist in the sense that it was written down and put in a book. The Winona Giant, as Dewhurst (2014) calls it, comes from an 1883 book entitled *The History of Winona County*. The book (and many other local history books like it) is available for viewing online (www.archive.org). The Preface in the Winona book explains that a collection of stories was gathered from interviews, recollections of stories from "old pioneers," extracts of files and papers, and "other such sources." There is no author listed, but 8 resource people are cited in the Preface. The Preface cautions that the failing memories of some people have certainly caused some errors but they wanted to present the history as told to them. The first page of the text states that absolutely "nothing is known about the Indians or Mound Builders." With that as a starting point in the 1883 book, many readers can guess where this is leading.

On page 564, the book discusses the town of Dresbach and says that there are mounds in it. It then continues: "while some men were digging in Mineral Bluff, one hundred and fifty feet above the river, a skeleton of unusual size was unearthed. On measuring, the giant skeleton was found to be ten feet in length... another skeleton, nine feet long, was found in the village of

Dresbach, while some were digging a road or trench." Such reports are impossible to evaluate for reasons that should be obvious. But the term "some men" indicates that the person telling the story had sketchy details. The statement "digging a road or a trench" means the same thing. It is a dead end. People can choose to accept it as factual or not. Skeptics will scoff at it and others will believe.

Another report that "vanishes" when scrutinized is one that is often begun with the title: "It is unknown why scientists have remained silent about the discovery of 18 giant human skeletons" found in a Wisconsin mound in 1912. The internet articles on this case assert that Beloit College supervised the excavation and that skeletons 7.5 to 10 feet tall were found and reported. The widely-cited internet article relies on a brief *New York Times* story published May 4, 1912.

The actual *Times* article does not claim that Beloit College supervised the excavation nor that the skeletons were 7.5 feet to 10 feet tall. The article stated that a couple brothers dug into a mound on a farm and found big skeletons. The story was also secondhand, told to a *Times* writer by a traveler from Wisconsin. Beloit College excavated and restored some mounds on its campus, and reported no skeletons at all. It seems to be a jumbled story. The Beloit College website has a large article posted about their work on campus mounds—but no skeletons were found.

Still another "giant" report circulated on the internet touts an 8-foot skeleton found in 1822 in Bradford County, Pennsylvania. My mother's parents were born and lived there on a farm, and I grew up in the area. The internet asserts that, "men digging a cellar" hit a stone grave and found "a skeleton, measuring, as it lay, eight feet two inches in length (this measurement was made by Dr. Williams, late of Troy, now deceased)."

The book, *History of Bradford County, Pennsylvania* (1878—no author listed) was the cited source of the article with no page numbers listed. The book is available online (www.archive.org). On pages 291-292, one significant difference between what the internet "quotes" from it and what is actually written in the book is revealed. The sentence relating that a "Dr.

Willams" measured the skeleton simply isn't there. It is likely that having a doctor measure the skeleton gives it more credibility than just saying "men digging a cellar" found it.

Several other newspaper reports of giants more than 10 feet tall simply went nowhere when followed up. When the actual archaeological report about some finds was found and examined, there was nothing in the report verifying the newspaper account. Most of the more fantastic claims were reported to newspapers by someone who had "heard about the discovery." Almost all of these reports were attributed to unknown workers, diggers, or some men. We followed up on a couple of widely-cited newspaper reports about giants and continued looking through the same paper for weeks after the original article was published. What we found in one case was that about a week later, another article came out saying the prior story about giants wasn't true. Some of the newspaper articles were factual accounts of excavations by the Smithsonian or other professionals, but none of them cited any skeleton much over 7 feet in length.

There is another rather amazing newspaper report on giants that became intriguing—to a point. The most cited article about it was supposedly published by the *St. Joseph Herald* (Michigan) on September 9, 1880. On the internet and in some books, it is touted as "Giant Skeletons from Serpent Mound." Serpent Mound is in the Brush Creek, Ohio area, but the mound mentioned in the actual article is unrelated to Serpent Mound and is on a farm about a mile away. I'm not sure why someone decided to link it to Serpent Mound. The newspaper article reported that a mound had been opened in Brush Creek, Ohio under the supervision of Dr. J. F. Everhart. A total of 11 skeletons measuring between 7 feet and 10 feet tall were excavated along with an engraved tablet. A search for the newspaper article revealed it had actually been published on September 4, 1880. The article cited the *Kansas City Review of Science* as its source. A search (www.online.org) turned up the article from that publication (Case, 1881). On pages 149-150 the full article appears. In essence, it basically *confirmed* the *entire* newspaper account of the discovery of the 11 large skeletons and the tablet. In the *Kansas*

City Review of Science, the tablet was said to be Greek and the giants were described as "sun worshippers" (150). Somewhat amazingly, an abbreviated form of the same report confirming the giant skeletons was published by the *Scientific American* on August 14, 1880 (106). In his book *This Land* (2009), Wayne May found a signed document about the mound excavation and giant skeletons in the Muskingum County Township files. Six names appear on the document's signature line, but Everhart's name isn't one of them. However, Dr. Everhart is cited as the author of the document. It repeated the story about the giant skeletons and tablet and also revealed that 7 of the skeletons were badly burned.

Still more digging into the story turned up a curious letter from Dr. Everhart that was published in the *Proceedings of the Numismatic and Antiquarian Society of Philadelphia* (1881 volume) dated November 4 (17-18). In the letter, the "tablet" was described as an 18-pound, unpolished, red sandstone piece, 12 inches long, 11 inches wide, and 4 inches thick. There were two "sharp and distinct" lines inscribed on it. Strangely, Everhart's letter stated that "he was not personally present when it was found" (18). The society determined that the "tablet" was a historic inscription made by French missionaries. As to the skeletons, Everhart's letter only stated that there were "some human bones" found scattered in the mound and that a "female skeleton and child's skeleton" were found. No sizes of the skeletons were listed at all. Whether or not Everhart was present when the bones were found wasn't mentioned. There the trail ended.

In various books and websites, a host of photos of large skeletons allegedly excavated at Serpent Mound are shown. In addition, books and websites often use photos of skeletons to enhance articles and stories. I have run down the source of many of these, and they have been copied from various books from the 1800s. Several Serpent Mound "giant" photos actually come from Ohio excavations at Chillicothe, and they are described as normal-sized skeletons in their original source. The conical burial mounds adjacent to Serpent Mound were excavated by Frederic Ward Putnam for Harvard's Peabody Museum in 1887. A lot of skeletons were found, but only one approached 6 feet in length (Randall, 1905). The jumbling presentation of unreferenced and wrongly-labeled photos is a perplexing issue that proponents of the giant skeletons should somehow address if they want to be taken seriously.

What does all of this mean? Honestly, I don't know. A skeptic would immediately dismiss it all as rubbish. A believer in the giant skeletons will immediately accept it as evidence. To me it's interesting, but it clearly shows why archaeologists fully document excavations and don't trust amateurs. In essence, perhaps the best conclusion to reach is that there isn't much evidence to substantiate the skeletons typically described as "giants." But there is solid evidence, from archaeology itself, that there were a lot of people who were 7 feet tall in ancient America. The numbers of these exceptionally tall people were far higher than one would expect. But they seem to have been concentrated in the West Virginia area.

The large skeletons recovered by the Smithsonian in the Kanawha Valley appeared to impress Cyrus Thomas. In the May 23, 1884 issue of *Science*, Thomas published an article specifically detailing the large skeletons recovered from the Great Smith Mound. More than 12 feet down from the mound's surface, a stone vault 7 x 4 feet was found. Inside the vault was a large skeleton—but its skull was missing. Only a spear was found with this skeleton. About 20 feet down from the surface, another large, timber-formed tomb 12 feet square and 7 to 8 feet high was found. In the middle of the vault, an unusually large skeleton was found, "measuring 7 feet six inches in length, and nineteen inches between the shoulder sockets" (619). It was surrounded by 8 other skeletons. The large skeleton was on its back and wrapped in bark and textiles. It had six large and heavy copper bracelets on each wrist and another four bracelets under the head. A copper gorget was on the chest. In each hand were three black, flint spear points with many others spread around the skeleton. Two large, hematite celts were found by the right hand, and three large, mica plates were near the shoulder. Small shells and numerous beads were located under the remains. The Kanawha mounds were excavated by Col. Philetus Norris, who rose to the rank of

Smithsonian map of mounds and earthworks in the Kanawha Valley area of Charleston, South Charleston, and Mound, West Virginia (Powell, 1887). In the Great Smith Mound two skeletons over 7 feet in length were found. Mound #7 was also excavated revealing a 7-foot skeleton. In Mound #31, called the Institute or Poor House Mound, two large skeletons were found.

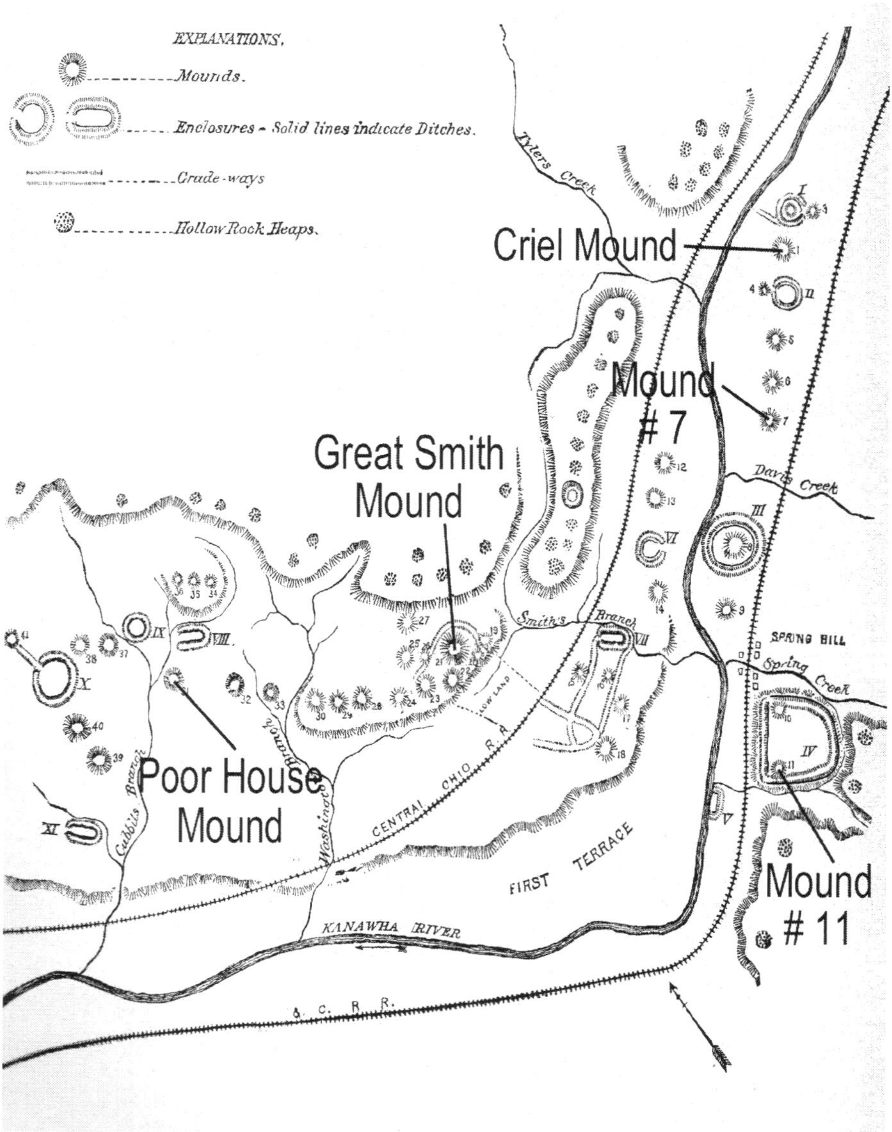

Colonel during the Civil War. Norris became a member of the Ohio state legislature and became the Superintendent of Yellowstone National Park in 1877. Norris excavated in West Virginia in 1883 and 1884 and died in 1885 of a heart attack while working for Smithsonian in Kentucky. The Great Smith Mound was completely destroyed, but the burials seem to be very similar to those found in the Criel Mound (schematic shown on next page).

In April 2014, my wife and I went to the Criel Mound with Brent and Joan Raynes. At the local museum we viewed "pictures" of a lot of the artifacts recovered from the mound by the Smithsonian. A local photographer had gone to the Smithsonian and was allowed to photograph some of the artifacts so that the artifact *photos* could be displayed. We were told that the Smithsonian refused to allow even a single artifact to go to the South

Col. Philetus W. Norris *circa* 1864: National Park Service photo.

Charleston Museum devoted to the mound for display there. Perhaps the most curious fact found on that visit was that neither the display at the Criel Mound nor the museum had any information on the size of the skeletons found in the local mounds. We picked up several brochures at the museum, all of which highlighted the area mounds. All of them mentioned that skeletons were excavated there, but there was no mention of the sizes of them.

"Spreading" and Archaeology's Disdain for Large Skeletons

The "spreading" of skeletal remains is a way some skeptics have tried to explain away the Smithsonian's large skeletons as well as other reports of giant skeletons. McMichael & Mairs (1969) excavated the Murad Mound in 1962 and 1963, which is located near St. Albans in the Kanawha Valley. Their paper also discussed the Smithsonian's earlier excavations at nearby

Display at Criel Mound shows the unusual arrangement of the skeletons found during Col. Norris's excavation. Photo—Lora Little.

sites. Several tombs were found in the Murad Mound along with some artifacts. In one tomb a skeleton was found measuring "6 feet 4 inches long by 16 inches wide in situ" (9). The authors asserted that earth pressures had "probably" spread the bones. Spreading is caused when tombs collapse and earth and stone falls on unattached bones of a skeleton causing them to gradually push apart from pressure. It doesn't always happen, but with collapsed tombs and when skeletons are buried in earth, it can occur. Using a tibia from the skeleton they calculated that the individual was probably 5 foot 10 or 11 inches tall. It was a 6 percent reduction. Another skeleton found in a tomb was measured at "6 feet 1 inch" (20). The authors wrote, "much spreading had probably occurred" (20) so they estimated that the actual height of the person was "5 feet 6 and a half inches tall" (a 9 percent reduction).

In their discussion, McMichael and Mairs describe searching the records of the Smithsonian and the National Museum for artifacts and information on the Kanawha excavations conducted in the 1800s. They related that there was so little detail and provenence made on artifacts and excavations that "it is impossible to make sense of the information" (39). They also mention the 7-foot skeleton removed from Mound 11 in the Spring Hill enclosure and called it "a supposed 7 foot long skeleton" (33).

Making the questionable assumption that the 7 large (7+ foot) skeletons recovered by the Smithsonian in the Kanawha area were all "larger" due to spreading, I reduced their height by 7.5 percent, meaning that they were about 6 feet 5.5 inches tall. I then recalcuated Fisher's Exact Probability test and a Chi-squared analysis based on the standardized population figures mentioned earlier. This assumes that all the skeletons reported by the Smithsonian were male—which, of course, there were not. Both results showed statistical significance at the probability = .01 level. In summary, the number of exceptionally tall skeletons found by the Smithsonian in the Kanawha area (even if they were all subject to spreading) exceeds what would be expected by chance.

Conclusion on America's "Giants"

In sum, there actually is a mystery here. It is not as spectacular as many might claim, but it is a mystery nonetheless. There were some hoaxes and a lot of exaggerations in some newspaper accounts, especially from the laborers who helped at excavations and from newspapers eager to gain readers. There are also a lot of reports that are essentially impossible to verify. But the fact remains that quite a few unusually tall skeletal remains were found in mounds and detailed in formal reports. The numbers of these far exceed what would be expected in a population where height fits a normal distribution. In order for the Smithsonian's 17 tall skeletons to fit what would be expected by chance—in a normal height distribution—they would have to excavate 2.5 million skeletons. These were not giants, but they were exceedingly tall. If you have ever stood next to a person 7 feet tall or more, it's easy to understand why someone might call them giants. In fact, as will be explained later, American academic archaeologists have recently published articles calling skeletons less than 6 feet tall, "giants."

We know too that the Native Americans had legends telling of giants and that these tales were believed by them to be literally true. We also know that de Soto and other explorers encountered several tall people. Tall people, it seems, tended to rule. Despite my friend's statement that, "there were some tall people back then as there are now," there certainly seems to have been a somewhat higher percentage of them "back then." And they appear to have been important enough to have their remains buried in prominent tombs in mounds. They were the elite—the people whom we now know exerted a great deal of social control over the mound-builder cultures. This elite group appears to have exerted their control through secret knowledge shown in specific symbols which magically helped to control the death journey to the Path of Souls.

Chapter 7

Symbols From the Mounds

Until the mid 2000s, if you asked archaeologists and museum staff what the "eye in hand" symbol meant, you'd hear something like, "It's a universal symbol." Even in 2014, during our visit to Spiro Mounds in Oklahoma, the site archaeologist used those very words to explain the meaning of the "eye in hand" to us when we asked about the symbol on one of the displayed artifacts in the museum. (He does not accept the more recent interpretation by other archaeologists.) But archaeologists have been studying the issue and have come to some amazing conclusions.

Archaeologist Kent Reilly has been interested in the symbols for decades. When asked about the first time he saw the symbols, Reilly stated in an interview, "I looked at all the artifacts in the museum and wanted to know what they mean, and nobody could tell me" (Friou, 2008: 44-45). Reilly is now a Texas State University archaeologist who was one of the key people who eventually unraveled the symbols' meanings. When I was writing the *Illustrated Encyclopedia of Native American Mounds and Earthworks* in 2005 to 2008 (Little, 2009), I had become aware of several possible interpretations of the symbols, but didn't have the time to really look carefully at what the archaeologists were then proposing. The underlying meaning of all of these symbols has now been deciphered. It is one of the most incredible, solved mysteries in all of American archaeology, and it actually tells us a great deal about other mysteries in the world.

The Eye In Hand—The Rattlesnake Disk & Giants

No one knows for certain when the famous "Rattlesnake Disk" was found in Moundville, Alabama, but its discovery was an important link in a chain of events leading to an understanding of what it depicts. Sometime around 1865, a farmhand—thought to be an African American worker—was walking behind a mule-pulled plow. It was in the small town of Carthage, Alabama, which is today in Moundville, Alabama. The plow hit a stone, lifting it out of the ground. When the stone was brushed off, it was a finely-polished stone disk, 12.5 inches in diameter. Around the outer edge, at regularly-

The famous "Rattlesnake Disk" showing "eye in hand" from Moundville, Alabama. Credit: Jeffrey Reed, Wikipedia Commons.

spaced intervals, were 17 small, carved indentations. On one side of the disk there were circular lines etched into the surface. But the other side revealed a mystery. Carved into the stone surface were two intertwined rattlesnakes curving around the outer edges of the disk. In the center was a carving of a hand with what appeared to be an eye in the palm. The farmhand gave the stone to the landowner who put it on a mantle, where he showed it to a steady stream of gawking visitors.

In 1873 a geology professor at the University of Alabama, Eugene Smith, dropped by the farmer's house and asked to see the disk. Smith had also been appointed the Alabama State Geologist that year and had begun trips around the state surveying sites and gathering artifacts. While showing Smith his prize, the farmer asked Smith about the many newspaper reports of giant skeletons being excavated from mounds around the country. At that time, of course, people were excited about the possibility that an exterminated race of giants had built the mounds, something that newspapers routinely touted. It is not known exactly how Smith answered, but he supposedly told the farmer that the U.S. Congress was providing funds to "settle the matter of the mounds" (Blitz, 2008). He convinced the farmer that allowing his disk to be examined would help, and Smith was allowed to take it. Not long after, the disk was sent to the Smithsonian where it was put on display. Oddly it was initially thought to be a fake artifact.

As many people who follow American archaeology know, artifacts that are not "discovered" by archaeologists are always suspected of being fakes. And artifacts that have unusual aspects such as unrecognized symbols or "writing" of some kind etched into them are typically branded as frauds. In truth, at the time there were a lot of frauds and fakes presented as genuine.

The Rattlesnake Disk was discussed in the *Second Annual Report of Bureau of Ethnology* (1880-81). In a section discussing it, geologist William H. Holmes concluded that it could be a hoax, writing, "There is not sufficient assurance of its genuineness..." (278). In 1890, after numerous other artifacts showing similar snakes and the "eye in hand" had been excavated from many

different sites, Gates Thruston wrote that it was "a genuine artifact" (Thruston, 1890: 334). The Bureau of Ethnology immediately changed its opinion on the disk officially accepting that it was genuine. Another "eye in hand" symbol on a stone disk from Moundville is the *Willoughby Disk*, named for the person who first made a sketch of it. Among its images are two "eye in hand" symbols and two skulls twisted together.

The Willoughby Disk from Moundville, Alabama. It displays two "twisted skulls" and two "eye in hand" symbols along with other symbols of the Southeastern Ceremonial Complex. Photo—Lora Little.

Clarence B. Moore: The Most Prolific Mound Excavator

It was in 1873 when one of the most lauded and criticized figures in American archaeology first dug into mounds. At the age of 21, Clarence Bloomfield Moore dug up a few artifacts and skeletal remains from a couple of shell mounds near Palatka, Florida. C. B. Moore, as he is commonly called, was the son of a wealthy paper company owner in Philadelphia, PA.

His mother, Clara Jessup Bloomfield Moore, was a famous author who wrote books on "manners" for women, usually under a pseudonym. She was also a major supporter of the work of John Keely, a Philadelphia inventor who made numerous vibrational machines using what he called "etheric forces." Clara wrote many articles and a biography on Keely, and gave him $100,000 to support his ongoing research projects along with a monthly salary of $250 (which would be $5,400 a month today). She later increased Keely's monthly stipend to an astonishing $2,000 (Fowler & Wilcox, 2003).

C. B. Moore did not support Keely's projects and considered him to be a fraud, and Moore clashed with his mother frequently. The family's

John Keely in his Philadelphia laboratory with his "vibrodyne"—*circa* 1881. Photo in the Edgerton Sykes special library collection in Virginia Beach, VA.

disagreement over Keely was the major factor leading to an estrangement between C. B. and his mother. Keely died in 1898 and Moore's mother died in early 1899. Moore was so incensed by his mother's involvement with Keely that after her death, he had his friend, Dr. Milo Miller, dismantle Keely's entire work building to search for hidden pipes Moore suspected that Keeley had used to run his machines (Fowler & Wilcox, 2003). Keely is generally considered today to have been a fraud.

C. B. Moore graduated from Harvard in 1873 and visited Florida in January where he found artifacts in a shell mound by digging with a stick. On the same trip, he used a knife to dig into another shell mound—finding even more artifacts. He then traveled the world as was the custom of the rich aristocracy of the time. He visited Egypt, Europe, and Asia, and he also took a trip down the Amazon River. His father unexpectedly died in 1878, and C. B. was made President of the family paper company while his mother lived in Europe. The assets left to Moore and his mother were then estimated at over 5 million dollars. By 1889 he had amassed many more millions of dollars and he turned his attention to archaeology after ceding control of the company to others (Fowler & Wilcox, 2003).

By 1891, at the age of 39, Moore had become totally devoted to the excavation of mounds. It appears that one motivating factor was his interest in the newspaper accounts of giants. Moore made an official agreement to represent the Academy of Natural Sciences in Philadelphia on his excursions. While he shared artifacts with landowners, the vast majority of the finds were eventually given to the Academy for display. At the end of each excavation season, Moore wrote articles about his finds in various archaeology journals. He also published a series of large books that the Academy published at Moore's expense. From 1891 until about 1918, Moore spent virtually every winter traveling by boat to every mound site in the southeast that could be reached by a navigable river. That was his stated goal, which he completed by 1917. He continued to do limited excavation work until 1920. He excavated at an astonishing 850 sites and probably opened far more mounds than the Smithsonian did (Fowler & Wilcox, 2003).

After finding that chartered boats didn't give him what he needed, Moore built and outfitted a stern-wheel boat named the *Gopher of Philadelphia*. He kept the boat until 1926. His spending on the boat and excursions was extravagant, and he was quoted as saying, "economy at any cost" (Swift, 1903). Each summer he sent the boat's Captain to explore rivers and stop at every landing. The Captain would inquire at each site about the presence of mounds; find the landowners; and make arrangements for "excavations" at identified sites. In September of each year, Moore would travel from Philadelphia by train with Dr. Milo G. Miller to the starting point, where he joined up with the Captain and the boat's crew. Miller, a Philadelphia physician 10 years younger than Moore, is usually described as an inseparable companion who accompanied Moore on all of his expeditions. Miller was married, had two children, and commented that he enjoyed archaeology more than medicine. Moore never married. They typically excavated until the middle of spring when they would return to Philadelphia, write their reports, and illustrate and photograph artifacts. Miller helped in all aspects of the excavations including the analysis of burial remains and preparation of maps and illustrations (Fowler & Wilcox, 2003).

Accompanying Moore and Dr. Miller on most of his expeditions were the boat Captain, a cook, an engineer, several stewards, and waiters. In addition, Moore typically hired 8 to 20 "colored gentlemen to do the excavating." They accompanied Moore on the boat and apparently appreciated his loyalty to them (Swift, 1903: 48). Over the next 20 years, he changed boat Captains only once and tended to hire the same workers each year. They became efficient excavators. In Arkansas and in several other locations, Moore and his crew were threatened by local segregationists who did not want the blacks with Moore in the river or on land. Moore died in 1936 at the age of 84 (Fowler & Wilcox, 2003).

No one has calculated how many mounds Moore excavated or obliterated, but it is in the thousands. If the landowners requested it, Moore's workers would backfill mounds, but in many cases they leveled mounds to the surface, which, to the farmers, was often seen as desirable. Moore's Captain convinced

many of the landowners to allow the work by "sharing" some artifacts found. It is known that when Moore's crew worked, if anyone came to watch, they all simply sat down and ceased work until the visitor left. He didn't want any outsiders to see what was excavated.

In his initial years, Moore seems to have been keenly interested in skeletons—especially the reports of giants. As the years passed, his driving goal was obtaining specimens for the Philadelphia Museum. His later works give fewer descriptions of skeletons or their sizes.

Starting in 1891, Moore excavated in Florida. In subsequent years he excavated in Georgia, South Carolina, Alabama, Mississippi, Arkansas, Louisiana, Tennessee, Kentucky, Texas, and Missouri as well as doing small excavations in Illinois and Indiana. He ended his seasonal excursions in Florida in 1920. He visited almost all of these states numerous times. The University of Alabama Press has in recent years reprinted Moore's publications in a series of oversize volumes.

Moore's Conclusions On Giant Skeletons

In one of his first reports (Moore, 1892), C. B. Moore addressed the issue of the height of the mound builders and the many reports of giant skeletons swirling around in popular publications (138-139). His conclusion was that the mound builders were of normal, average height. He stated that he had made several trips to personally inspect the skeletons of "giants" that had been reported in the media of his day. In each case, he found that the people making the claim simply did not know how to arrange bones to allow for the interlocking of joints. They consistently overestimated the height (139). He also found that exaggeration was an issue. In one of his "giant skeleton" investigations, Moore explained how a Professor George Piersol visited a "professional man" in a Florida town which Moore chose not to name. He was initially told by this man that a 9-foot skeleton had been found nearby. He asked the name of the individual who had supplied the information.

He then visited *that* person who told him that it was only a 7-foot skeleton. But that individual supplied the name of the actual skeleton "finder" as well as his location. Piersol then went to this person and was showed the skeleton. Piersol found that the skeleton was smaller than average (139). Moore's conclusion was that exaggeration and the inability of most people to accurately articulate a skeleton led to most reports (138-139). It is probably important to note that Moore didn't excavate mounds in West Virginia, Pennsylvania, Ohio, Wisconsin, or North Carolina—the states where the Smithsonian found most of the large skeletons.

Florida & Moore's First Discovery of Frequently-Found but Mysterious Symbols

Moore was keenly aware that the Bureau of Ethnology had excavated some mounds in Florida, and he commented that they found very little and missed many sites. The first area which Moore's crew visited was in northeast Florida where the Bureau had never been. Shell mounds were excavated in the area of the St. John's River. Actually, the term "excavated" isn't completely accurate. His crew often "demolished" mounds, and that descriptive word is the one he occasionally used. Since a lot of the mounds that Moore "demolished" can't be found today, it may be even more appropriate to say he "obliterated" them. From 1891 to 1895, Moore explored mounds in Florida, extending from extreme northeast Florida south to Lake Okeechobee using a digging crew of 20 or 21 men. Almost immediately he started finding mysterious symbols on various types of artifacts.

One of the first mounds nearly obliterated by Moore was the Mt. Royal mound by the St. John's River where it leaves Lake George. The mound was 16 feet in height with a circumference of 555 feet—too big he related for total demolition (Moore, 1894: 19). He found hundreds of artifacts including a copper sheet, 10.6 inches square. In the center of the sheet were 7 depressed concentric rings. Surrounding the rings were curious symbols Moore would later find engraved on many other artifacts. He wrote that it was of "great

Unusual copper plate found by C. B. Moore in a Florida sand mound. The object was 10.5 inches square. From: Moore (1894).

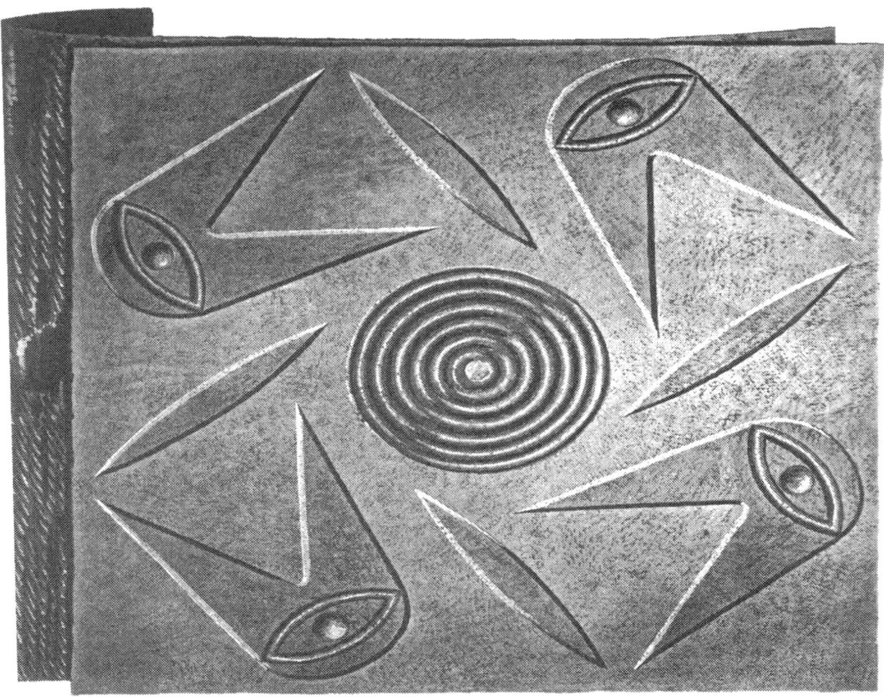

interest" but had no explanation for it. It is a kind of symbol that looks "alien." In Volusia County, Moore found a 4.25-inch shell gorget. In the center was a cross with a hole in its center. The cross was surrounded by a two-ringed circle and an eight-pointed star. He eventually found many more of these cross symbols (Moore, 1894).

More Symbols Are Revealed

The "cross" symbol, looking somewhat like a plus sign (+), has been found on countless pieces of pottery and other artifacts throughout the entire Southeast. They are sometimes circled, and sometimes a star or the sun surrounds it. It was long-interpreted as a sun symbol and is partly the reason

Gorget depicting a cross surrounded by concentric circles and a sunburt found by C. B. Moore in a Florida sand mound. The two holes at the top were used to suspend the gorget around the neck. Note the curious hole in the center of the cross. From: Moore (1894).

the "Indians" were held to be sun worshippers. Recall that when de Soto first encountered Chief Tuscaloosa atop a mound, above Tuscaloosa was a banner with the cross sign on it.

Moore also discovered many artifacts depicting an odd, ovoid shape nearly everywhere he went. The symbol had also been found by many others and is shown on many types of artifacts in a consistent form. Moore found the symbol curious but only said that it had an "unknown meaning" (Moore, 1911: 459). Today it is known as the "ogee." It is considered to be a portal or "slit" in the sky. Moore is to be credited for discovering that the opening at

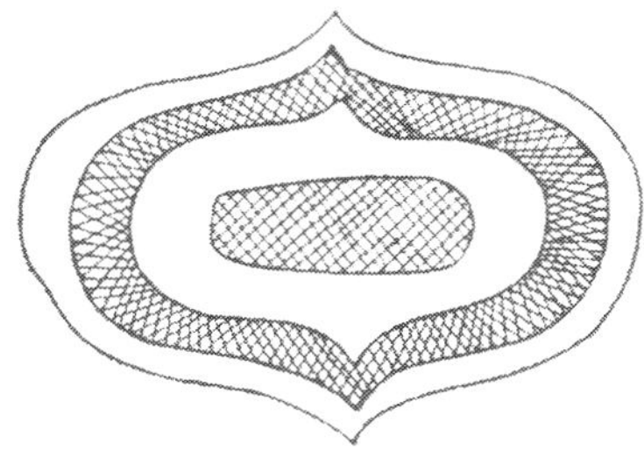

C. B. Moore found numerous artifacts displaying a curious symbol we now know as the "ogee." Moore simply stated that the meaning was unknown. From: Moore (1911).

the top of many jars and pots was formed into an ogee. As we shall see later, the highly decorated vessels displaying the symbols were not everyday cookware or containers. They were used for specific ceremonies.

In his several trips to Moundville, Alabama, Moore discovered pots and other vessels displaying the "eye in hand" symbol. Bones attached to a hand were seen on many pots. He also found many examples of a "feathered serpent," which had a forked eye with what appeared to be an ogee-like symbol in the center of the eye. Raptor bird symbols with a forked eye were found on many objects. He excavated several copper pendants showing the downward-pointing "eye in hand" displayed at the bottom of the pendant. Above the hand's wrist was a split with two sets of three star-like dots leading to an ogee symbol inside a six-pointed star. Other pendants had a swastika-like cross in the top of the pendant. In a shell mound in Georgia, Moore found a gorget with an unusual rattlesnake motif. The head of the snake was

Pot found at Pecan Point, Arkansas by C. B. Moore. It shows three symbols of the Southern Death Cult: the hand, a bone (ulna), and a skull alternating around the outside. From Moore (1911).

Right: Drawing of winged serpents with horns, found on pottery vessel at Moundville by Moore (1907). These are also representations of the ruler of the underworld, Scorpius, when seen in the southern sky.

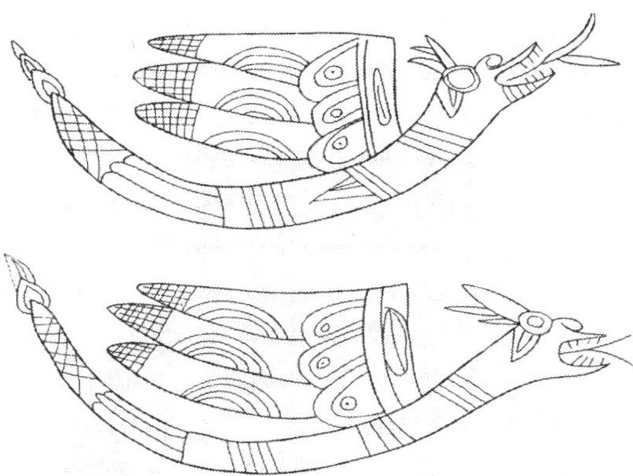

Below: Drawing of a raptor bird with forked eye found on vessel at Moundville by Moore (1905). This image represents the "Adversary" encountered on the Path of Souls located at Deneb at the junction of the Dark Rift of the Milky Way. The Forked Eye probably represents the split at the Dark Rift, with the ogee-like "eye" probably representing Deneb.

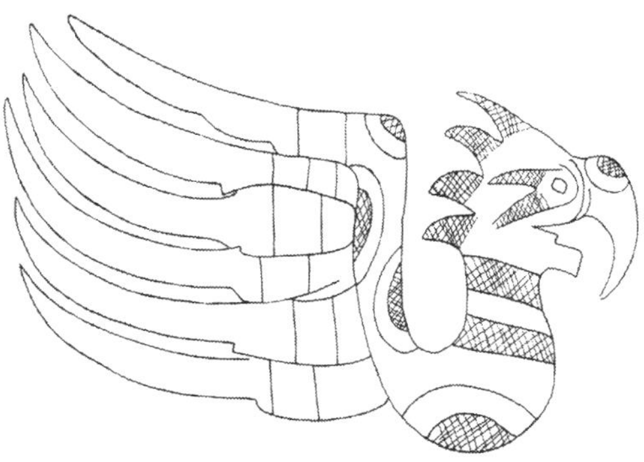

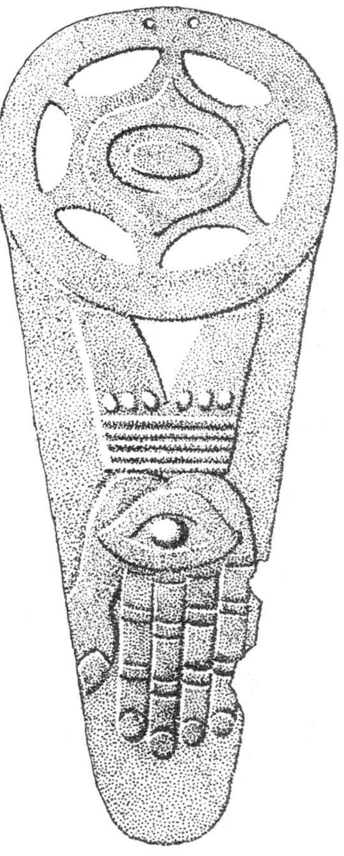

Right: Copper pendant found with an adult skeleton by Moore (1907) at Moundville. The eye in hand (Orion's Nebulae and Orion's Belt) leads upward to a split (the Dark Rift). At the top is a 6-pointed star with an ogee in the middle—representing Deneb.

bird-like with a forked eye, and concentric circles were engraved in the eye. In sum, Moore excavated artifacts showing almost all of the major symbols of the Southeastern Ceremonial Complex—the Death Cult.

The value of C. B. Moore's investigations are so wide-ranging and important that it's not possible to do them justice in a simple summary. In addition to showing the incredible artistry of the people who built the mounds, Moore developed some of the first techniques used in professional archaeology. But he is also widely criticized by the same people who appreciate his fieldwork and findings. Moore destroyed a lot of mounds. Paradoxically, both the Smithsonian and Moore often discussed and lamented the rapid destruction of mounds by farming, road and railroad construction, buildings, and looting. In some ways, it seems that these early excavators wanted to obliterate mounds before others did the same. But it's also clear that Moore and the Smithsonian were on a quest to discover who the mound builders were—and accumulate as many artifacts they could—but not for themselves. In a twist of fate, most of the thousands of artifacts Moore excavated are now at the Smithsonian.

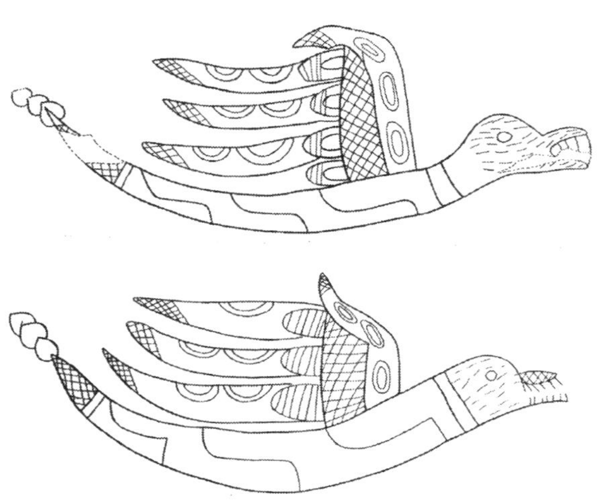

Drawing of winged serpents found on vessels at Moundville by Moore (1907). They are representations of the constellation of Scorpius, and the eye of the serpent is the star Antares. The serpent is the ruler of the underworld. When it is seen in the southern sky during summer months, it has feathers. In the winter, the serpent remains in the underworld.

Chapter 8

Key Symbols of the Southern Death Cult and Native American Cosmology

The key symbols of the "Death Cult" or the Southeastern Ceremonial Complex were essentially known by the time C. B. Moore and the Smithsonian ceased major excavation work. But precisely what most of these symbols meant was a great mystery. Over the ensuing years, efforts were made to match actual birds or other animals to some of the imagery, but this led to many contradictions and arguments.

The raptor bird images some archaeologists asserted were just simple depictions of the actual birds.

The rattlesnakes were just rattlesnakes.

It was assumed that many of the images of dancing "warriors" were showing just that. They were supposedly images of warriors of different clans in a celebration. In some cases the images were said to depict an important corn ceremony known as the *Busk*.

Skulls and bones were just trophies of war displayed by warriors and tribes.

Some images, such as spiders, were ways to show the story of the water spider bringing the first fire to humans—a simple mythological tale.

It was asserted that crosses always depicted the sun to the "sun worshipping" natives.

The "eye in hand" was just a symbol circularly explained as a "universal symbol" (Hudson, 1976).

And it's all wrong.

Archaeology is a plodding academic discipline that changes its beliefs very slowly. In general, American archaeology tends to pay attention to findings that support what is already accepted and believed by the mainstream. Findings which dispute the accepted beliefs are discounted and often ridiculed. It is a type of psychological process called *perceptual bias* and *confirmation bias*. It means that people have a strong tendency to notice and support things that confirm what they already believe. When evidence is presented that contradicts our beliefs, we tend to dismiss it as simply wrong or discount it as a single exception to our beliefs and therefore unimportant. In general, people are seldom aware when these strong processes are at work—they almost always take place at an unconscious level of cognition. A large and clinically important area of psychology specializes in this topic.

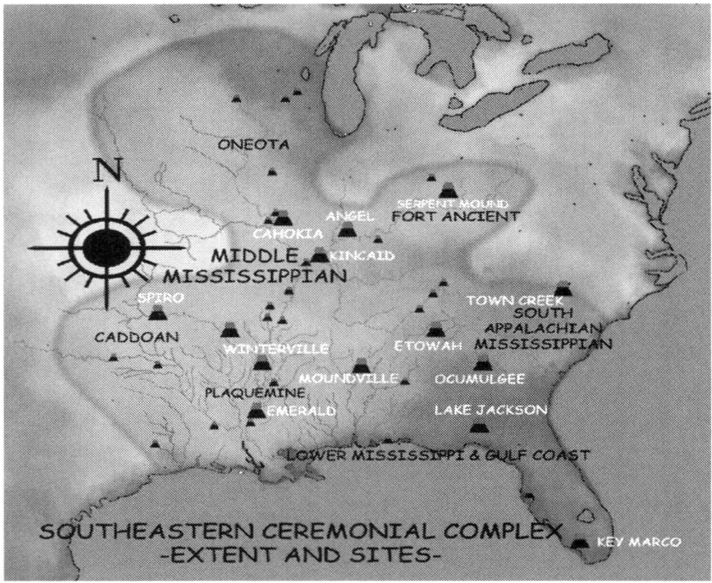

Map of main areas of the Southeastern Ceremonial Complex.
Credit: Heironymous Rowe, Wikipedia Commons.

Andrew Collins Points to Cygnus

The story about the Death Cult symbols that unfolds here actually began for me with an unexpected realization by Andrew Collins, a well-known British researcher and science writer. Collins found that a large number of ancient structures appeared to be built to focus attention on the Constellation of Cygnus, also known as the Northern Cross. Cygnus is typically represented by a bird, often a swan, eagle, or other raptor bird. In 2004 Collins visited the immense Hopewell site in Newark, Ohio with my wife and I. One of the earthworks we visited was the "Great Circle" which is only one major component of what is the largest and most complex set of ancient earthworks

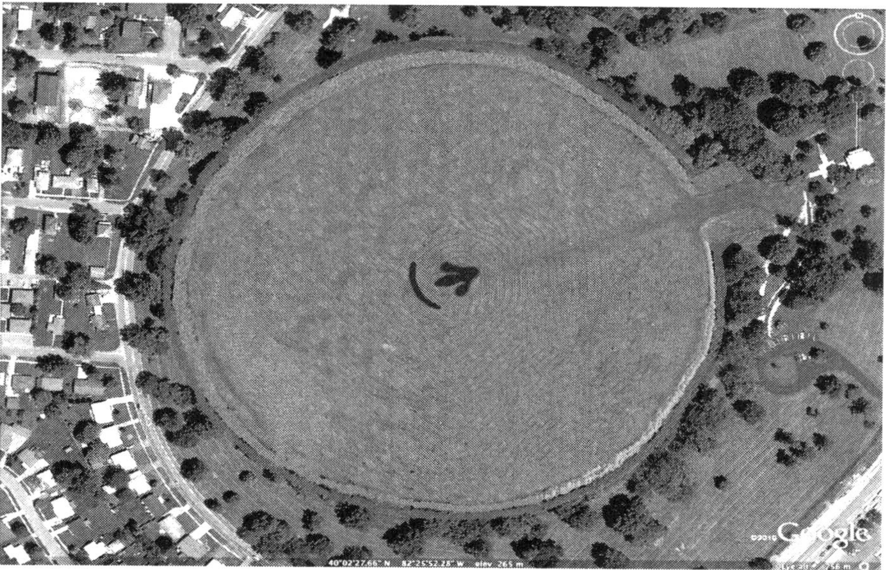

Altered Google image of Newark's Great Circle, which encloses 30 acres. It is the same size as England's Avebury. All of the trees have been removed from the circle's interior. Around the inside edge of the outer earthen embankment is a 7-foot-deep moat. The outer wall is a 9-foot-high earthen embankment. Eagle Mound has been blackened in the center of the circle. It orients toward the only opening located on the northeast side. Andrew Collins found that viewed from Eagle Mound on the Summer Solstice in 100 B.C., the Milky Way was seen as a vertical band rising from the opening. Directly overhead was Cygnus.

in the world. It is an incredible site once extending over tens of miles. Huge portions of it are well preserved today.

Great Circle is a circular "henge" enclosing a flat, 30-acre area. A low bird-shaped mound known as *Eagle Mound* stands in the exact center of the circle. The size and formation of the outer wall and inside moat is essentially identical to England's famous site of Avebury. This was one reason we wanted Andrew to see it.

In his book *The Cygnus Mystery* (2006: 47-49), Collins wrote, "For me, it was Eagle Mound that kept drawing my attention . . . I suggested that it was [a place where] those about to journey beyond death to the sky-world" could be sent off on their journey. Collins concluded that the Milky Way, which was described in Native American verbal traditions as a "River of Souls," "Wolf Trail," or a "Ghost Trail," may well have been the ritualistic focal point of many Hopewell sites, including Newark's Great Circle. He also found that a Kansas State University archaeoastronomer (Thaddeus Cowan) had speculated that many eagle effigy mounds (including the one in the center of the Great Circle) were representations of Cygnus. Using different computer star position programs, Collins and I both found that at the accepted time of the creation of the Newark site—100 B.C. and in mid-summer—the Milky Way was seen as a vertical band rising up from the only opening of

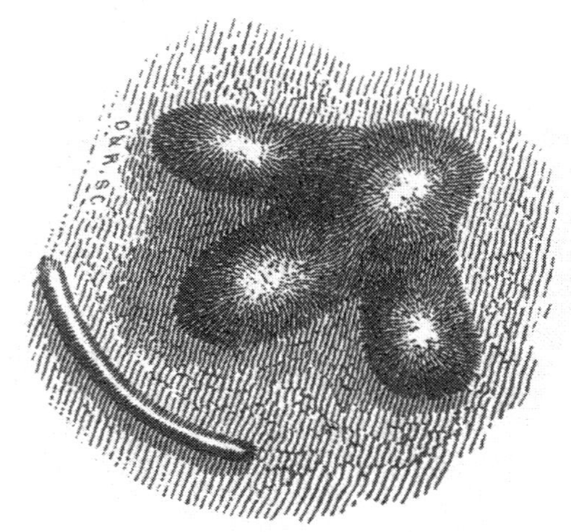

Enlargement of Eagle Mound in Newark's Great Circle. There is controversy regarding whether the mound is an actual eagle effigy or a representation of a bird's foot. Cygnus was sometimes seen as a bird's foot. Image from Squier & Davis (1848).

the massive earthwork as viewed from Eagle Mound in its center. At that precise time, after midnight, the constellation of Cygnus was located directly overhead of Eagle Mound. This finding suggested that the circle was constructed for rituals which would send dead souls to the Milky Way where they could then make their way to Cygnus. Of course, in his 350-page book *The Cygnus Mystery*, Collins also found many other sites around the world that were aligned with Cygnus. One of these sites was the pyramid complex at Giza in Egypt.

Orion *versus* Cygnus in Egypt

Unexpectedly, while Collins was working on *The Cygnus Mystery*, the British engineer Rodney Hale discovered that the layout of the three main pyramids of Giza matched the position of the three stars of the Cygnus constellation that form its cross bar. This finding caused a major controversy

Left: The stars of Orion's Belt positioned on the three pyramids at Giza. The stars have to be turned upside down to make them get close to fitting. *Right:* The cross stars of the Cygnus Constellation positioned on the three pyramids of Giza *circa* 2600 B.C., with proper motion calculated. In truth, you can choose any three stars in the sky and by adjusting their relative distance, make two of them fit perfectly. The important issue is how closely the third star fits. Cygnus is a better match.

because many people had accepted that if the pyramids at Giza matched a star formation, it was the Belt of Orion. In truth, Orion has never really matched the alignment of the pyramids as Rodney Hale also found. Orion looks like a good match if two things are done. First, you have to greatly magnify the size of the three stars. And then, only by turning either the three belt stars or the north-south layout of the pyramids upside down does it look like a close match. But even then, one of the stars of Orion doesn't "perfectly" match the pyramids as it was once claimed to do. That, of course, has never bothered the Orion supporters who asserted that it was close enough and that the "upside down" issue was not an important criticism. In addition, they often countered that one of the airshafts of the Great Pyramid has long been thought to target Orion. That assertion is considered by most Egyptologists to be accurate.

Undaunted by the criticism of Orion supporters, Collins went on to discover a cave complex under the Giza Plateau that had essentially been unknown to modern Egyptologists (*Beneath the Pyramids*, Collins, 2009). The location of the cave complex, called by Zahi Hawass "Collins' Caves," supported the contention that the ancient Egyptians used Cygnus as the template for the pyramids' layout. But there was still the issue of the Great Pyramid airshaft that targeted Orion. How could the issue be resolved?

Collins has expanded the research on Cygnus in a recent book entitled, *Göbekli Tepe: Genesis of the Gods* (Collins, 2014). While one of the originators of the Orion theory suggested that the Göbekli Tepe site was built to target Orion, Collins has thoroughly demonstrated that Orion was not the focus of this almost 12,000-year-old site. It was built to focus on Cygnus. He also showed how both Cygnus and Orion could have been used together in ancient death rituals by including evidence from Native American sites.

Texas State University's Mississippian Iconography Conference

In 2006 a former professional excavation archaeologist handed me a copy of the book, *Hero, Hawk, and Open Hand* (Townsend & Sharp, 2004). I was astonished to see in it the recent conclusions about the symbols' meanings that were made by mainstream archaeologists. It explained that both Orion and Cygnus were central components to Native American beliefs about death. As time passed, I located several more of the publications explaining the symbols and was a bit upset at myself for not keeping up with this research.

Beginning around 1993, a series of conferences were held at Texas State University that directly focused on unraveling the mystery of the symbolic images. The annual meetings were called the "Mississippian Iconographic Conference." The results of these conferences, attended by many archaeologists, anthropologists, and folklore experts, were eventually released in a series of books, virtually all of which have been published by major university presses. Many mainstream professionals have been involved in the findings and conclusions of their work. Their findings are not guesswork. They are partly based on long-ignored ethnological studies conducted in the 1700s, 1800s and early 1900s published by Schoolcraft, the Bureau of Ethnology, and many others. They also used interviews of various tribes' shaman, medicine men, and storytellers. The archaeologists compiled beliefs and legends from a large number of tribes, and partly through statistical analyses they gradually formed a set of consistent beliefs and statements about the symbols' meanings that were present in the majority of the tribes' lore. In brief, they have found that the symbolic images describe the journey of the soul after death including the path taken and what is encountered along the way.

It is important to note that various archaeologists specialized in specific aspects of certain symbols while others formed a more overall composite

view. It should also be noted that among the group, not all of them would agree with every interpretation of each symbol's meaning. However, it appears that all of them are in agreement that the overall view of the death journey that came from their research is an accurate depiction of the beliefs.

The information that follows comes from *An Archaeology of the Soul* (Hall, 1997), *Hero, Hawk, and Open Hand* (Townsend & Sharp, 2004), *Ancient Objects and Sacred Realms* (Reilly & Garber, 2007), *Reachable Stars* (Lankford, 2007), *Looking for Lost Lore* (Lankford, 2008), *Visualizing the Sacred* (Lankford, Reilly, & Garber , 2011), and *Native American Legends of the Southeast* (Lankford, 2011). The books and various chapters had contributions from 24 different archaeologists and anthropologists. A brief synopsis of the meaning of key symbols is presented first, followed by the composite story of the soul's death journey.

The Meaning of Key Symbols in the Death Cult

Not all of the symbols encapsulated in the Southeastern Ceremonial Complex (or the Southern Death Cult) will be presented here. Only those that are directly related to the soul's journey at death will be briefly explained. Those who want a more detailed explanation are referred to the books listed above.

Skulls & Bones

There are two forms of skulls that represent the two souls that human beings have. One skull has a wide-eyed lifeless look. Both this skull and individual bones (such as an ulna) represent what Native Americans called the "life-soul." The life-soul is a mindless force that animates the body. The other type of skull shows what looks like "fire" coming from the mouth. It depicts the "free-soul" leaving the body. The free-soul has self-awareness and retains memory. The free-soul takes the journey on the Path of Souls.

Left: Drawing of skull from pottery bowl depicting the "free soul" leaving the body. From: Moore (1905). Right: Ceremonial vessel from Moundville, Alabama showing bones and skull. The wide eyes are thought to indicate death. Photo—Lora Little.

Eye in Hand

There are numerous examples of the "eye in hand" symbol from widely-scattered Mississippian sites. The hand is severed at the wrist and represents a constellation known to many Native American tribes as "The Hand." Three stars form the severed wrist—they are the three stars forming the Belt of Orion. The "eye" in the hand is an ogee.

Eye in hand symbol depicted on two ceremonial vessels from Moundville, Alabama. Photos—Lora Little.

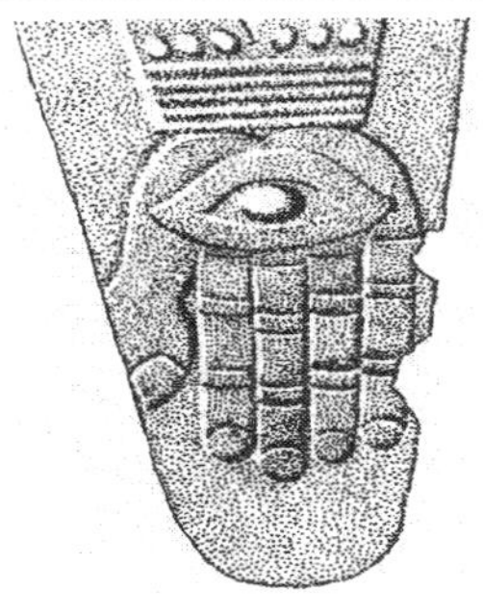

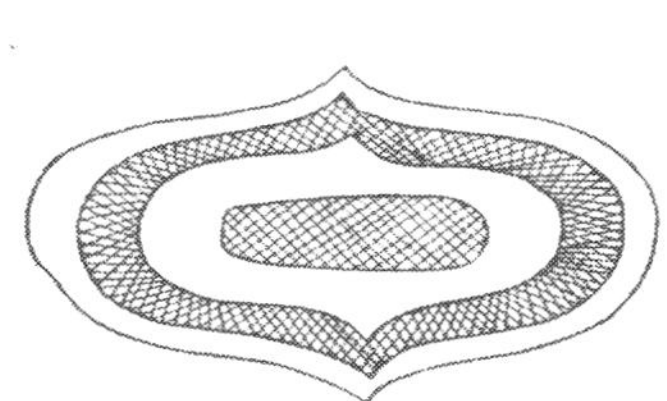

The ogee is depicted as the "eye" in the "eye in hand" symbol on Moundville pendant (left) and has been found on numerous ceremonial pottery pieces (right). Source: Moore (1905; 1911).

Ogee

The ogee symbol has been found at virtually all major Mississippian sites and many smaller sites as well. It is a portal or slit in the sky that gives access to the Milky Way. The Milky Way is the "Path of Souls." The ogee in the "eye in hand" symbol is a nebula known as Messier-42 or the Orion Nebula. It is located below the three belt stars.

Paired Twisted Skulls—Paired Warriors

There are many examples of "paired warriors," paired skulls, and other symbols. They sometimes depict a story of cosmic twins and parts of the cosmos. The "twins" story is similar to twin stories in various cultures around the world. The warrior depictions are key characters involved in the death journey and show the struggle between life and death, which is sometimes

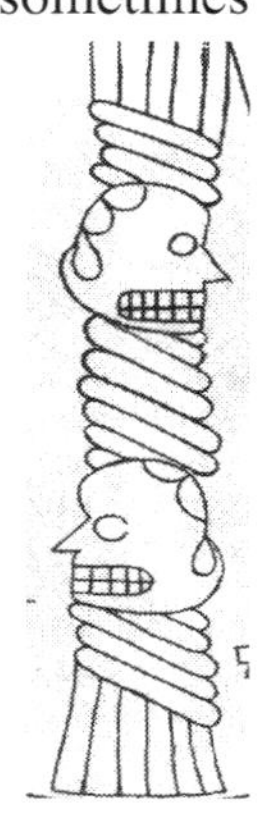

Left: Illustration from gorget showing twins splitting from a striped pole, the axis mundi. Note the three dots. Source: Heironymous Rowe, Wikipedia Commons. Right: Twisted skull image from the Willoughby Disk.

symbolized by a game in which the head of one's opponent is a trophy. Moundville's Willoughby Disk is, to my knowledge, the only symbol depicting two skulls twisted together. It may depict the two souls twisted together in a living person—or dead twins.

Raptor Birds—Hawk, Eagle, Falcon

The depiction of fierce-looking raptors usually symbolizes an important "adversary" encountered at a key point on the journey across the Path of Souls (the Milky Way). The star Deneb in the Constellation of Cygnus is the point where the adversary is located. At this spot, souls also make a choice to continue their journey using one or the other side of the Milky Way's split at the Dark Rift. Some tribes saw the adversary as an eagle, hawk, or falcon. However, at the point where the decision on direction is made, there are other beings and tasks encountered. At some point near the Great Rift is the "Path of Awakening," a spot where souls can be sent back to earth to reincarnate.

Eagle head from pottery. The raptor shows a forked eye and is the Adversary encountered at Deneb. From: Moore (1907).

Eagle depicted on various artifacts excavated at Etowah, Georgia. From: Moorehead (1932).

Top left: Engraved shell from Spiro burial mound. The numerous "ogee" symbols on the body of the figure are identical to the forked eye. This means that they depict the same thing: the Dark Rift of the Milky Way and an opening at Deneb. Photo—Lora Little. Top right: Effigy vessel from Nodena Site (Arkansas) at the Hampson Museum. Note the forked eyes. Photo—Lora Little. Lower left: Copper plate from Spiro, Oklahoma. Photo—Lora Little. Lower right: Thunderbird image with 3-forked eye (J. G. Braecklein).

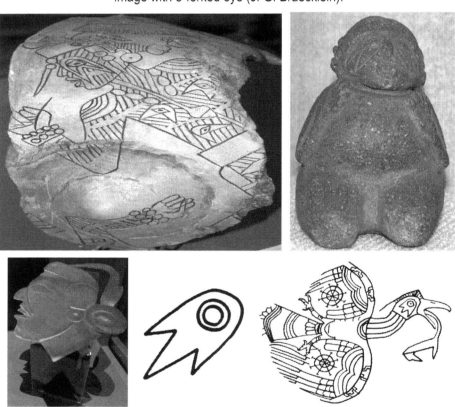

The Forked Eye

The forked eye is complicated and has more than one meaning. In some cases where it has three extensions, it is thought to represent thunder from the Thunderbird, a power in the Upper World. When it has a double split, it may represent the place in the Milky Way where the Dark Rift splits. In that case, it has an ogee for the eye.

The Cross with or without Outer Sun/Stars

Long considered to be sun symbols, the cross or + signs often represent the earth suspended on 4 corners by ropes that attach to the sky world. These relate to the four cardinal directions. Earth is in the middle world. Surrounding Earth is a watery surface that extends down into the underworld. Above Earth or the middle world is an upper world—the sky world. There are forces or "beings" that exist in each of the three levels, and each of the three levels has various levels within them. Thus, the universe as they saw it, was a 3-layered sphere—with a top, a middle layer, and a bottom. The outer sphere rotated causing night and day. In some instances the sun was shown around the inner cross. In other cases it is likely that the cross symbolized the point where the four ropes joined together and were suspended from the upper sphere. That joining point of the ropes holding the middle world appears to be Cygnus in some tribal beliefs.

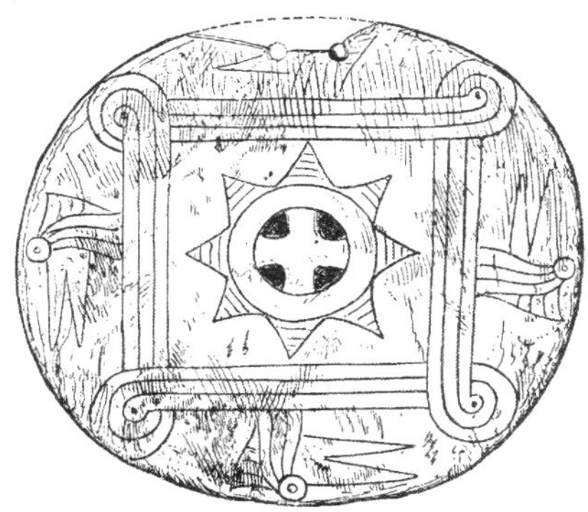

Above: Shell gorget from Wayne County, TN. The looped square represents the middle world, the birds represent the four winds/directions, the cross represents the axis mundi connected to a point in the sky dome. From: Thruston (1890). Right: Double-circled cross symbol on Moundville vessel. Photo—Lora Little.

Feathered Serpents & Water Panther

The ruler of the underworld was believed to be a large snake that was often called a "water panther." But this ruler was also at times seen flying in the upper world. When it was flying over the southern horizon, it had wings and was called the "feathered serpent." The feathered serpent is the constellation of Scorpius, which is seen in the southern sky during the summer. It has a large red eye, the star Antares. When it was seen in the sky during the summer, tribes were banned from telling stories because the serpent was listening. Free souls could not make the Path of Souls journey while the feathered serpent was visible. A common practice was to store the bones of the dead until the right time (winter) for death ceremonies and rituals to be held.

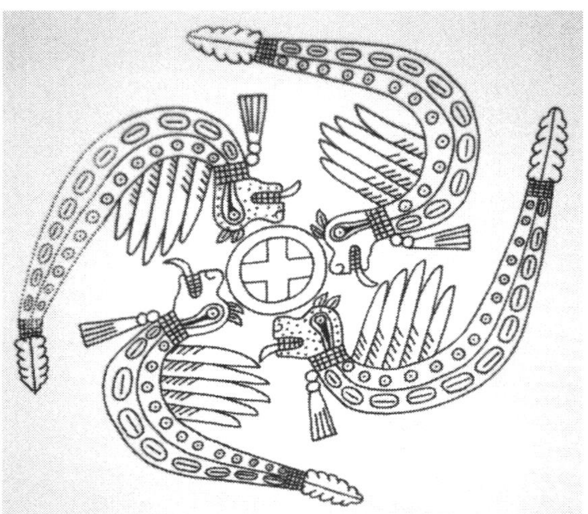

Left: Image engraved on shell cup found at Spiro, Oklahoma. It depicts feathered serpents (the ruler of the underworld) moving around the axis mundi or the point where the middle world connects to the sky. Credit: Heironymous Rowe, Wikipedia Commons. Top right: Water Panther bowl from the Nodena site. Photo: Lora Little. Lower right: Feathered serpent found on Moundville pottery. From: Moore (1905).

Examples of swastica symbols (swirl crosses) found on various artifacts from mounds.

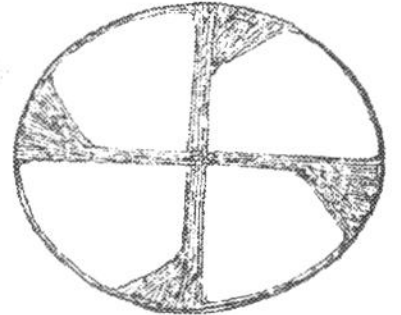

Swastikas—Swirled Crosses

Numerous swastika-like images have been found on pottery and other artifacts. Archaeologists prefer to call them "swirl crosses" because of the implications related to the term *swastika*. They are thought to represent a column (sometimes represented by a tree) that connects the three-layered universe—at the point where the lower world connects to the middle world. It is the *axis mundi*, but it refers mainly to the point connecting the middle and lower worlds.

The Striped Pole with Twin Turkeys

This is a curious design that shows two turkey cocks facing each other. In between them is a striped pole often represented in historic times by white and red stripes. It depicts the three-part universe seen from a side of the middle world—where humans reside. The turkeys represent the upper world; the bottom horizontal bar depicts the Earth's surface; and the pole is the *axis*

"Hixon" style gorget from Etowah, redrawn from Hamilton (1952). Note the striped pole—the pole that connects the three worlds.

mundi connecting the three major layers. The pole is important because it can be vibrated by the methods used in some rituals. The vibration allows a sort of mental access between the three worlds.

Spiders

Spiders have been depicted on 35 gorgets and various other artifacts found from mound sites. Many of these have crosses on their back. They have a wide-ranging meaning but nearly always relate to the middle world. They sometimes symbolize the bodily or physical enclosure of the soul. Some spider motifs depict the "Spider Woman." She is said to be near the portal beneath Orion's Belt where she waits for some souls to be caught and taken into the underworld. In this case, she functions to capture souls which do not successfully make the leap into the ogee.

Spider gorgets found in Missouri and Tennessee. From: Thruston (1890).

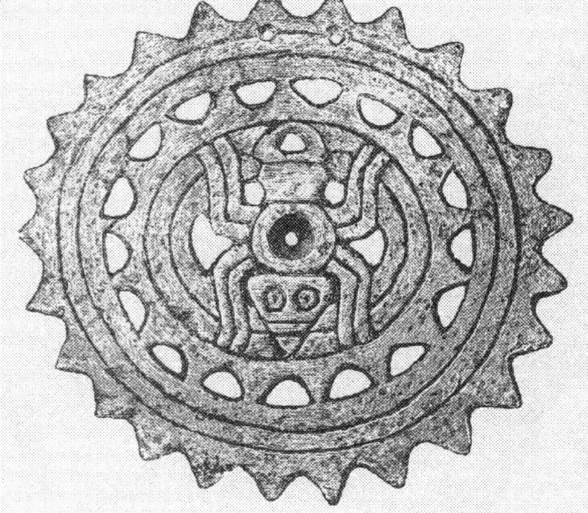

Birdman—Falcon Dancer, Dances With Heads, and Others

In 1885 John Rogan recovered two brass plate figures depicting what was long thought to be warriors or clan members dressed as "Birdmen." Known as the "Rogan Plates," they were removed from a stone chamber burial at Etowah Mounds in Georgia (where the Smithsonian found a 7-foot skeleton). The plates' origin has been traced to Cahokia. Similar depictions were found on shell gorgets excavated at Etowah. The "Birdman" symbol, also called "Falcon Dancer" in some variations of the motif, has been found on artifacts from Spiro, Oklahoma. From a wide range of Mississippian sites, several variations of the symbol have emerged. These include ones depicting a Birdman with a moth, severed heads, stars, the game of chunkey, and more. Another curious form is the "Double Birdman," called by archaeologists a "Hightower" style. They have long been accepted as depictions of actual warriors or various clans celebrating or preparing for war. They often depict warriors dressed as hawks or falcons. They are actually images showing the cosmic struggle between life and death with important characters in their legends depicted. There are also many huge, carved stone effigy pipes which depicted these characters. The figures display the actual costumes worn by the elite during rituals and ceremonies. The costumes showed the elite's

Illustration of image on one of the "Rogan Plates" excavated by John Rogan at Etowah. It was made from copper and was recovered from a mound burial where a 7-foot skeleton was also found. It depicts an elite member of the society in costume mimicking a raptor bird. Note the "beaked" nose. The ceremonial mace in the right hand and the severed head in the left hand represent the power of life and death. From: Powell (1894).

connection to the upper world and were displays of their power and authority. The rituals were a magical way that elite members of tribes could control the society.

Famous engraved gorget from Spiro, Oklahoma. Note the three encircled dots on the lower vertical striped bar—they represent Orion. The horizontal bar represents the Milky Way. The swastika-like center is the connector of the middle world to the axis mundi. The two figures are shown in ceremonial garb and holding maces to display their power over life and death.The racoon on the top pole is a representation of a power in the sky world—a being that can be hidden, serve as a trickster, and a shape shifter. These objects were worn by the elite as obvious displays of their connection to the mysteries of life, death, and reincarnation. Photo from a replica displayed at Spiro, Oklahoma—Lora Little.

Ceremonial Mace

Ceremonial maces—polished axes cut from a single piece of stone—have been recovered from many Mississippian sites. They are impressive-looking weapons but are useless for that purpose—except for perhaps a single use. They are often depicted on Birdman images. They were exquisitely-made, symbolic artifacts carried by rulers that showed the power of the elite. In sum, the elite or a priestly class used many of the symbols during rituals where they dressed as specific "sky people," or various upper world powers, to show their influence and connection to the cosmos. It is thought that the rituals they performed were public ceremonies intended to maintain social control. Their costumes, the wearing of symbolically magical artifacts, and the possession of ceremonial maces were all designed to show the public their power and direct link to the upper world. The populace believed that it was necessary that they be given authority so that the rituals of death and the renewal of the tribe could be accomplished. In some tribes, the elite were also believed to have the ability to control a soul's reincarnation.

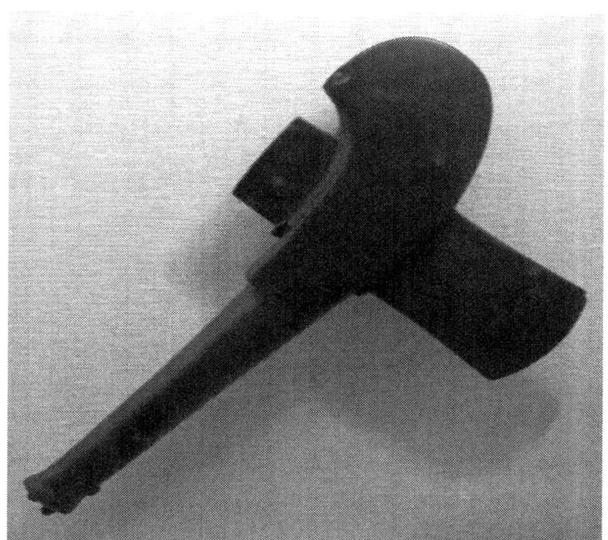

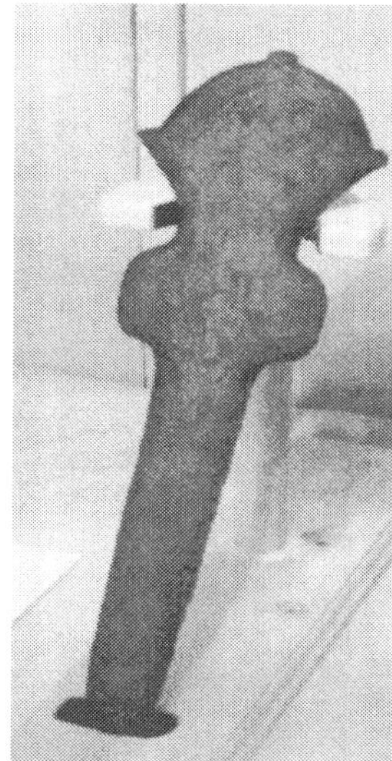

Left: Ceremonial mace from Moundville, Alabama. Photo: Lora Little. Right: Ceremonial mace from New Madrid, Missouri. Photo: Greg Little

Orion, Cygnus, and the Path of Souls—What Ancient Native Americans Believed About the Death Journey

This section represents a narrative composite summary of the death journey to the Path of Souls and many of the important experiences which occur on the path. It is based on the information in the previous section and is found in 6 books (Townsend & Sharp, 2004; Reilly & Garber, 2007; Lankford, 2007; Lankford, 2008; Lankford, Reilly, & Garber, 2011; and Lankford, 2011). Many Native American tribes shared this basic idea about the death journey, especially those from the areas of the Mississippian mounds. An earlier book not as widely-known as the 6 listed above (Hall, 1997) is entitled *An Archaeology of the Soul*, which gives many detailed descriptions of tribal legends collected from the 1600s to the early 1900s. It also explains how many basic details were distilled from various tribes. In the legends that are detailed in Hall's book, the fundamental beliefs about death and religion were shared not only across the North American continent but also in Central America. Ideas about Orion, the nebula below it, the two souls of humans, The Milky Way as the Path of Souls, reincarnation, the adversary encountered on the path, the tree or pole connecting the three worlds, and how the elite utilized rituals and costumes to maintain social order are all included in these legends.

According to the Native American beliefs, humans have two souls. One of these is attached to the body (or the bones) and serves only to animate the body. It is called the "life-soul" and is described as a mindless force that can be dangerous. The other soul is a "free-soul" that leaves the body at death. The free-soul has a self-aware personality and is what we typically identify as the soul—after death it retains a sense of identity and memory and separates from the body. The free-soul often stays in the vicinity of its body until it starts the journey.

It was believed that certain magical rituals were necessary to assist souls to make the death journey. But the journey of the free-soul to the Path of Souls could only take place in the winter months. It was also believed that

the bones of the dead had to be carefully handled due to the presence of the life-soul. The life-soul was thought to be dangerous, so a class of the elite—a mortuary-related priestly class—gave instructions and managed the overall series of rituals and the handling of the body. This could involve excarnation where the body would be placed in such a way that the flesh would be removed by carrion birds. Individuals who died during summer months often had their bones stored until winter when a series of rituals could be held to help the life-soul transition to the sky. Only the elite were seen to have the power to conduct the rituals. They wore ornate bird-like costumes, various symbols on gorgets and containers, ceremonial maces, feathers, a variety of medicine pouches, and used fire in the rituals. In the winter months, during a prescribed time after the sun sank beneath the horizon, the necessary rituals were performed. Bones were sometimes burned (to banish the life-soul) or buried and at times reburied again later. In some cases, the bones of dead members of the elite classes were collected and stored to facilitate reincarnation.

Individuals who died in winter months were given the same ritualistic ceremonies, but their journey to the sky world could commence within a few days after death. With the rituals releasing the free-soul performed, the

Bones and skulls with tongues found on artifacts from Spiro Mounds. The tongue coming from the skull represents the "free soul." The tongues from the bones represents the "life soul." Redrawn from Phillips and Brown (1978).

free-soul began a journey to the west. The length of this journey varied among tribes, but it may have been determined by the proximity of large bodies of water to the tribe's location. In general, the journey to the west was described as taking three to four days, until the free-soul reached a vast watery edge. The water represents the underworld. Here the free-soul waited through the night until the Hand Constellation (Orion) was seen to descend toward the horizon—just before dawn.

There is a widely-cited story in tribal lore about the hand that reveals it was cut off when an attempt was made to block the portal. The "eye" in the hand, or the ogee, is a portal found just below the hand. This portal represents a slit through the sky vault that gives access to the Milky Way. The severed hand is the Native American constellation obviously known as "The Hand."

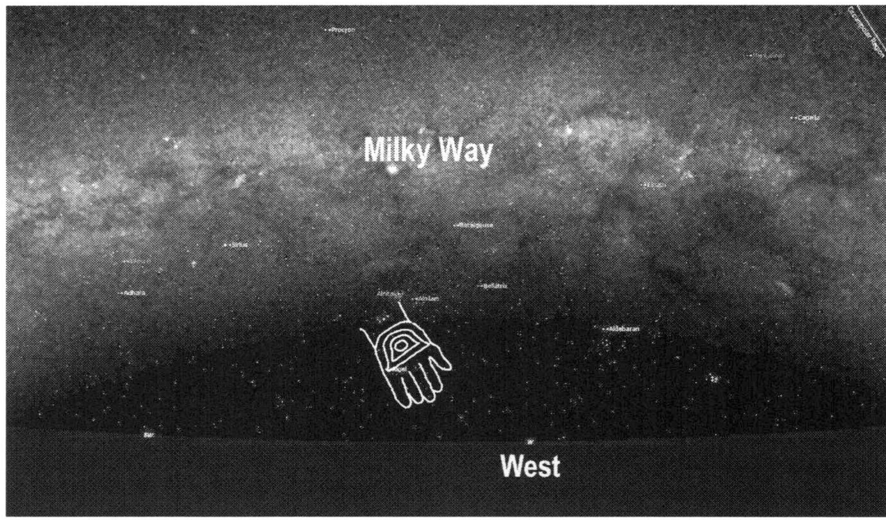

The "Hand Constellation" with the severed wrist formed by the three belt stars of Orion. During the winter months, the hand sank into the western horizon just before sunrise. Below the wrist is the "ogee"—the portal that leads to the Milky Way. The ogee is Messier-42. The free soul had to make a leap to the Hand just before it set in the morning. The Milky Way was a horizontal wall above it, and it sank below the horizon just as the sun rose. Once a soul reaches th Milky Way, the trip on the Path of Souls began, leading to Cygnus. The image above depicts 4:00 a.m. at Spiro, Oklahoma on December 1, A.D. 1200 and was generated from *Starry Night Pro*.

The three belt stars of Orion form the severed wrist, and in the morning just before sunrise, it was seen to set on the western horizon—but only during the winter months. The Hand pointed down.

At the moment before it sets, the soul makes a leap toward the Hand, actually aiming at a fuzzy "star" below the three belt stars. The fuzzy star is a nebula called Messier-42 or Orion's Nebula. It is a slit or portal in the sky—the ogee. As the Hand constellation sets into the horizon in the winter, the Milky Way is seen as a horizontal wall that falls below the horizon in the west not long after the Hand disappears. The belief was that if the soul made the leap to the portal successfully, it would then transition to the falling Milky Way to start its journey on the Path of Souls. The movement from the ogee to the Path occurred because the Milky Way sank below the horizon immediately after the Hand.

Once a soul had successfully entered the ogee in the sky and safely reached the Milky Way, it could remain on the "path" during the trip through the underworld to the south. The next night, the Milky Way appeared in the south and the Hand appeared in the southwest sky. The soul then began a journey to the north across the Milky Way toward the realm of the ancestors. Native American tribes called the Milky Way by several names: the Path of Souls, River of Souls, Ghost Trail, Wolf Trail, or similar terms.

Souls that failed to make the leap to the Hand's ogee successfully could be caught by a "Spider Woman" or simply fall into the watery underworld and lost forever. The Spider Woman could send the caught soul back to Earth for reincarnation or send it to the underworld. The underworld was ruled by a powerful Great Serpent. In some of the Mississippian cultures, the underworld ruler was a "water panther" with the ability to shape-shift.

The lord and guardian of the underworld—the Great Serpent or water panther—was not seen in the night sky during the winter. It is the Constellation of Scorpius. In the summer months, Scorpius, with its giant eye (the star Antares), floated above the southern horizon. When Scorpius was seen in the sky in the summer, it was seen as a feathered serpent, an image depicted on numerous artifacts.

Scorpius in the summer sky during the summer months. It was seen as a feathered serpent. The image below depicts 1:00 a.m. at Spiro, Oklahoma on July 1, A.D. 1200 and was generated from *Starry Night Pro*.

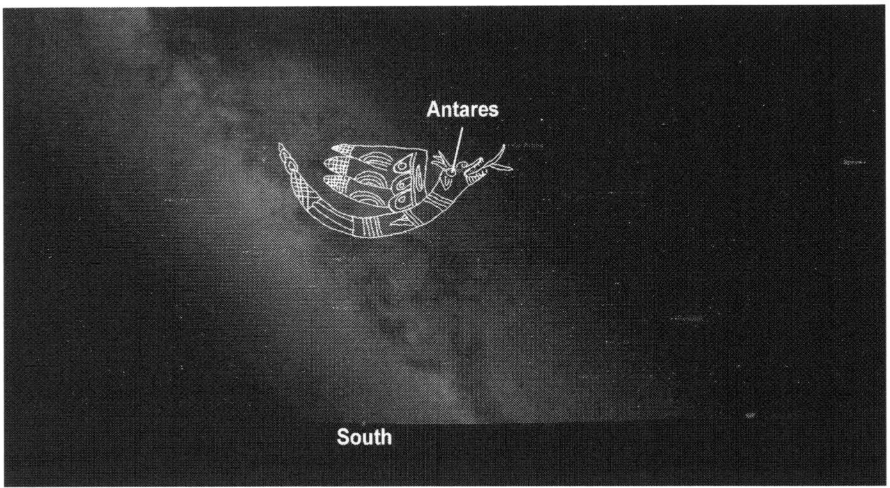

Souls that successfully made the transition to the Path of Souls experienced various trials on their journey, but the most significant one involved an adversary. The adversary could trick the soul, scare it off the path, make a judgment that deprived the soul of its existence, or allow it to pass. At this point each soul also made a decision.

The adversary was located in a spot in the sky where the Milky Way splits into two sides or paths. The spot of the split into two paths is the Dark Rift of the Milky Way. The star Deneb, the brightest star of the Cygnus Constellation, was the point where the Raptor/Adversary was encountered. A river, log, and other elements which tested the soul are found around the Dark Rift.

The adversary is described in a couple different ways by various tribes. Many tribes descending from the larger Mississippian sites saw it as a Raptor Bird (usually an eagle or a hawk). A few western tribes described the adversary as an old man or old woman dressed in a buffalo robe. Some tribes added another trial at the location involving a dog, several dogs, or a coyote. These animals could scare the soul and cause it to fall or turn back.

A successful leap to the ogee allowed souls to make a safe journey through the underworld and on to the Path of Souls. The soul then made its way to a key point on the Milky Way where it encountered an Adversary—a judge. The Adversary was usually seen as a raptor bird located at Deneb and the Dark or Great Rift of the Path of Souls. It is at this point that a judgment is made on the soul, and it chooses one of two paths. The image below depicts 10:00 p.m. at Spiro, Oklahoma on December 2, A.D. 1200 and was generated from *Starry Night Pro*.

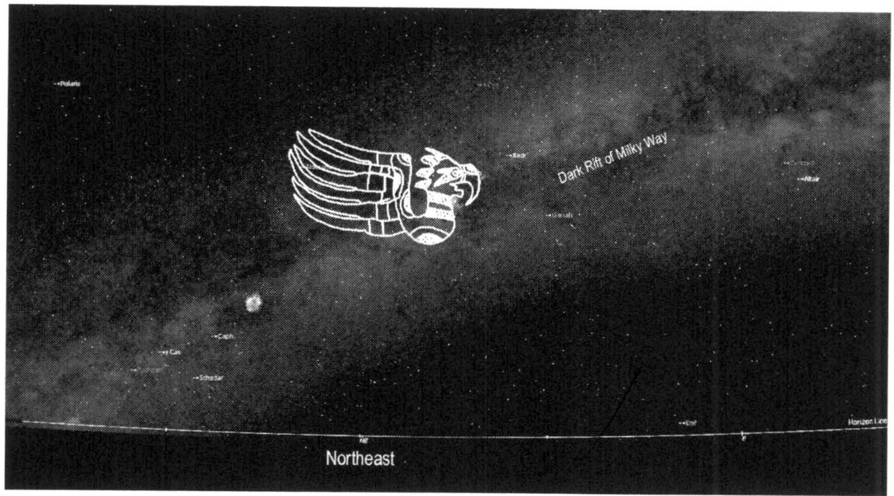

There was a river at this spot that had to be successfully crossed. A "log" across the river was used, but some souls fell back to earth at this point to be reincarnated.

In many tribal versions the adversary is described literally as a "Brain Smasher." Another tribe describes a creature that sucks the brain from the soul that does not pass the judgment. It was a way of describing "blotting the soul out of existence." The judgment was not necessarily about good and evil, it also concerned bravery, family, and other factors. The term "brain smasher" implies blotting out memory and identity.

If the adversary makes a favorable judgment on the soul, the soul then chooses one of two paths around the Dark Rift. One path is a dead-end where the soul is trapped or falls back to the world for reincarnation. The other path continues unbroken across the Milky Way. It eventually leads to a portal into the true sky world where the ancestors live.

The final destination of souls which successfully make the journey is more muddled. It is the realm of the ancestors and is usually described as at the top of the sky world. But it is mostly said to be somewhere in the north. Some tribes saw it as the North Pole star area, but others did not. Some apparently thought it was located at the point where the adversary was encountered—the Cygnus Constellation. This is an interesting component to the story that gives us clues about the actual timeframe when these beliefs were developed.

The Elite's Power

The astonishing level of social control exerted on the Mississippian people was done through an elite group of people who maintained the population's belief that they were connected to the powers in the upper world.

Birdman image redrawn from a Spiro, Oklahoma shell engraving. Credit: Herb Roe, Wikipedia Commons. Long thought to represent a dancing warrior or a representation of a sky power, Birdman more likely represented a costume worn by the elite during ceremonies to graphically demonstrate their link to the sky world.

It appears that the elite were defined by their lineage extending back into time when they came from the sky world or from some powerful group. Some of these elite were probably unusually tall people. They utilized the artifacts displaying the sacred symbols during the various rituals and ceremonies they conducted. They dressed in costumes that mimicked some of the powers of the upper world. They carried ceremonial maces to display their power. They were the holders of magical knowledge, and they closely guarded their secrets. Finally, as related by many of the archaeologists who distilled this remarkable set of ideas, the Mississippian people believed in the literal meaning of the death journey and the Path of Souls. The "literal belief" in the death journey was a critical component in maintaining social control (Hall, 1997; Lankford, Reilly, & Garber, 2011).

Hall (1997) explains, "the leaders of ranked societies in the Southeast during the Mississippian period acquired their authority by descent from previous leaders and that this relationship was symbolized by the mortuary aspect of the temple" (146). Hall provides several instances where the knowledge of the elite was closely guarded and how other members of the overall society had no knowledge of the secrets. In one example, a Winnebago Medicine Rite member, Sam Blowsnake, stated that when he entered the society, they "preached to me and told me that the most fearful things imaginable would happen to me if I made public any of this... The world would end, they said... if I told anyone, I would surely die" (68). But perhaps

Braden-style gorget found in Tennessee. It shows a member of the elite with a forked eye. He holds a ceremonial mace and a severed head demonstrating his power over life and death. Credit: Herb Roe, Wikipedia Commons.

the most telling power of the secret rituals over the populace is seen in Paul Radin's recording of the actual Winnebago Medicine Rite.

Radin arrived in Winnebago, Nebraska in 1908 to perform an ethnology study. At that time peyote rituals were just starting in the area and the Ojibwa Medicine Rite society didn't approve of it. But fewer tribe members were seeing the elite secret society and its rituals as important. One member of the Medicine Rite society, Jasper Blowsnake, the older brother of Sam who is mentioned above, had moved to the side of the peyote users. Radin arrived at the right moment and Jasper and two other former members dictated the deepest secrets to Radin who recorded them. Before the recording took place, it was stated that someone must die if the information was revealed. It took Radin two months to transcribe the story word for word. When Radin completed that part of the task he received a telegram stating his father was ill and near death. His father died shortly thereafter.

While Radin attended his father's funeral, Blowsnake checked Radin's manuscript for complete accuracy and came to believe that preserving the secrets on paper was his life's destiny. Radin's resulting book, *The Road of Life and Death*, was published in 1945. But the most interesting part of the story is the tribe members' response. After the secrets had been told to Radin and he transcribed them, all the tribal members became aware it had been done. They demanded to hear the secrets, every word as it was told to him. Radin was forced to agree, and in a small room, 40 tribal members surrounded him. "Radin read slowly from his transcribed texts to an audience that uttered not a word while listening in awe and with great respect to sacred knowledge, which until then only members of the Medicine Rite had known" (Hall, 1997: 70).

Hopewell Rituals to Moundville and Spiro

As related earlier, mainstream American archaeology seems to slowly plod along and resist new ideas. One good example of this is the response to archaeologist William Romain's theories about various mound and earthwork

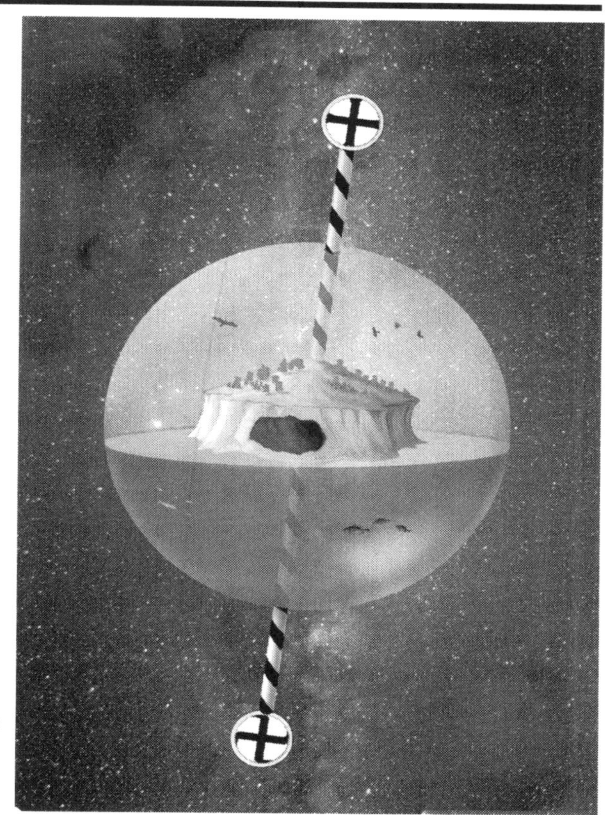

Native American Cosmos—by Duncan Long. The cosmological beliefs of Native Americans conceptualized the universe as a sphere divided into three worlds. In the middle was the Earth. Above was the sky world, which was populated by various powers. The lower world was in watery depths and was ruled by a serpent or Water Panther. A striped pole, or a cedar tree, connected the worlds together as the axis mundi. Vibrating the pole allowed shaman access to all three worlds.

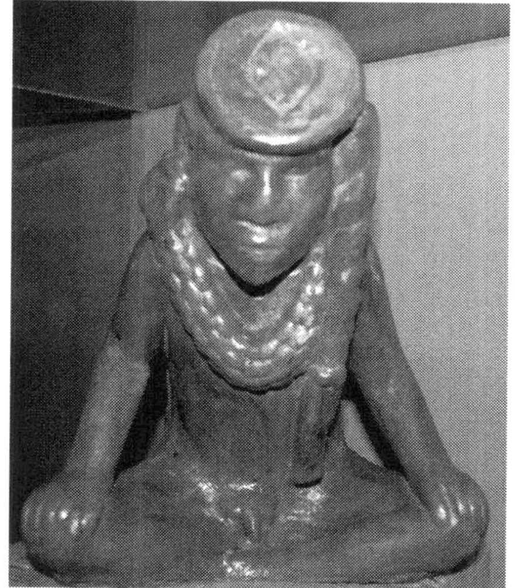

Red Horn (replica) depicted in an effigy pipe recovered at Spiro, Oklahoma in the 1930s. Photo: Lora Little. Red Horn is one of many mythical characters in the detailed cosmology of the Southeastern Ceremonial Complex. To the Sioux, Red Horn was fashioned by the Creator and sent to Earth to battle the giants and evil spirit forces plauging early humans. Other myths relate he had twin sons, a story which parallels Mayan mythology. Red Horn was also seen by some tribes as "Morning Star," typically Venus or any planet seen in the morning sky. One tribe believed Red Horn was Orion.

alignments and their purpose. Romain has written several books and articles regarding Ohio and Hopewell sites. In his 2000 book, *Mysteries of the Hopewell*, Romain theorizes that square Hopewell enclosures represented the sky while circular enclosures represented the earth. He also believes that the moon and Milky Way were also represented in various earthworks. Romain has also proposed various stellar alignments at the sites. In a chapter in a large Hopewell-archaeology oriented book, *A View from the Core* (Pacheco, 1996), Romain presented some of his ideas and concluded that Hopewell earthworks were used for ceremonies and rituals intended to help souls pass from this world to the next.

The last chapter of the 1996 Hopewell archaeology book was an invited commentary by Olaf H. Prufer. Prufer was a mainstream Ohio archaeologist who received his Ph.D. from Harvard. He died of cancer in 2008 at the age of 78. Regarding Romain's speculations in the book, Prufer wrote, "I am unable to follow the author [Romain] into this almost mystical and numerological interpretive jungle. ... All this is beyond the realm of verifiable archaeology" (415).

I personally don't necessarily believe all of Romain's speculations, but there is a lot of careful reasoning and solid facts attached to many of them. The comments from Prufer are a good example of how American mainstream archaeology maintains a status quo. Some ideas and some people are not allowed in the realm of mainstream archaeology. Still, there are some good signs from the field.

Oddly, at the Moundville, Alabama site we encountered something quite unexpected. In February 2014 Andrew Collins, my wife Lora, and I went to the site and its museum. We were the only visitors there as the excursions we took to mound sites were during the coldest and harshest winter in the south for nearly 30 years. At Moundville you now stop at a building located at the main entrance before entering the mound complex and driving to its museum located some distance away. In the entrance building you pay a fee, can view a few artifacts, and see their brief film. When you enter the building, the first thing you see is the "eye in hand" symbol. I immediately asked the site manager (an archaeologist) about it. Without any hesitation she related that it was "actually the Constellation of Orion. The three belt stars form the severed wrist." "The eye," she continued, "is a portal into the sky. It is a nebula," she added. "It takes you to the Path of Souls—the Milky Way." It was unexpected and told us that the ideas had reached the mainstream and were being accepted—at least in some of the mainstream.

A week later we visited Spiro Mounds in Oklahoma. Again there were no other visitors at the site or the museum. Scott Peterson, the site manager and site archaeologist, was a bit surprised that anyone had come in the weather conditions but was very friendly and helpful. Andrew, Lora, and I asked him a lot of questions. I initially asked him about the "eye in hand" symbol displayed on some of the museum artifacts. "It is a universal symbol," he immediately replied.

"But a symbol of what?", I asked.

"It's a universal symbol," he again said.

"Could it be Orion's Belt?", I asked.

He only smiled and shook his head, scoffing at the idea.

Andrew asked about several shell gorgets showing Birdmen in various poses. Peterson explained they were warriors and the different poses and ornamentation on them were symbols of different clan affiliations, dances, and games. He explained a few other symbols as the corn (busk) ceremony. Peterson cited only the long-held archaeological explanations of the artifacts. He then began to tell us the truly important background information about the Mississippian era. "Spiro," he said, "was the capital of the entire Mississippian Culture. All the larger sites like Cahokia, Moundville, and Etowah were ruled from Spiro." He made a comparison by relating that Washington, D.C. is the capital of America and it rules far larger cities like New York City. "Spiro was the same way," he said. "Spiro sent ambassadors to all of the other cities it ruled, and they made sure that the religious beliefs were being carefully followed."

We then asked Peterson about the skulls that appeared to have fire coming from their mouths. He related that what was being shown were "speech boxes," like the words spoken in a daily comic strip.

I was a bit amazed by this and will state that I don't buy any of it. I was hesitant to quote the archaeologist in this section but when I found the same ideas from Peterson quoted in Oklahoma newspapers, I decided that it accurately represented the way many mainstream American archaeologists think. A 2004 article in the *Times-Record* (Lovett, 2004) quotes Peterson as frequently saying that Spiro was the "Washington D.C." of prehistoric America. Maybe it is just a way to hype the hard-to-reach Spiro site that is vastly underfunded. But to me it showed the psychological processes of confirmation bias and perceptual bias. In archaeology, once a belief forms, it seemingly can't be disputed. But the problem isn't just with archaeology, it's found everywhere.

Left: Moundville, Alabama skull with "tongue" or fire coming from mouth. From: Moore (1905). Right: Bones and skulls with tongues found on artifacts from Spiro Mounds; redrawn from Phillips and Brown (1978). Are these just comic strip speech boxes as we were told at Spiro in 2014? Or do they represent the free soul and life soul leaving the dead person as modern archaeologists now assert?

Chapter 9

Pseudoarchaeology, Cult Archaeology, & Science

Alternative archaeology, fantastic archaeology, cult archaeology, fringe archaeology, and bullshit archaeology are a few of the litany of terms academic archaeology applies to ideas and people who challenge its accepted truths. The term *pseudoarchaeology* is also used to describe such efforts. Wikipedia's page on pseudoarchaeology bluntly defines it as "interpretations of the past from outside of the academic archaeological community, which typically also reject the accepted scientific and analytical methods of the discipline." The ideas of "too many" large skeletons, elite groups of people in ancient America, links between Egyptian and Native American beliefs, and rituals and stellar alignments with mounds would be dismissed as pseudoarchaeology.

Archaeologists seem to have come up with just two primary motivations they attribute to people who propose a different interpretation of the past than the academic community: 1) Nationalism characterized by racist beliefs or Nazi leanings; and, 2) Religious beliefs often linked to creationism or the Bible.

There is no doubt that both motivations have been present in some alternative history writers, but it's an uninformed psychological assertion to dismiss all alternative theorists as racists or creationists. In truth, such a callous dismissal of others with different opinions is a prime characteristic of a cult that attacks outsiders. In a brilliant synopsis of the tension between mainstream academic archaeology and "outsiders," Cornelius Holtorf, a

Professor of Archaeology at Sweden's University of Lund, wrote, "Archaeologists do not serve as a special state police force dedicated to eradicating interpretations that are considered to be false or inappropriate by a self-selected jury" (Holtorf, 2005: 549). He argues for "critical understanding and dialogue" with those who propose alternative ideas (550). He related that he sees the antagonism against what one mainstream archaeologist described as "bogus archaeology" astonishing: "Views about the past that do not sit well with his own fairly narrow, scientific approach are dismissed as 'ideologically driven pseudoscience'" (545). The idea that all the people who don't agree with mainstream archaeology are "ideologically driven" (by their racist or creationist beliefs) is the type of sweeping generalization (of outsiders) that often characterizes a cult. It is a method of mind control. Few people will think of mainstream American archaeology as a cult-like belief system, but it indoctrinates its new members, aggressively proselytizes, and judges outsiders who disagree with their beliefs as enemies. In addition, a lot of what archaeologists call their science is more like pseudoscience.

Physics Has Learned How to Engage the Public Rather than Alienate It

I've never seen a documentary about some aspect of physics that had to say the words, "The science of physics has found..." What is strange about this is that some of the most popular physics documentaries tell the general public that things like quarks, dark matter, wormholes, and black holes exist. They'll use good animation to represent these ephemeral "realities" but the actual "things" they tell us about have never really been seen and probably never will be. Instead, the proof of these rather exotic realities consists of massive, complex mathematical equations completely and utterly indecipherable to nearly everyone. We readily accept that dark matter makes up most of the universe—but it can't be seen. Black holes exist, but if you look at them you can't see anything. Okay, makes sense, right? Physics doesn't remind anyone over and over that, "we are a science." But when physicists tell us it's a fact that there are things that exist that are exotic, unseen, and impossible to ever see—we tend to just believe them. Or we are just entertained with what is truly a vast unknown. Physicists have learned how to engage the public and not insult it.

Imagine for a moment what we might think of physics as a science if in 1863 they told us the speed of light was 186,000 miles per second. Then 100 years later said, "Oops. We were wrong; it's really only 90,000 miles per second." Just 25 years from then they said, "We don't really know what we measured. But maybe it's really closer to 175,000 miles per second; we're not really sure." That hasn't happened with physics, but it's frequently the reality in archaeology.

Serpent Mound Was Built in ... ?

If you visit many of the museums associated with mounds and watch their films, you'll probably hear over and over, "The science of archaeology has found..." and then some small detail about the food or environment is revealed such as, "They ate nuts and berries." Then you'll hear some date for the particular site revealed. But as related earlier in this book, those dates change, and they actually change quite a bit. One example is given here, and it's actually recent.

In 1883 and 1886, Frederic Putnam investigated the Serpent Mound for the Peabody Museum. After cutting trenches in the mound, Putnam concluded that the mound was built sometime between 800 B.C and A.D. 100. Over the next 100 years, that was the accepted date for the mound in mainstream archaeology. In 1991 archaeologists obtained charcoal samples from areas thought to be the same places where Putnam's trenches were located. They concluded that Serpent Mound was constructed around A.D. 1130 (Pickard, 2011). So from 1991 to very recent times, Serpent Mound's date was about A.D. 1130.

Bradley Lepper, Curator of Archaeology for the Ohio Historical Society, was one of the archaeologists involved in the 1991 study. In November of 2013, Lepper wrote in the *Columbus Dispatch* that the charcoal they dated in 1991 came from a mixture of soil that could have come from the mound's time of construction *or* something intrusive that happened later. He related, "That means we're not really sure what we dated." Lepper's 2013 article went on to describe the results from a newer study. In 2012 a team of archaeologists from several universities, including William Romain, took several core samples from different areas of the mound. They found that the

Serpent Mound near Locust Grove, Ohio shown from the viewing platform at the site. It is a 1,348-foot-long effigy mound depicting an uncoiling snake. It is formed from a 20-foot-wide, 4 to 5-feet-high embankment of earth with a line of stones under the earthen mound. It appears to be aligned to Polaris and has various solar alignments incorporated into the undulations. There are several conical burial mounds located nearby and many more mounds in the area. Photo: Lora Little.

mound was probably constructed sometime between 400 B.C. to 80 B.C., which was within the dates first proposed back in 1886.

Confused by all this? Here's more to add to the confusion. The official Ohio Historical Society marker at Serpent Mound, updated in 2003, relates that the mound was built around 1000 A.D. In his profusely illustrated book on Ohio archaeology, Bradley Lepper (2005) tells us that the mound was constructed "about 850 to 990 years ago," which puts it between A.D. 1155-1015 (217).

Pseudoarchaeology: Misleading and Defrauding the Public

One of the primary reasons archaeologists say they need to attack pseudoarchaeology is that pseudoarchaeologists are misleading and somehow defrauding the public. There have been attempts to defraud; mainly through the sale of fake artifacts. But most of what archaeologists call pseudoarchaeology simply entertains people and proposes alternatives. Because television shows and books create revenue, some archaeologists and skeptics argue that misleading information presented as fact is defrauding the public. But for about 70 years, archaeology textbooks sold to countless students, films that generated revenue, and paid academic archaeologists insisted that the Clovis culture was first in the Americas. They were wrong. They still don't know the answer. There are also a lot of examples similar to the Serpent Mound dating problem. In essence, the "facts" seem to shift around. That's somewhat true in all disciplines, but most genuine science areas have learned how to adjust to new information and use it to their advantage in keeping the public interested. Archaeology feuds with outsiders and even those inside the field who assert their accepted beliefs might be wrong. It's a huge mistake based on jealousy, esteem issues, and deep-seated doubts.

There are reasons why archaeologists remind you over and over that they are scientists. It's not because they are scientists. They are a tightly-

knit group with an underlying motive to maintain a belief system. It's an exclusive group that functions a lot like the elite priests of the mound-builder cultures. There are plenty of examples from mainstream archaeology where anyone from outside their field is ridiculed and attacked for making claims that go against the mainstream view—even when the claims are based on scientific evidence.

Cult Archaeology, Pinson Mounds, and Skeptics on Göbekli Tepe

In the late 1980s and 1990s, I was a member of the Tennessee Anthropological Society partly because I liked receiving their publications. In 1991 an article by mainstream archaeologists (Mainfort & Kwas, 1991) appeared in the *Tennessee Anthropologist* that refuted an article about the Bat Creek Stone in a prior issue of the same journal (McCulloch, 1988).

The Bat Creek Stone still exists and was sent to Cyrus Thomas of the Bureau of Ethnology in 1889 by Field Agent John Emmert after it was excavated from a mound in Tennessee with a group of burials and other artifacts. In the Bureau's 12th Annual Report, Thomas concluded it was probably a Cherokee inscription. The object was just a curiosity, and there the issue remained until the 1970s, when it was proposed through carbon dating and other evidence that the tablet was a Paleo-Hebrew inscription (McCulloch, 1988).

In their 1991 article, attacking the tablet and the author of the prior article, Mainfort and Kwas wrote twice that the stone was "reportedly excavated" (1, 3), "allegedly recovered" (5), and "allegedly found" (14). They also mentioned several times that other artifacts associated with the tablet were "reportedly" and "allegedly" found. Finally, the mainstream archaeologists used the term "cult archaeology" 14 times in their 12 pages of text attacking McCulloch's earlier article. The term "rogue professors" was also used, along with a quote stating that people making such claims have the ability to defraud the public. Mainfort and Kwas won the battle. In 2014 the Smithsonian formally announced that they concluded the artifact was a fake largely based upon allegations made by Mainfort and Kwas.

Ridiculing and attributing questionable motives to those who present evidence contrary to mainstream beliefs is a standard ploy in archaeology and is the major method used by many of the online skeptics. It works. Archaeology does utilize some scientific techniques; it also utilizes reasoning and logic, but it cannot tolerate those who disagree with the mainstream view. In that sense it is more of a cult and religion than it is a science.

On a related sidenote, in 1987, Robert Mainfort (then the Tennessee State Archaeologist) told me in a formal interview that the Pinson site in Tennessee had 12 definite mounds (Little, 1987). But in 1916 a Smithsonian survey showed 34 or 35 mounds there. Currently, the Wikipedia entry on Pinson relates that there are 17 mounds there. The Tennessee State Park site on Pinson relates that the site "contains at least 15" mounds. Tennessee's "History for Kids" website states, "There are known to be at least 17 man-made mounds there."

An archaeology textbook chapter on Pinson (Mainfort & Sullivan, 1998) states that Pinson has "a minimum of twelve mounds" (57). A 2002 book (Anderson & Mainfort: 27) relates that Pinson, "includes more than twelve mounds." And in the recent book *Pinson Mounds* (Mainfort, 2013) it is stated, "the Pinson Mounds complex includes at least thirteen mounds." The 2013 book costs $47.36; the 2002 book is $36.58; and the 1998 book is only $52.25. I don't think charging so much for the constantly shifting facts is defrauding the public, but perhaps Mainfort should simply say that there are "allegedly" 12 or more mounds at the site. I bought all of the books listed above, have been to the site more than a dozen times, and I'm still confused about how many mounds are at Pinson. But I don't have a degree in archaeology so that may be the problem.

I personally respect both Bob Mainfort and Bradley Lepper and admire their work greatly. Both of them have made significant contributions. One has to admire Lepper's honesty and frankness about the Serpent Mound dating issue. And in truth, Mainfort's waffling on the number of mounds at

Pinson reflects the way archaeological information is processed and evaluated over time. But the attacks on outsiders are not smart. Still, the worst offenders are the self-described skeptics who are "true believers" in their own way.

The skeptical archaeological bloggers are often a bit worse at discerning facts than actual archaeologists. On his blog (Colavito, 2013d) Jason Colavito wrote about how and when alternative researchers became aware of the Turkey site of Göbekli Tepe: "It's been all the rage for the past five years because *Smithsonian* magazine had an article about it in November 2008, which is where all the alternative researchers first learned about something scholars had been working on for a very long time before." That is a rather clear-cut and understandable assertion: *All the alternative researchers first learned about Göbekli Tepe after the 2008 Smithsonian article*. Is this assertion about Göbekli Tepe true?

More than a year before Colavito made his assertion (Colavito, 2012a) he "reviewed" Andrew Collins' book *The Cygnus Mystery* and even mentioned the dvd documentary based on it. The documentary has has over one million views. In his commentary, Colavito called the book a "silly foray."

The point is this. Chapter one in Collins' book, *The Cygnus Mystery*, published in 2006, is entitled "The oldest temple in the world." It is about Göbekli Tepe. The book contains many other sections on Göbekli Tepe as well as several photos of the site Collins took on his 2004 visit. On *The Cygnus Mystery* dvd (2006) Collins stated in his first interview, "The Cygnus Mystery began for me when in 2004 I visited Göbekli Tepe." The film then shows images of the site Collins took on his 2004 visit there as he describes it on film. In truth, most "alternative researchers," as Colavito calls them, first became aware of the site when Collins' 2006 book was published. In the Introduction to Collins's new book on Göbekli Tepe (2014: 7) Graham Hancock wrote, "there is little question that Andrew was one of the first writers to realize the greater significance of Göbekli Tepe, bringing it to the attention of the mysteries community as early as 2004." After his first trip to the site in 2004 Collins began issuing articles on it. It is an easy fact to check

out, and readers can decide for themselves why Colavito presented the false information.

Still another skeptical website is operated by Edwin Hodge, who relates he is a doctoral student at Canada's University of Victoria. The site is called the *Skeptical Cube Farm*. In July 2011, Hodge wrote that Collins had asserted that the "Biblical beings known as 'Watchers' came to the earth from the Heavens to impregnate human women..." (Hodge, 2011). Of course, Collins has never written that the Watchers were aliens or from the heavens. In fact, Collins has written in several books that he believes the Watchers were a group of advanced humans who left the area around Turkey's Lake Van and moved to the lower regions of Mesopotamia where some of them merged with less advanced races. (I personally found Andrew's assertion both intriguing and disappointing at the same time. I wish they *had* been aliens.) It was Andrew's book on the Watchers (Collins, 1996) where I first became aware of his remarkable research on this topic.

Hodge (2011) also derided Collins writings about Göbekli Tepe and falsely stated, "He's [Collins] never been there, nor has he apparently spoken to the researchers who have." As stated previously, Andrew first visited Göbekli Tepe in 2004 (Collins, 2006) and his new book (Collins, 2014) devotes many pages to his interviews with Klaus Schmidt, the archaeologist in charge of the site. I'm fairly sure that the skeptics never read Collins' books and I assume that explains why they cite false information as being factual. They simply didn't know the facts and were driven by a belief system that blinds them from seeking the truth. It is a good example of perceptual bias at work and how pseudoscience erodes archaeology from within it.

As previously mentioned, when such psychological processes are active they are unconscious—not recognized by the individual. It is somewhat similar to the defense mechanism of *denial*, which most people misunderstand. Denial as a defense mechanism is not something of which the person is aware. It is an unconscious process where the person is perceptually blind to the truth. It is a way in which an individual can maintain a false set of beliefs. The fact that an "alternative historian" might be right

about something seems to be unbearable to the skeptics, so defense mechanisms come into play. In essence, some of the skeptics are themselves cranks who want to be true scientists, but are overwhelmed by their own incompetence, which they misinterpret as insight and personal brilliance. The truly sad part of all of this is that mainstream archaeology ignores the falsehoods put out by its own skeptical defenders who essentially police the boundaries they arbitrarily set. In so doing, they alienate the general public.

Alien Ideas, the Elite, & Elongated Skulls

Archaeologists and their always-active skeptics deride all mention of "Ancient Aliens" as well as European contact in the Americas before Columbus. However, many Native American tribes have mythology relating to sky people and that they came from the stars. In the *19th Annual Report of*

Left: This odd figure recovered from a mound at Spiro, Oklahoma looks a bit like a spaceman. Photo—Lora Little.

Above: Hightower-style shell gorget excavated from Etowah, Georgia depicting birdman theme. Credit: Herb Rowe, Wikipedia Commons.

the American Bureau of Ethnology (Powell, 1900), an ancient belief of the Cherokee was described. The myth related that, "The first man and woman, and the sun and moon were all created by a number of beneficent beings who came down for the purpose from an upper world, to which they afterward returned..." (440).

The Osage related that they too came from the stars naming the Pleiades as their place of origin (Lankford, Reilly, & Garber, 2011: 22). However, it is notable that of all the tribes of the Eastern Woodlands, only one had definite myths of their origin being in the stars. That was the Natchez who claimed that only their ruling class came down from the sky (28). Southwestern tribes have similar tales of star people as do so many others that a full summary is not necessary. It is accepted by anthropologists that the legends are there. Believing the stories as literally true is another matter. But ridiculing them seems biased and demeaning.

One of the History Channel's *Ancient Aliens* episodes suggested that the reason Orion seems to have been so important in the ancient world is because the aliens who came to Earth originated from there. Of course the Path of Souls death journey indicates that Orion was a way station used to jump to the Milky Way and then to Cygnus. On April 17, 2014, NASA released a statement to the press that their Kepler Telescope had discovered the first Earth-sized planet in a habitable zone—not too close or too far away from

Area where the Kepler Telescope has been focusing in its search for planets capable of sustaining life. The area of Cygnus is where 186f was found. Credit: NASA.

its star—where the conditions are ideal for life as we know it. They named this Earth-like planet Kepler-186f. There are 4 other planets orbiting the central star. The planet is located in the Constellation of Cygnus (NASA, 2014). It is "only" 500 light-years from Earth.

I see nothing to definitively support the pervasive "Ancient Aliens" idea that hordes of ancient astronauts came to earth and created, well, everything. I have earlier written and still support the idea that it is probable that sometime in the past, there was a visit or two to Earth made by wandering explorers from out there, somewhere. I believe it's statistically probable. Anything beyond that simple probability is to me speculation. But I don't see such speculation as *harmful* in any way. In fact, it is interesting to a lot of people. Physicists learned this fact and have produced a lot of documentaries hypothesizing on how aliens might get here, what they might look like, how their craft would function, and so on. That fantastic material holds an audience's interest, but they manage to reveal a lot of physics in the process.

I don't see any alien influence in ancient America, but the key point here is that it's completely clear that there was an elite group of people in these ancient cultures who rigidly maintained social control. There had to be something profound in their knowledge, appearance, and behavior so that they were able to exert such a influence on the masses. The knowledge

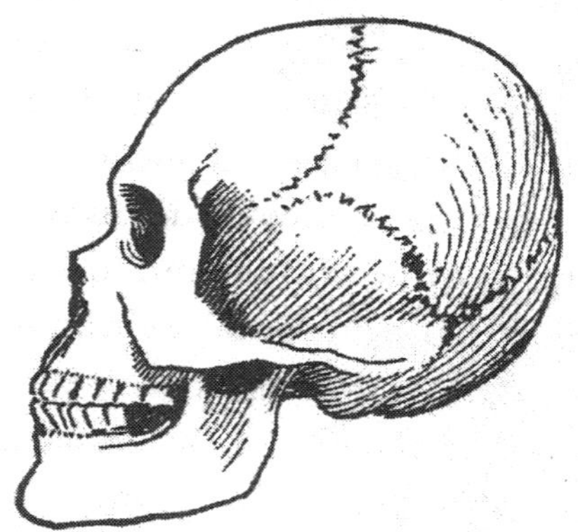

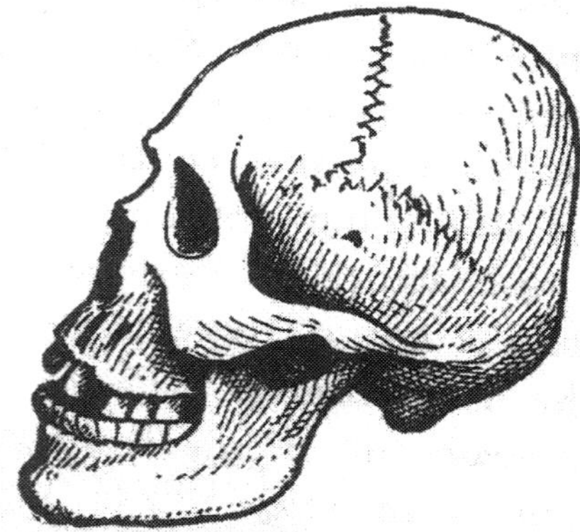

Elongated skulls found in stone graves near Nashville. From: Thruston (1890).

Elongated skulls were once displayed at the Moundville, Alabama museum. Photo: Greg Little, 1987.

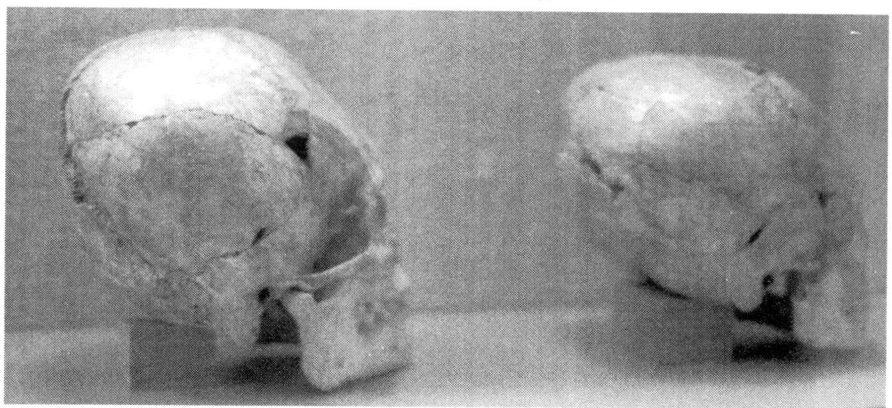

was about the death journey, but where these beliefs came from or how they developed is a mystery.

Another widely-touted discovery from excavations conducted in various parts of the world is that many "elongated" skulls have been found. Excavations in South and Central America, North America, and even at Neolithic sites in Asia have found deformed, elongated skulls. While it is known that many Native American tribes and some in South and Central America deliberately deformed the heads of babies to elongate them, nothing has ever been found that conclusively shows that they are aliens—in the real sense of the word.

DNA?

The vast majority of people do not know the difference between mitochondrial DNA and human nuclear DNA. It is also claimed at times that the entire DNA genome of various ancient skeletal remains has been successfully sequenced.

Mitochondrial DNA (or mtDNA) is *not* human DNA. It is DNA extracted from tiny organelles found in almost all cells in the human body. The mitochondria are a vestigial form of bacteria (called organelles) that convert

sugar (glucose) into usable energy for cellular functions. As specialized bacteria, the mitochondria reproduce on their own. Everyone's mitochondria came from their mother (Little, 1997). Studying mtDNA is far easier than studying human DNA, and it has been found useful to trace the movements of ancient people because the mtDNA mutates at a fairly regular rate. But again, it isn't human DNA to start with.

When an "unknown" type of mtDNA is found, it only means that a different female lineage has been found, implying that a mutation in the mitochondrial DNA happened and was then passed on to the descendants of the first female with the mutation. The daughters of this new mtDNA mutation pass it on to their daughters and so on. Many "extinct" variations of mtDNA

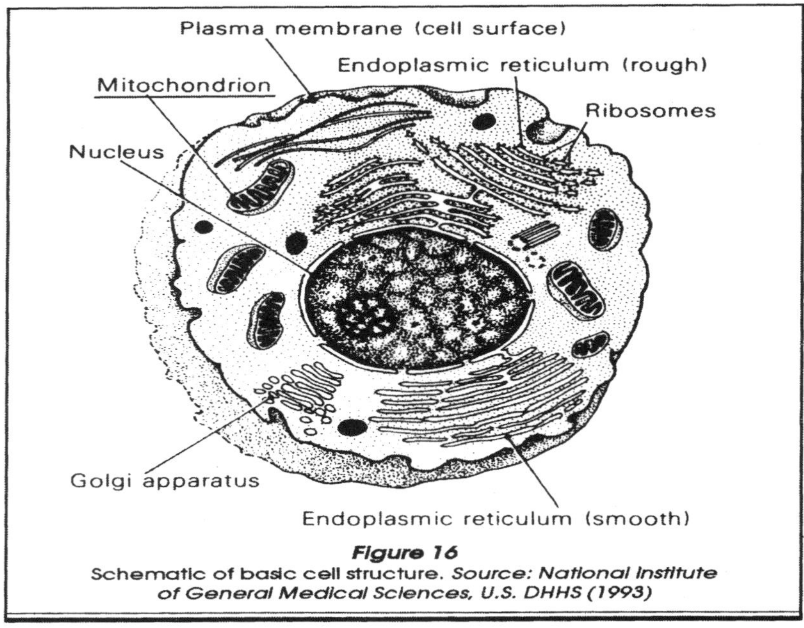

Figure 16
Schematic of basic cell structure. *Source: National Institute of General Medical Sciences, U.S. DHHS (1993)*

Schematic illustration of a human cell. The mitochondria are small football-shaped organelles found in nearly all cells—in the hundreds. A single one is called a mitochondrion. They ingest glucose (sugar) and produce adenosine triphosphate (ATP), which is the energy used by cells. The mitochondria are inherited from the female side. Human DNA, or nuclear DNA (nDNA) is found in the nucleus. Human DNA is much more difficult to sequence than mitochondrial DNA (mtDNA). Human DNA has 3 billion base pairs while mtDNA has only 16,000. Credit: US DHHS (1993).

A single mitochondrion magnified by 228,000 times by an electron microscope. Credit: Little (1997).

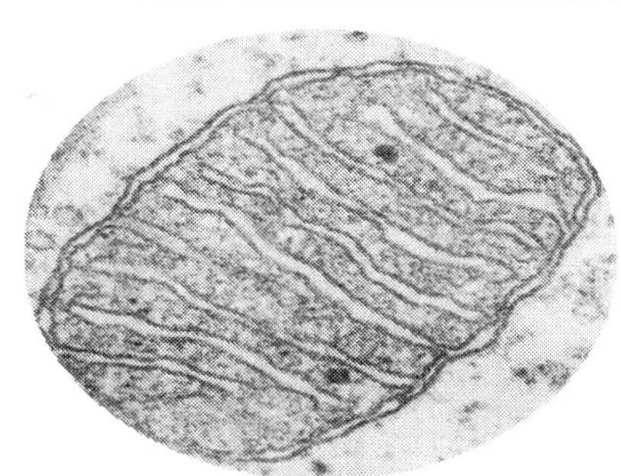

have been found, especially in South America (Little, Van Auken, & Little, 2002). An extinct version of mtDNA simply means that it was a hereditary lineage that eventually died out on the female side. Mitochondria are also present in plants, fungi, and other living organisms.

In 2002 (Shimada, et al., 2002) a group of researchers extracted mitochondrial DNA from teeth removed from 55 individuals buried in Moche pyramids from three pyramid sites in Peru. A total of 40 of the mtDNA samples fit into the expected types—called *haplogroups A, B, C, & D*. However, 15 of the individuals' mtDNA types did not match any known haplogroups. I contacted the head researcher, Izumi Shimada, Professor of Anthropology at Southern Illinois University. Shimada told me: "Nobody can specify what the 'other' haplogroups were—at least not yet. Although the four defined haplogroups (A-D) seem to effectively account for the present-day indigenous populations, there are a variety of reasons to think there were other haplogroups in ancient times" (Little, Van Auken, & Little, 2002: 56).

What does this mean? In brief, it means that there were now-extinct (female) hereditary lineages who lived in ancient South America. It does not mean that they were aliens. It means their female family side died out and became extinct. Were they the elite? It isn't known. A claim that an unknown type of mitochondrial DNA proves the individual it came from was an "alien," is essentially baseless.

Human DNA (nDNA or nuclear DNA) is far more difficult to study, and when sequencing is done on the three billion amino acid links in DNA taken

from ancient remains, a lot of sequencing errors can occur. In general, sequencing errors are just skipped or "corrected" by simply substituting the linkages that are known to be correct. A lot of "discoveries" are said to come from a successful, complete DNA analysis of ancient bones. But journalists and writers describing the results seldom read the important "fine print": the actual methodology and limitations. With rapid advances in technology, the genetic research of ancient remains will be greatly enhanced. For the moment, nothing that can be truly called "alien" has been found in human DNA. But it might one day be found. As for mitochondrial DNA, it is "alien" or nonhuman in the sense it comes from vestigial bacteria.

I've taught psychopharmacology at several colleges and have written a textbook on it. In general, I have found that the majority of people can easily

Spiro, Oklahoma (replica) pipes. The one on the right is called the "Lucifer Pipe," but its origin has been traced to Cahokia, Illinois. It depicts a naked man with an oversized head holding down a deer with one hand while holding an unknown fringed object in the other. The pipes are thought to have been used in ceremonies. The back of a different pipe on the left shows the opening and bowl. Photos: Lora Little.

get confused about nDNA and mtDNA. It is almost useless to explain the difference as many writers seem to confuse mitochondrial DNA with human DNA.

There have been several successful recent efforts by geneticists to sequence DNA in Denisovian remains (see Andrew Collins' Afterword in this book). These may help bring an understanding of where the elite originated and where the ideas about the Path of Souls started.

It is unknown why the practice of elongating heads was done, but it is usually explained by anthropologists as being performed to make the person more attractive. A more likely explanation is that the people were attempting to mimic the appearance of an elite group. The Egyptian pharaohs are an example of an elite group. But for the moment, most archaeologists consider that idea far-fetched.

While skeptics and archaeologists claim that the widespread belief in alien intervention is harmful to "science," it's difficult to agree with the "harm" aspect. It is an exciting idea to a lot of people and keeps them interested in archaeological findings. I'll again mention that I do not accept any alien intervention claims, but I can't see it as a harmful idea. In the 1960s, mainstream archaeology saw beliefs that challenged the Clovis-First idea as harmful. It was harmful in that it threatened cherished beliefs.

Archaeologists also see the wide interest in giant skeletons as harmful to science. They appear to see themselves in some sort of battle with people who believe "crazy ideas" which are in some way harming their "science." It's not really harmful at all and could be turned into something beneficial to archaeology. Scientists and the "masses" have long believed a host of crazy ideas. Not everyone who is interested in extremely tall skeletons is a creationist or a racist Nazi. Believers in ancient aliens are not holding an Inquisition or subjecting archaeologists to torture. Nor are they withholding funds for research. Archaeologists also view esoteric beliefs about the mystical powers of mounds as something harmful, but again, there is no real harm produced from the beliefs. Perhaps more harmful is mainstream

archaeology's pronounced tendency toward confirmation bias and serving as the police in order to maintain their accepted truth.

One more fact is relevant here. Archaeologists and skeptics both make money from books, talks, and articles where they get to discuss ideas about Ancient Aliens, giant skeletons, UFOs, lost continents, and mystical beliefs. Skeptics ask for donations on websites, ask you to buy their books so they can continue to do battle with the crazy side, and try to get on television to promote themselves. From a Jungian perspective, on an unconscious level they are fighting with their own shadows and making money from it. The ongoing battle with the enemy—their own shadow—keeps their field moving along at a snail's pace. Sadly, it is doubtful that they will ever understand or care about what this means.

The rituals involving the Path of Souls were ways to honor the dead and an attempt to assist the soul of the deceased in making a successful journey to an afterlife or to reincarnation. Some mounds were essentially funeral mounds or mortuary mounds used to prepare the dead. This illustration of a mortuary atop a mound depicts the site of Ocmulgee, Georgia, another key mound site in the Southeastern Ceremonial Complex. Credit: National Park Service.

Chapter 10

Origin of Mound Building & the Death Journey Beliefs

The primary purpose of this book has been to present ancient Native American beliefs about the death journey. In particular, there are widespread ideas about the roles of the constellations of Orion and Cygnus in a journey to the stars made by the dead. Many ancient sites around the world seem to have alignments that target one or both of these constellations and the Native American death journey to the Path of Souls. Pieced together only in recent years by mainstream American archaeologists, they may have found the real answer to the Cygnus-Orion issue. The relationship between the Native American death journey and that found in Egypt is hopefully obvious, but it will be addressed briefly.

In moving toward the answer to the Cygnus-Orion issue, a range of topics became relevant. For example, how and when the artifacts displaying the death symbols were excavated needed to be described. Since the majority of these artifacts were found in Mississippian era mounds, a brief overview of the various eras of mound-building cultures was presented. Another important topic that was explained was how the Native American tribes developed a sort of "cultural amnesia," wherein their knowledge of their own symbols and beliefs were lost and forgotten by many tribes. The stories about the 1500's expeditions into America's Southeastern mound-building regions provided several pieces of important information. The details from these well-documented stories showed that the mound builders were far more advanced than most people typically believe, that the population of Native

Americans was far greater in numbers than most people realize, and that the natives were nearly exterminated by the spread of diseases to which they had no resistance. We also know from the early encounters between Europeans and mound cultures that the society was highly stratified and controlled by hereditary chiefs and an elite class of priests.

The Smithsonian's involvement in the 1800's excavations of mounds is an important topic in its own right for several reasons. First, the Smithsonian's stated goal was to determine whether the mounds were built by some "lost race" or by the ancestors of the Native American tribes who were present when Europeans began exploring and settling America. Second, at the time the Smithsonian began their mound project, the most widely-held belief about the mounds was that they were built by a lost race of advanced "giants" who had been exterminated by the "savage Indians." In addition, a real investigation into some of the "giant skeleton" newspaper reports was conducted. Some Native American myths and legends about the "giants" were also presented. Finally, there are many people who have asserted that the Smithsonian has been involved in a long-running conspiracy designed to cover up the real facts about America's mound builders. To answer the "conspiracy" issue, it was necessary to look at the facts about the large skeletons and carefully review the Smithsonian's own reports.

There are several conclusions that we can draw about America's mound builders, the issue of giants, the Smithsonian's involvement, and the evolution of the idea of the death journey to the Path of Souls. I have always accepted that the mounds were constructed by the ancestors of the Native American tribes which were present when the first Europeans came to the Americas. However, it is known that ancient America was a melting pot, just as it has been in historic times. That may or may not be an important issue in tracking the origin of the Path of Souls idea. Some skeptics claim that all attempts to reevaluate ancient American history are racist. There is no doubt that some agendas are driven by biased underlying belief systems—on both sides of the issue. But seeking the truth isn't racist nor is it unscientific.

Origin of the Ideas of the Path of Souls & Mound Building

We do not know where the ideas about the death journey originate. Nor do we know the origin of mound building—an almost universal burial practice in the ancient world. But both issues are moving toward answers. It is interesting that in ancient Egypt, both Orion and Cygnus seem to have been important in the death journey. But evidence about the Egyptian ideas of death dates to no earlier than 3000 B.C. Andrew Collins has found that Cygnus was a focal point of many other ancient religious sites including Göbekli Tepe in Turkey. The site dates to at least 9600 B.C. and *could* have been *a* starting point of the death journey beliefs. Perhaps it is no coincidence that the Clovis culture in America is believed to have begun at the same time by migrations into America from Asia.

Many mainstream archaeologists readily admit that the archaeological record of ancient America is unclear and that several migrations to the Americas may have happened as early as 40,000 years ago (Dillehay, 2000). It is acknowledged by some American archaeologists that the first sites of occupation may have been in South America (242) and that it is possible Neanderthals could have been the first to arrive if the first migrations were 40,000 years ago (242). The problem is that no skeletal remains that old have been found in America, and little definitive evidence has been found at sites dating that far back in time. And there is no evidence whatsoever of Neanderthals ever being in ancient America. Also acknowledged is the strong possibility that migrations to America by the (18,000 B.C. - 14,000 B.C.) Solutrean culture of Spain and France could have occurred (243). The Solutreans are sometimes suggested as the people who brought the Clovis Culture to the Americas around 9600 B.C. But the timeframes of the two cultures are widely separated.

Archaeologist David Meltzer summarized the accumulated genetic studies of Native American populations and explains that the evidence points to migrations to the Americas somewhere from 42,000 to 21,000 years ago

(Meltzer, 2009). More recently, a host of geneticists and linguists have concluded that people migrated to America from Siberia starting around 25,000 years ago (Stromberg, 2014). The study upon which the 25,000-year-ago migration theory is based, with an astonishing 54 authors, concluded that there were three distinct waves of migrations, all from Asia (Reich, et al., 2012). It is clear that nearly all of the genetic evidence points toward Asia as the source for the past migrations of large groups of people into the Americas. There may have been some other intrusions, but in terms of total population, if other groups entered the Americas, their numbers were relatively small. There is no clear-cut evidence of large migrations to America by European-based cultures, but some contact by pre-historic European people is not only possible, but is probable. It is a fascinating mystery to many people, a fact which archaeologists seem to completely misinterpret.

None of these hypotheses about migrations to ancient America tell us much about from where the ideas related to the Path of Souls originated. Nor do they explain the origin of mound building—if in fact the practice

England's Silbury Hill. Standing at 131 feet in height with a base of 5 acres, Silbury Hill is taller than any American mound. It was constructed starting around 2750 B.C. and has never been completely excavated. It is one of hundreds of mounds in the U.K., many of which have circular earthworks and moats. Photo: Lora Little.

had a single origin. Some of the most interesting mounds I have seen are in Sweden, and mounds in the UK are essentially identical to American mounds. Mound building may simply be a natural progression of ideas related to handling and honoring the dead. However, it is likely that the importance of Deneb, Cygnus, and the Dark Rift extends back to the time when Deneb was the closest star to the north pole and the Dark Rift was seen to rotate above it—some 16,500 - 18,000 years ago. Whether the idea originated in America at that time or was carried into America by a group of elite people simply isn't known. But is clearly an area where one can speculate.

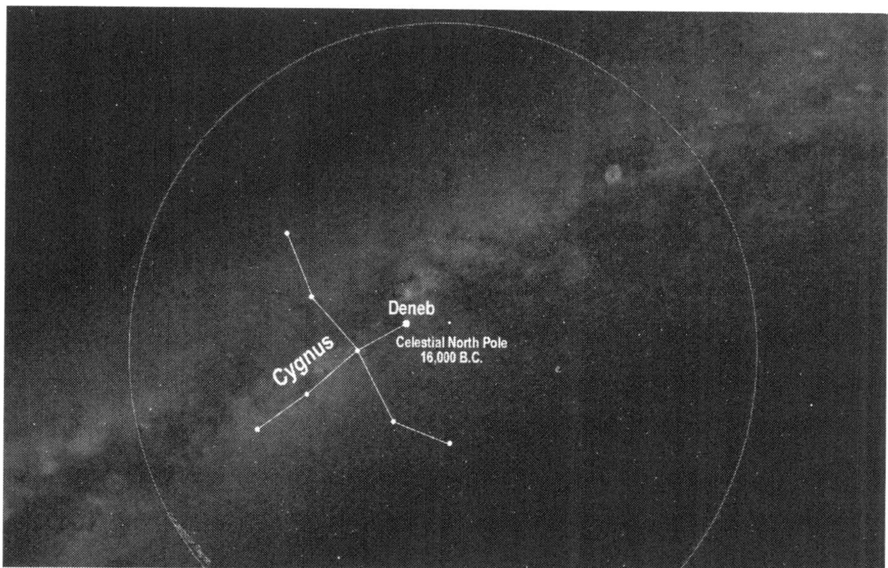

Cygnus as the location of the pole star, circa 16,000 B.C. For several thousand years, the stars of Cygnus served as the north pole stars. Around 16,000 B.C., Deneb, the brightest star in the constellation of Cygnus, was very close to the precise spot of the north pole. The illustration above, generated from *Starry Night Pro*, shows the celestial north pole as it would have been viewed from Spiro, Oklahoma in 16,000 B.C. The Dark Rift would have been seen to slowly rotate around Deneb in a counter-clockwise fashion. The "imperishable stars," as the Egyptians called them, were the stars that never set in the northern sky. This could well be the origin of Cygnus as being a key spot on the Path of Souls, as Andrew Collins has suggested. How or when it came to be incorporated into Native American ideas about the death journey isn't known.

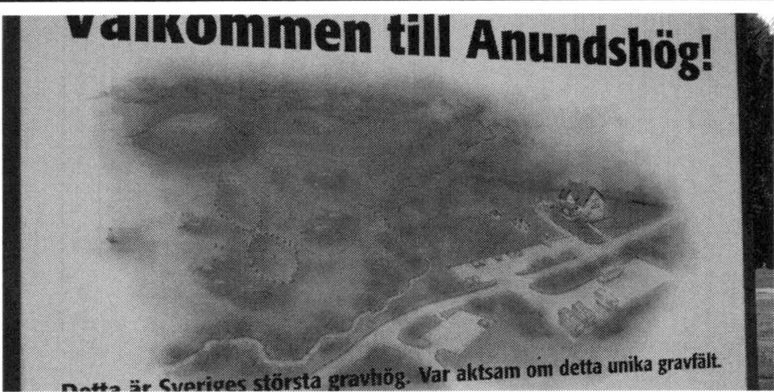

Sign leading into the Anundshög, Sweden mound complex and stone ship site. There are at least 8 mounds at the site and many more in the surrounding area. In addition, there are 4 “stone ships” in the mound area formed by upright stones. The site is dated to A.D. 210-550. Photo: Lora Little.

The largest mound at Anundshög, Sweden is a platform mound 30-feet tall with a diameter of 200 feet. Below the mound is a row of standing stones that forms one of the four “stone ships” at the site. Photo: Lora Little.

Photo of mounds at Gamla Uppsala, Sweden. Odin and his two sons, Thor and Loki, have direct links to the site and it is believed that Thor and Loki may both have been buried here. There once were somewhere between 2000 to 3000 mounds in the immediate area, but today, about 50 remain. Photo: Lora Little.

Chapter 11

Giants in Ancient America, The Smithsonian Controversy, & the Elite

The use of the term "giant" is a bit more complicated than skeptics assert. The Smithsonian spokesperson's statement that, "there was no prehistoric race of giants" (*Science News*, 2012) was meant as a slap at the proponents of giant skeletons. However, archaeologists use the term "giant" too. A 2008 report by two American university archaeologists was entitled "Forensic iconography: the case of the Moche giants" (Cordy-Collins & Merbs, 2008). In their study, they examined five "giant skeletons" (their terminology) excavated from lavish tombs at a Moche pyramid in Peru. Their "giants" ranged in height from 5' 10" to 6'—quite a bit taller than the populace. But the intention in this book was to look at the evidence of what might be more accurately termed a "giant."

We found no support for the assertions that a race of "giants" once ruled America—using the underlying meaning typically attributed to the term *giant*. But it is clear that exceptionally tall people were present in ancient America and that some of them held an elite status. It's likely that these tall people had other body proportions that matched their height. They seem to have ranged in height from well over six feet to nearly eight feet tall. It's also possible that some of these people were even taller, but the evidence for that assertion relies on accounts that are likely exaggerated or at the least are not verifiable. There were a lot of these tall people, far more than would be

expected by chance. In short, those who believe in the idea will continue to do so, and skeptics will continue to deny it all. But there was an exceptionally large number of tall people during the mound-building eras, and for whatever reason, they seem to have been buried in prominent mounds. These exceptionally tall people seem to have been most concentrated in the Adena and Hopewell areas around Ohio and particularly in West Virginia, but there is evidence of these tall people scattered nearly everywhere in America. The Kanawha Valley in West Virginia is clearly the area where these tall people were most concentrated. It is very unlikely that any of these tall people had the disorder of gigantism, but of course that will be a way skeptics will dismiss it. As stated earlier, actual gigantism is very, very rare.

It should be stressed that the many Native American tribal legends about giants have been passed down as if they have a literal meaning. The stories are told as true stories, not as a children's tale. In sum, the stories state that at a remote time in the past, a tall and fierce group of people invaded America. The tall people became the chiefs and priestly class. Over time they became increasingly corrupt until the populace rose against them.

Combined with the knowledge that Europeans encountered many tall chiefs and leaders, there should be little doubt that there was a group of people who, probably through heredity, became the elite. In a society where

Illustration by Theodor de Bry (from *Grand Voyages*,1591) of Spanish explorers meeting tall chief during their encounters in Florida.

the average height was 5' 6", it is easy to see how people standing 7 to 8 feet in height could be seen as giants. The height which the tallest of these people reached is debatable, and their origin is unclear.

The Smithsonian Conspiracy

It is an easy leap of logic to claim that the Smithsonian's 1800's mound survey project had determined the answer to its question of "Who built the mounds?" before the project began. Whether or not it was a true scientific search is also debatable, but there is no doubt that as far as mainstream archaeology is concerned, the answer they gave, remains the answer today. ***But they most certainly reached the correct conclusion. There should be no doubt that the Native American tribal ancestors built the mounds and earthworks.***

Skeptics cite the fact that the Smithsonian never displayed skeletons from giants as a way to assert that such skeletons were never found. On the other hand, those who support the giant skeleton reports cite the fact that the Smithsonian never displayed such skeletons (and denies ever actually having them) as evidence for the idea that the Smithsonian conspired to hide them. Both of these ideas are essentially misguided. The goal of the Smithsonian's mound survey project was not to collect full skeletal remains—only skulls that could be displayed. Cyrus Thomas' letter of instructions to his Field Agents (presented in Chapter 4 of this book) makes that clear. In addition, it was consistently reported by the Field Agents that skeletal remains often crumbled when attempts were made to remove them. In some of the descriptions of the large skeletons found by the field agents, they reported trying to remove them. These efforts failed because the remains were at times spongy and fell apart or were brittle and crumbled to dust. C. B. Moore found the same thing with his excavations.

The Smithsonian's conclusion about mound building could have been more appropriately worded, but that can probably be said about virtually

every written conclusion. The biggest failure of the Smithsonian, in retrospect, was ignoring the issue of "giants" that was swirling in the newspapers when the mound survey was conceived. The fact that they reported on the excavation of many large skeletons certainly shows that they were not trying to hide them. However, the Smithsonian could have dealt with the entire "conspiracy" issue by making a few statements directly addressing the issue. They should have stressed that their excavations did find several tall skeletons in mounds and that their earlier ethnological studies indicated that there were some tall people referred to in the Native American legends. Even the recent comments from the Smithsonian regarding "giants" could have easily dealt with the issue. Instead of stating, "there was no prehistoric race of giants" (*Science News*, 2012), they could have admitted that there were, in fact, a fair number of skeletal remains found that measured from 6.5 to nearly 8 feet in height. The lack of being scientifically open and honest isn't just the Smithsonian's failure; it is a colossal and ongoing failure of mainstream archaeology. Rather than taking advantage of the public's fascination with mysteries, mainstream archaeology attacks and ridicules it (Holtorf, 2005), thus alienating a large number of people who are already interested in their field. It also needs to be acknowledged that some conspiracy theories are manufactured, often for the benefit of the small group of people who create them.

The Elite

There is no doubt that the mound builders recognized several types of elite classes or special people who held distinctive roles and power in society. The status of the elite appears to have reached its peak during the Mississippian era. The elite groups appear to have come from a long hereditary line extending well back into prehistory. There appear to have been three types of elite. One of these, shaman and healers, were probably not entirely chosen through heredity. This is known through ethnological studies.

The most powerful elite group was the ruling class including the chiefs. In almost all known cases, the chiefs of the mound-building cultures all appear to have claimed a hereditary link to their status. They sometimes claimed to have been descended from the stars, the sun, or from the realm of the sky people. The elaborate tombs constructed in large mounds were often their burial places. These tombs are where most of the large skeletons were found.

There was also a very powerful class of priests who held the secrets of death and controlled mortuary rites. It is clear that the populace saw this as so important, that they allowed the extreme social control that was exerted on them. The people erected monumental mounds and earthworks under the direction of their rulers, probably the priests. The elite dressed and acted the role of their status. They wore ceremonial outfits that displayed their power and connection to the upper and lower worlds. They reenacted cosmic characters who were seen as important players in the struggle between life and death. They carried and manipulated magical symbols in rituals and ceremonies that displayed their power and secret knowledge. The possibility of reincarnation, making a successful journey to the sky world, or being lost in the underworld were some of the secrets controlled by the priests.

The evidence of attacks on Mississippian cities like Cahokia, the defensive nature of some Hilltop Forts, and the legends of overthrowing the

Right: Henry Farney's (1903) painting of *The Sorcerer*. Photo: Greg Little. Above: *Indian Conjuror* by by John White (1590). Credit: Wikipedia Commons.

The power and esteem Native Americans had for their rulers can be seen in several illustrations made by the Spanish. Mound builders carried their chiefs and rulers on "throne-like" chairs in a manner similar to the way the Inca and Mesoamericans did. Below is an illustration of Atahualpa, the Inca ruler who was encountered by Pizarro. From: Cady (1890).

The Natchez Chief, known as the Sun, was carried on a throne. Natchez chiefs were determined through hereditary and were encountered as late as the 1700s by the French. The Chiefs claimed a star origin. Credit: du Pratz (1758).

ruling classes all point to a social uprising against the elite. The uprisings were regional conflicts, but the legends from tribes tell us that the elite became corrupt. However, in some places, the control of the elite over the society continued—as evidenced by de Soto and others.

In *Looking for Lost Lore* (2008), Lankford describes several old Cherokee legends about their elite leaders. There was a special group of "superior" priestly people who functioned as an "order" in the tribe. Elite members of the order possessed knowledge of heaven and creation that was used to both conduct rituals for the entire society, as well as maintain a rigid social structure. These elite leaders were certainly the ones who utilized the sacred symbols of the Death Cult. According to Lankford's research, the priestly elite became so rigid in maintaining their control that "it became disagreeable and oppressive to the people" (15). They were called the *Anikanos*. The masses rose up against the elite and annihilated them. In another telling of the story from the 1800s it was revealed that the elite were a "priestly class" and a "hereditary clan." They were "massacred in a public uprising in response to their corruption and sexual impropriety" (16). The Muskogee

Hopewell shaman conducting rituals. From: National Park Service, Mound City.

also had a priestly class who held esoteric knowledge. There are dozens of similar stories in various tribes' lore. It is a clear and accepted fact that among the people of the Mississippian Culture and even among the earlier Hopewell and Adena cultures, there was an elite class based on heredity. With the Mississippians, we know that their leaders and priests were chosen based on heredity. Somehow, the elite individuals in these tribes were different from the masses. Physical size may have been one of the most obvious differences.

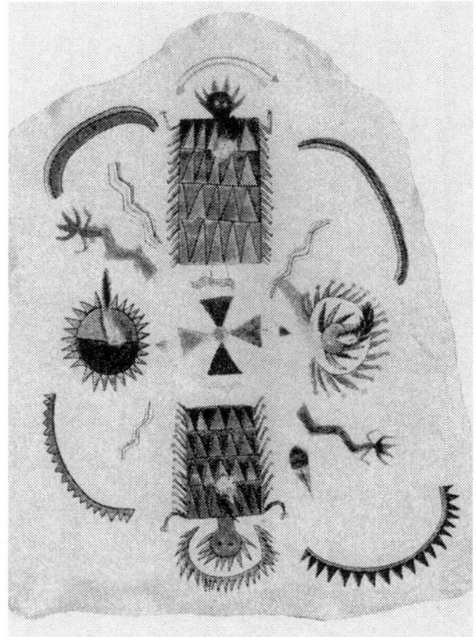

The Bureau of Ethnology's 9th annual report (Powell, 1892) contained an 150-page paper on the Medicine Men (and Women) of the Apache by Captain John Bourke of the US Army Third Cavalry. The article noted that some tribal medicine men were hereditary and very clannish, while others were more self-selected. They claimed a variety of powers and the ability to commune with spirits. Their dress, objects of power, and symbols were individually chosen and played a role in their specific techniques and specialties. These two Apache Medicine shirts were presented in full color and depict a variety of symbols related to the Southeastern Ceremonial Complex, showing that some of the ideas of death persisted into historic times.

Chapter 12

Path of Souls, Magic Machines of Earth, Cygnus versus Orion, & Dark Skies

It is apparent that the Hopewell and Mississippian cultures believed in the literal meaning of the death journey on the Path of Souls. It can be suggested that this literal belief was responsible for the extraordinary coordinated efforts made by large groups of people to construct many of the Hopewell geometric earthworks, mounds, and the earthen features that connected sites. The earthworks were definitely used in rituals, but some of these rituals were a means to assist the dead souls on their journey.

The Mississippians appear to have taken the ideas of social control to another level by making large platform, pyramid-shaped mounds for both chiefs and priests to live on, thus demonstrating their status in a more obvious way. But the mortuary rituals continued, and the symbols and regalia used by priests and leaders became even more important. The ideas embedded into the soul's journey are not yet fully understood, but the leap to the portal or ogee below the Hand, the transition to the Milky Way, and the movement of the soul to Deneb and the Dark Rift are clearly identified and accepted. So too is the idea of an Adversary encountered at the spot where the Dark Rift begins—at Deneb. However, it needs to be stressed that there were regional variations about the identity of the Adversary as well as the exact place where

the soul exits to the realm of ancestors. It was often thought of as toward the north.

Magic Machines:
Geometric Earthworks of the Hopewell

For decades I have pondered the incredible geometric earthworks made by the Hopewell. Exactly how were they used and why were they constructed into such specific shapes isn't known. All we can really do is guess. There are many, very unusual Hopewell sites, but those at Newark and Portsmouth in Ohio rival anything built in the ancient world. These geometric earthworks cannot be easily described or comprehended without seeing them firsthand.

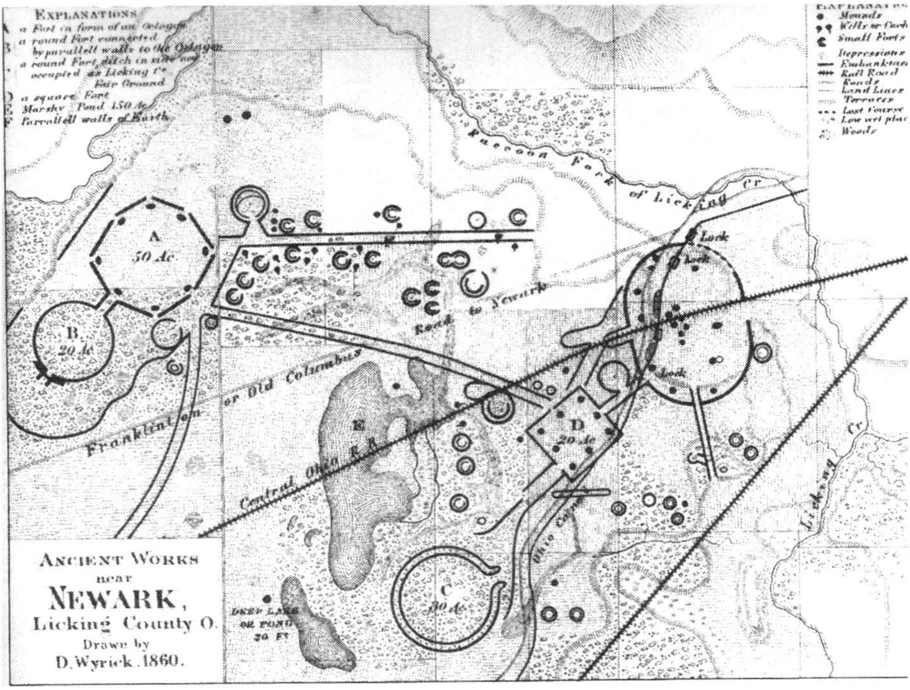

David Wyrick's little-known (1860) survey of the Newark, Ohio earthworks and mounds. Wyrick shows more detail than did Squier & Davis (1848). It is clear that the earthworks were made to control and channel the movements of people from one site to another and that rituals related to the Path of Souls were employed.

But even then they are so vast that it is difficult to get a true grasp of their significance.

William Romain's many publications claiming that many Hopewell earthworks were "ritualistic machines used to assist souls to journey to the sky world" are certainly correct. Archaeologist Bradley Lepper, who is about as mainstream as archaeologists get, wrote that the earthworks "were likely to be conceived to be more like machines. The giant enclosures were enormous engines of ceremony and ritual intended to do something. They not only symbolized the cosmos, they may have allowed the Hopewell shamans to draw on the energies of the cosmos" (Lepper, 2005: 165).

Back in the 1980s, I described these sites as "magic machines of earth" (Little, 1988) utilized in rituals that involved complex ceremonies where groups of people moved from one area of the mounds and earthworks to another. "The sites were sacred circles used to commune with and call forth spirits" (Little, 1990: 175). "Rituals that stressed the participants both

Right: Part of small circular earthwork just to the right (East) of the Circle and Octagon at Newark. Below: Entrance into the Octagon showing truncated mound at center of opening, Photos: Lora Little.

physically and mentally" were used during the ceremonies, and drumming, "rhythmical hypnotic dances, songs, and chanting" increased the mental effects (175). In a 2001 book chapter entitled "Magic Machines of Earth," I wrote, "Rituals literally manipulate symbols. This is, according to ancient sources, the very essence of magic. The magic, if it can really be called that, is the opening of passageways between the physical world and the spiritual world" (Little, Van Auken, & Little, 2001: 244).

Some things are known about the rituals of the Hopewell and the Mississippians. It is known that at the Newark site, rituals involved following the moon's movements, the use of hallucinogenic mushrooms, and dressing in animal costumes (Romain, 2000). From the Mississippian tribes, it is known that dancing, rhythmic drumming, whistle-blowing, and singing were thought to vibrate the *axis mundi*. Conceptualized as a striped pole or more often a tree, the axis mundi held together the three-layered cosmos. The rituals they used to vibrate the axis allowed participants to access different layers of the cosmos (Reilly & Garber, 2007). All of these would have been important processes in the journey of the dead to the Path of Souls. But there is an element to these rituals that few people today truly comprehend. It is the importance of living in the elements and watching a truly dark sky.

Parallel earthen walls that connect the Circle and Octagon at Newark. In the upper center, the large circle can be seen arching in the distance. Photo: Lora Little.

Right: Illustration by Dee Turman depicting a shaman at Newark during eclipse. It is known that the shaman dressed in animal skins and that Newark's Circle and Octagon complex was a lunar eclipse predictor.

Below: Reconstruction of Portsmouth, Ohio earthworks adapted from Portsmouth floodwall murals—by permission. The walkway shown that descends to the Ohio River and into Kentucky was 6.5 miles in length.

The only remaining horseshoe-shaped enclosure in Portsmouth. The earthen walls are 10 feet in height. Photo: Lora Little.

Cygnus & Orion in Egypt

For some time I have considered the moment when Robert Bauval says he came to realize that the three main pyramids at Giza were made to mimic the three belt stars of Orion. While camping in the desert one night, an Egyptian accompanying Bauval pointed to the three stars and mentioned that they were not in a straight line. He mentioned that one of the stars was offset a bit. That was the moment Bauval concluded that Orion and the three pyramids matched. It was his "eureka" moment: The pyramids were built to match Orion! The pyramids were made to create Heaven on Earth. Various supporters of the idea also asserted that it was a perfect match and that the other stars of Orion matched other important Egyptian sites.

While I agree that one of the shafts in the Great Pyramid probably does target Orion, the fact that you have to turn either the pyramids or the belt stars upside down has always bothered me. So too did the fact that it wasn't a "perfect match" and the fact that the other stars of Orion did not fit on important sites as was initially claimed. The idea that Orion essentially explained everything wasn't something I accepted nor has it been accepted by a lot of others. But its simplicity did have a great appeal to many people. And once a belief is formed, it is extremely difficult to change. Just considering that the Orion match could be wrong is a nearly impossible task for the people who invested so much of themselves into the idea.

Back in 1999 (or maybe it was 2000) I attended a conference where I watched Graham Hancock effectively present the idea about Orion matching the layout of the Giza pyramids. He used two transparent overheads. The first one showed an aerial of the three pyramids. He then laid a picture of Orion's belt stars on top of the three pyramids. The audience gasped loudly and instantly comprehended the concept. It was so simple and seemed to explain it all. It was a sort of presentation magic and was one of the most effective ways I have ever seen of taking a topic that is exceedingly complex (Egyptian beliefs about the death journey) and making it exceedingly simple: The soul went to Orion and the pyramids are a representation of Heaven on

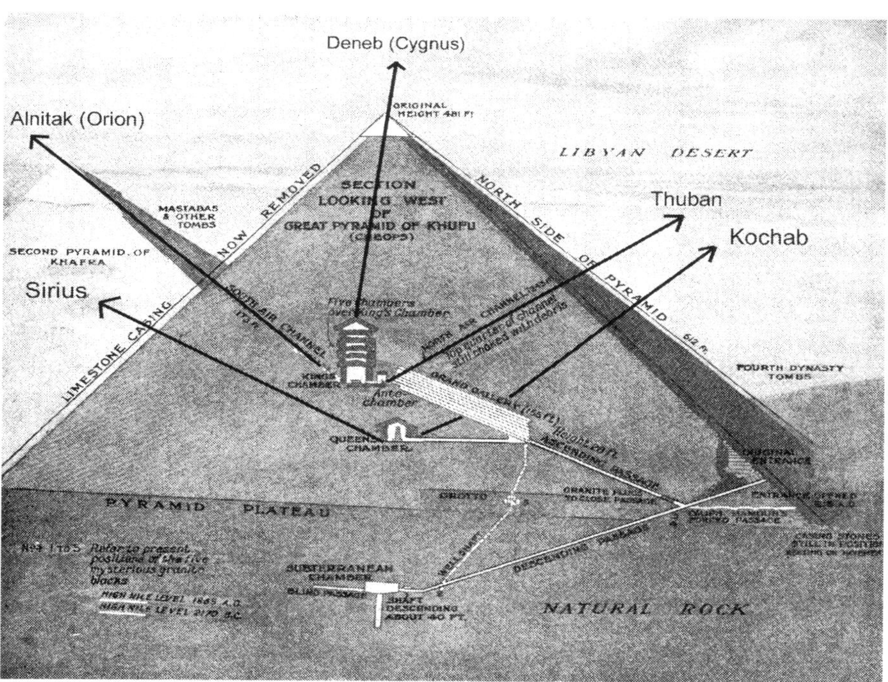

Schematic of the chambers and air shafts in the Great Pyramid. One of the main arguments made by supporters of the Orion theory cites the generally-accepted idea that one of four "air shafts" in the Great Pyramid (southern shaft in the King's Chamber) was aligned to the nightly passing of Orion's Belt around 2600 B.C. However, Andrew Collins also found that the vertical line from the apex of the King's Chamber through the apex of the pyramid itself aligned with Cygnus. Image adapted from Hammerton (1923).

Earth. To a great extent, such things excite the general public and fulfill underlying needs. I don't believe the simple idea explains it all, but I do think that the method that was employed has a message for archaeology in how to connect with the public.

Carefully reading Andrew Collins' book, *The Cygnus Mystery*, led me to conclude that in all probability, the pyramids actually mimicked the three cross stars of Cygnus, but it was also clear that Orion was a key component of whatever the Egyptians believed. When the Cygnus *versus* Orion controversy erupted in 2006, I had no explanation for the importance of both Cygnus and Orion, just an uneasy feeling that the real truth wasn't yet revealed. When Collins' team discovered the cave system running under Giza in 2008, it provided more support for the Cygnus connection to Giza, and the fact that the cave seemed to be a path through the underworld was intriguing. To me, the now-understood Native American beliefs about the death journey pull it all together. The Native American's beliefs about death may be somewhat similar, or even nearly identical, to what the Egyptians believed. The beliefs about Cygnus, Orion, the underworld journey, and the Path of Souls on the Milky Way probably extend far, far back into history as Collins has suggested: back to 18,000 years ago or so when Deneb was the north pole star and the Dark Rift of the Milky Way essentially seemed to rotate around it. It is logical to theorize that these beliefs were spread around the world as the elite migrated with their clans.

I have also thought many times that a "trickster" could be at work in all of this, especially with the idea that Orion explained everything. The Native American trickster, often depicted as a coyote, deceives people. More accurately stated, the trickster often allows us to deceive ourselves. Some of the ways it does this is through confirmation bias and perceptual bias. As previously explained, we tend to look for things that confirm what we already believe and we dismiss things which contradict or threaten our beliefs. The trickster concept just explains how our belief system works and how our belief system consistently maintains itself. One other psychological issue which directly relates to the trickster will not be so apparent to many people.

But it can be summarized in one sentence: *What we accept as factual often serves to meet our deep psychological needs.* I doubt that skeptics and archaeologists will understand—or care. But that's okay.

One thing that should be obvious by now is that the ancient sacred knowledge possessed by the elite classes of Native American tribes was, at least to them, meant to be kept secret. One might suspect that the elite priests of ancient Egypt intended for their ideas about death to remain a secret also. There is a reason why there is nothing in Egyptian writing of any kind that says, "The three pyramids were built to mimic Orion"—or Cygnus either, for that matter. There is a reason why it has taken several hundred years for the Native American ideas about death to be revealed.

When the huge controversy erupted on Cygnus *versus* Orion, I recall reading various comments that Cygnus was barely visible in the night sky. The reason that the comments were made is because of confirmation bias—it was a simple way to dismiss the ideas about Cygnus that had been proposed. The comment is true, of course; it is very difficult for people to identify Cygnus—at least now it is—especially if you look at the night sky from anywhere in the modern world.

Dark Skies

Deneb, the top star of Cygnus located at the point where the Dark Rift begins, is actually the 19th brightest star in the sky. However, a lot of people who will read this have never seen the night sky—or the Milky Way—as brightly as it appeared in the ancient world. The sky is obscured by so many modern lights that the Milky Way is barely visible. In addition, modern pollution has made the stars even dimmer. In fact, a lot of people have never actually seen the Milky Way at all. They may know what it is, but seeing it as the ancients did is simply not possible for most people. I recall seeing the Milky Way as a child while camping in the mountains of Pennsylvania. It was impressive, but it was not until a couple nights anchored on the ocean when I realized how dim the stars and the Milky Way now appear to us.

In 2006 my wife and I spent 10 days on a 4-deck, 78-foot research ship. We anchored for several moonless nights about 110 miles from Florida and about 100 miles from the nearest Bahamas' settlements. The top deck was a large platform and totally dark. No artificial light was visible on the horizons or from the ship itself. There was no visible pollution in the area. Several of us actually saw the sky for the first time while standing on the upper deck. It was a stunning view that showed the Milky Way clearly and how the sky can easily be seen as a gigantic dome that moves up and down as the Native Americans believed. The Dark Rift was extremely impressive. When you see the sky that way, it is easy to grasp what Deneb might have looked like back when it was the north pole star. Viewing the Dark Rift slowly rotate around Deneb would have been a very impressive sight.

In my earlier books I have discussed how ancient Native Americans really lived in a world we have trouble fully comprehending today. They saw a bright sky nearly every night, and the movements of the stars, the planets, moon, and the pole star area were exceedingly important. In the modern world, few people view the sky that way, if at all, and we exist in a sheltered, lighted world. The ancients were exposed to the natural world. Shelter from storms and the ravages of nature had a very different meaning to them. They were immersed in it (Little, 1990; 1994).

When Collins suggested that Cygnus was the template for the pyramids and many other ancient sites, I envision that a lot of people went outside and looked for the constellation. "It's too dim to actually see" is the reaction most believers in the Orion alignment probably had. That is a really simplistic way to dismiss an idea that challenges a deeply-held belief. People have a lot of emotion attached to their beliefs, so much that they will use whatever they can to dismiss anything that might show they could be wrong. I'm sure that many Orion supporters just concluded, "It can't be; therefore, it isn't." So Andrew faced an onslaught of criticism. And the criticism will probably continue.

Despite a rigid belief system that permeates archaeology, the work by the group that studied the Mississippian imagery should be congratulated and supported. Their methods were exemplary. They have explained one of the true mysteries from Ancient America. But while the conclusions reached by American archaeologists may well explain why Cygnus and Orion were so important in the ancient world, we are left with a host of other mysteries to ponder. Why, for example, were both Cygnus and Orion seen as important in areas of the sky across the world? How did this belief become so complicated? Did the priests who held the secret beliefs actually think it was true? Is the creation story of beings from the sky literal? We are also left with the important question of where and when did this belief first emerge? And how did it reach America and persist over so many years?

Several American mounds have incredible legends attached to them. Nikwasi Mound in Franklin, North Carolina was once the center of a large, thriving village. An ancient legend tells that the people were being invaded by a hostile force and that the outnumbered warriors of Nikwasi attempted a defense. As they were being overpowered by the larger force of invaders, a "stranger" appeared in their ranks. The stranger called to the chief to retreat to the mound. Once the Nikwasi warriors were on the mound, a doorway opened on the side of the mound. A horde of fierce warriors emerged from the opening and attacked the invaders. They were the *immortals*—the *Nunne'h*. They successfully repelled the attacking force and killed half of them. From: *The Encyclopedia of Native American Mounds & Earthworks* (Little, 2009). Photo: Lora Little.

Many of the creation and cosmological myths of Native American tribes that are known today came from storytellers who cooperated with the Bureau of Ethnology's early ethnologists. Shown on the left is Annie Ax Sadayí. On the right is Waliní. Both were Cherokee storytellers. From the *19th Annual Report of the Bureau of Ethnology* (Powell, 1900).

AFTERWORD—Part I
Of Stars And Giants: Guardians of the Starry Wisdom

By Andrew Collins

The cosmological iconography of the Southeastern Ceremonial Complex (SECC), which thrived during the Mississippian period (ca. A.D. 800-1500), was unquestionably a major influence on the funerary beliefs and practices of many Native American tribes. Yet aside from the concept of the Path of Souls as a visionary expression of the Milky Way, just two asterisms emerge as central to its cosmic geography. The hand and eye constellation, identified with the Orion constellation, acted as the entry point to the Milky Way, while the Cygnus star Deneb, personified as the birdman named *Brain Smasher*, judges the soul as it approaches a fork in the Path of Souls (Lankford, 2007). It is this supernatural being that determines whether or not the soul is free of sin. If it is, then it can enter the sky world proper via a log bridge, identified as the connecting arm of the Milky Way's Great Rift. Thereafter the soul enters the realm of the celestial beings and is reunited with its ancestral family.

The only other constellation to feature prominently in these star myths is Scorpius, located just below the other arm of the Great Rift, which peters out just before it reaches the stars of Scorpius. Many Native American tribes saw this asterism as the Water Panther, a Winged Dragon, or Feathered Serpent, all of which feature heavily in the carved art of the SECC. Very

Cygnus as the Judge (a raptor bird) at the Great Rift.

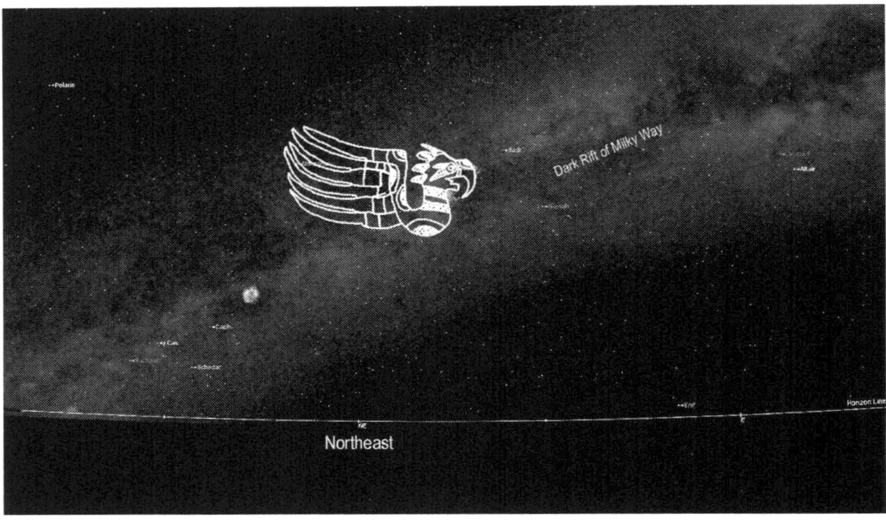

likely the gap between the end of the Great Rift's short arm and the stars of Scorpius signified the void into which the unclean soul is cast. Its final destination was the underworld or lower world, seen as located below or beyond the line of the ecliptic, the sun's path which crosses the Milky Way at this point.

We have seen also how these combined cosmological ideas, which were very likely present among the Adena and Hopewell cultures, *ca*. 1000 B.C. to A.D. 500, had existed on the North American continent since the arrival of its first permanent inhabitants towards the end of the last Ice Age. In addition to this, ruling elites who would appear to have preserved and perpetuated these star-based funerary myths, featuring the Milky Way, Cygnus, and Orion, might well have included individuals of extreme height, the "giants" or "Nephilim" of popular tradition.

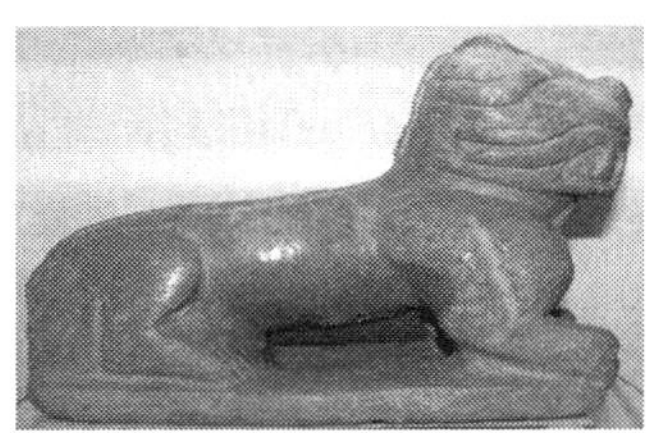

Water panther effigy from Nodena site, near Wilson, Arkansas. When it is beneath the horizon, Scorpius was thought to be the ruler of the underworld as a water panther. Photo: Lora Little.

Orion as the Hand Constellation as it sets in the West.

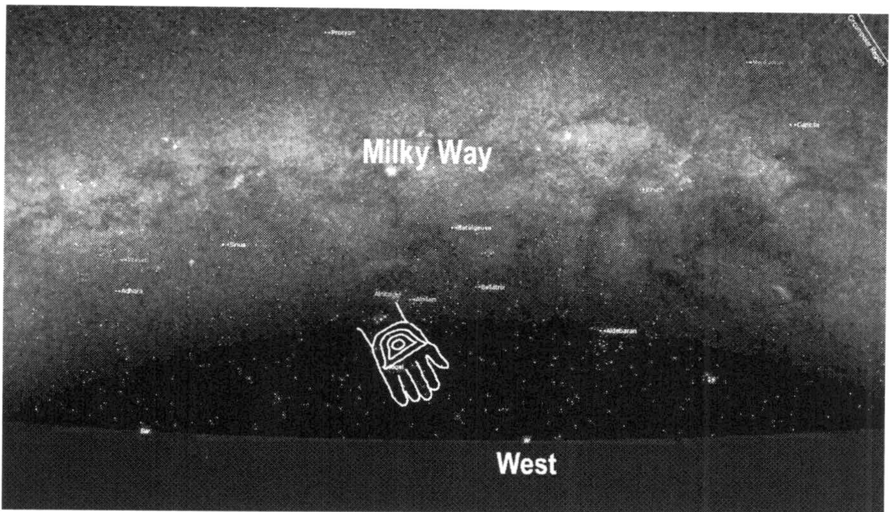

The Solutrean Hypothesis

Who were the *real* carriers of this starry wisdom? Where did they come from? Did these first peoples to inhabit the American continent really include individuals of exceptional height and striking appearance? More pressingly, did North America's first inhabitants come from Asia, as is currently believed by most academics, or did they arrive on boats from Europe? This second possibility we shall deal with first. It is a subject tackled admirably by Dennis J. Stanford of the Smithsonian Institution and Bruce A. Bradley of the University of Exeter in their ground-breaking book *Across Atlantic Ice* (2012). They propose that at the height of the final phase of the last Ice Age, some 20,000 years ago, highly advanced Paleolithic peoples known as Solutreans navigated the southern edge of the ice flow (which at the time covered half the North Atlantic Ocean) and stretched between the west coast of France and the east coast of the United States. The Solutreans produced very distinctive-looking projectile points known as bifaces (generally oval-shaped tools carved on both faces) that match very well the style and design of the characteristic "fluted" points produced by the Clovis culture. Clovis is North

America's first *recognised* human population, even though it thrived for as little as two to three hundred years between ca. 11,200 B.C. and 10,900 B.C. However, the discovery of much older bifacial points found at a number of "Pre-Clovis" settlement sites in the eastern United States, which match more closely those of the Solutreans, has made the transatlantic hypothesis even more appealing to some prehistorians (Stanford & Bradley, 2012).

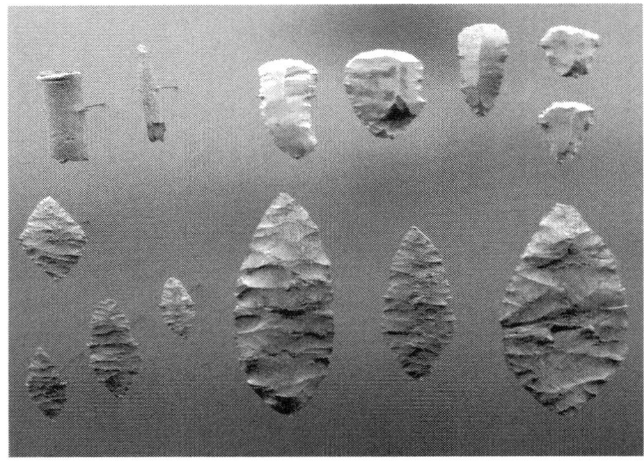

Above: Solutrean points from France. Credit: World Imaging, Wikipedia Commons. Below: Clovis points from Iowa's Rummells-Maske site. Credit: Bill Whittaker, Wikipedia Commons.

The major Solutrean Culture sites. Credit: Sémhur, Wikipedia Commons.

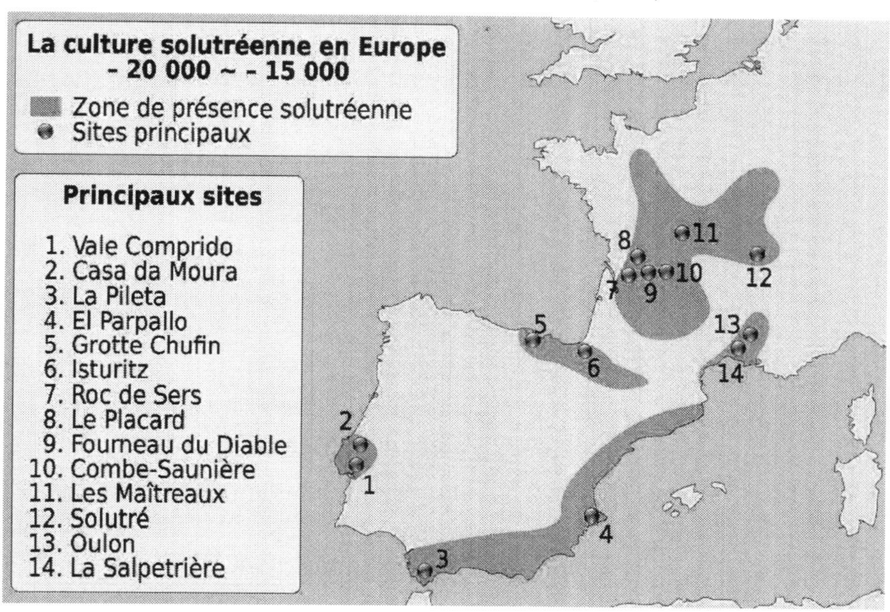

Paleolithic Birdman

The significance of the Solutreans is that in addition to creating a highly sophisticated and quite magnificent stone tool technology before vanishing from the archaeological record around 16,500 years ago, they were responsible for some of the earliest Ice Age art in Western Europe. This includes a strange painted panel in the deepest part of the Lascaux Caves in France's Dordogne region, which might well show one of the oldest representations of the Cygnus constellation. Within a vertical "well" shaft, accessible only from above, is a curious scene showing a bird-headed figure reclining backward, on the right of which is a charging bison, wounded by darts. Below the man is a bird with a similar-shaped head seated on a pole.

Dr. Michael Rappenglück, an expert in ancient astronomies with the University of Munich, has identified Lascaux's shaft scene as showing the area of sky immediately surrounding the Cygnus constellation (Rappenglück, 1999). Indeed, he writes that the birdman represents Deneb, with the bison

and bird on a pole signifying nearby stars. Yet the fact that this painted panel was created during the epoch, *ca*. 16,500-16,000 B.C. (Aujoulat, 2005), adds an extra dimension to its execution for it was at this time that Deneb was Pole Star.

Center of the Sky

The slow wobble of the Earth's axis across a cycle of approximately 26,000 years shifts the position of stars with respect to the local horizon by a rate of approximately one degree every seventy-two years, a process known in astronomy as *precession*, or backwards motion. What it also does is cause the perceived Pole Star (the star closest to the celestial pole) to change across the millennia. Today Polaris, a star in the constellation of Ursa Minor, the little bear, marks the location of the celestial pole. Between 16,500-14,500 B.C. Deneb played the same role. Even after it ceased to be the Pole Star,

Lascaux Cave image depicting bird on pole (Cygnus).
Credit: Peter 80, Wikipedia Commons.

another Cygnus star named Delta Cygni took its place, a position it held until around 13,000 B.C. Thereafter Vega, a bright star in the neighboring constellation of Lyra, became the Pole Star through until 11,000 B.C. After this time there was no star close enough to the celestial pole to act as the Pole Star until the beginning of the Pyramid Age, when Thuban, a minor star in the constellation of Draco, the dragon, assumed the role for a few hundred years.

So when Lascaux's shaft scene was created in *ca*. 16,500-16,000 B.C., the stars of Cygnus occupied the most important position in the night sky. To the Paleolithic hunter-gatherers who lived in the northern hemisphere at this time, it would have seemed as if this celestial bird, or birdman, was positioned on top of an imaginary sky-pole, revolving on its axis each night, something that led perhaps to it being featured in Lascaux's shaft scene. The painting was probably meant to convey the journey of the shaman from this world to the next—the birdman being the shaman and the bird on the pole being the Cygnus constellation.

As Cygnus was seen as a point of entry to the sky world among ancient cultures in every part of the world, from Peru to Egypt and from India to the British Isles (Collins, 2006), its incredible importance to the Paleolithic

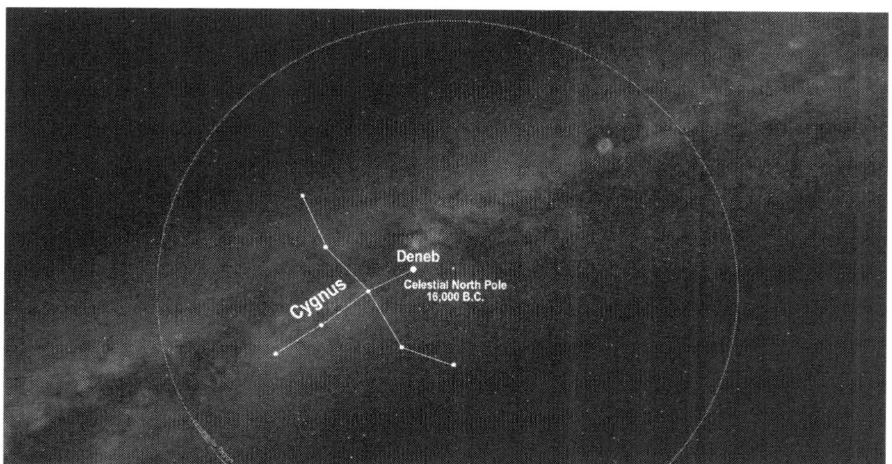

Deneb as North Pole Star in 16,000 B.C. Generated by *Starry Night Pro*.

mindset cannot be underestimated. That its stars also once marked the location of the celestial pole must have helped elevate its status in the mindset of the Upper Paleolithic peoples living at this time.

Such realizations help us better understand why the Native American peoples would appear to have considered Cygnus so important to their own cosmological beliefs, even though the disappearance of the Beringia land bridge in around 8500 B.C. meant they existed in virtual isolation from the outside world from then until the arrival of the first Europeans at the beginning of the historical period. Clearly, these stellar-based beliefs must have reached the American continent before this time.

Cosmic Mother

Even if Dennis Stanford and Bruce Bradley are correct and Solutreans did reach the eastern part of the North American continent (and the jury is still out on this possibility), to go on to assume that they had some impact on the cosmology of the earliest inhabitants of North America might not be the best solution to this enigma. As we see next, Cygnus' role in ancient astronomies was most probably widespread throughout the Eurasian continent *before* the emergence of the Solutrean culture around 25,000 years ago, for there is tentative evidence that their forerunners, the Gravettian peoples who thrived mainly in Central and Eastern Europe, held a strange fascination for the Milky Way. Moreover, there are indications that the starry stream was seen as a life-giving force (a Cosmic Mother) responsible for the creation of life on Earth. For example, within the deepest part of the Chauvet Cave in France's Ardèche region, Gravettian artists who visited here around 32,000 years ago left behind an abstract depiction of a female body. Overlaid on the woman's stomach is the head of a standing bovine, a male calf, which shares its right leg with that of the female's own left leg, showing the close relationship between the two figures. Since this is the only image of the human form in the entire cave complex, and is painted on a large stalactite hanging down from the ceiling, it emphasizes its significance to those who entered this subterranean world tens of thousands of years ago.

Chauvet's "Venus and the Sorcerer" panel, as it is known, may be the earliest representation of the Milky Way's Great Rift, for an examination of the legs of the woman mirror the appearance of the Great Rift's twin arms, which if correct places the calf's head in the region of her womb. As the current author outlines elsewhere (Collins, 2014: 108-110), there is good reason to suggest that in the past the crescent-shaped pattern made by the cluster of stars forming the extended wings of the Cygnus constellation (in its role as a celestial bird) were also once perhaps seen as the horns of a large bovine or horned animal, its elongated face composed of the asterism's remaining stars (interestingly, in Native American tradition, one of the alternative forms of the celestial guardian at the fork on the Milky Way was "an old man wrapped in a buffalo robe," see Fletcher and La Flesche, 1911: 590). It is thought that the bovine head as a symbol in prehistoric art was more often than not a metaphor for the human uterus complete with fallopian tubes (Gimbutas, 1989: 185, 265). If correct, it implies that cosmic birth was once thought to have occurred in the Cygnus region, with the opening of the Great Rift forming the loins of a universal Mother of Life, a creatrix, whose totemic form was that either of a swan or, occasionally a deer, most probably the reindeer.

The Mother of Life

The existence of this age-old Cosmic Mother is expressed in star-based myths and legends prevalent across the Eurasian continent. One of the most compelling traditions concerns the origins of the indigenous peoples of the Pannonian Basin, situated within the arc formed by the Carpathian Mountains of Central Europe. Here, in what is today the country of Hungary, folk legends talk extensively about the progenitor of the Hungarian or Magyar peoples as Tündér Ilona, with *tündér* meaning "fairy" and Ilona being a regional form

of the name Helena or Elena. Ilona's name derives from the Hungarian roots *él,* or *éle,* meaning "life," and *anya* (old Turkic *ana*), meaning "mother," making her the "Mother of Life" (Tomory, 2009b). Her zoomorphic or avataristic form is that of a swan, in which manner she is said to have laid the cosmic egg from which the sun emerged (Róheim, 1954: 63). Other accounts make Tündér Ilona the wife of the sun, whose earthly guise was Magor, or Magyar, the legendary founder of the Hungarian peoples (Tomory, 2009a).

Tündér Ilona's celestial origin is displayed also in the fact that she is the offspring of Csodaszarvas, a name which in Hungarian means "miracle stag" or "wondrous stag" (Tomory, 2009a). He is the personification of the starry vault, his antler tips bearing a thousand candles, an allusion to the countless stars of the night sky (Tomory, 2009b). Tündér Ilona's mother-in-law was the mysterious Enéh, whose name is said to mean either "cow/deer" and/or "pine tree," perhaps both. Yet Enéh is simply another form of Ilona or Elena, for she too is seen to have given birth to the sun-god Magor, while her name, like that of Ilona, most likely derives from the Hungaro-Turkic root *ana,* or *anya,* meaning "mother."

Island in the Sky

As the offspring of Csodaszarvas, the Miracle Stag, Ilona's homeland, and that of all tündér fairies, was the Cygnus constellation. Here were to be found two celestial islands lying within the opening of the Milky Way's Great Rift. The first, corresponding to the position of the star Deneb, was *Tündérek fordulója,* "the turning of the fairies," while the other, located in the vicinity of the star Albireo at the base of the cross-shaped asterism, was *Tündérek tanca,* the "dance of the fairies" (Magyar, 1991: 74; Tomory, 2009a). Tündér Ilona's role as creatrix, and the island name *Tündérek fordulója,* "the turning of the fairies," tell us that these stories stem from an age when the Cygnus stars marked the celestial pole, ca. 16,500-13,000 B.C. It is a fact confirmed with the knowledge that folk legends also talk about the Miracle Stag's journey across the heavens beginning in the Cygnus constellation, a point in time and space corresponding also with the foundation of the Hungarian peoples (Tomory, 2009b).

These facts make it clear that Ilona's true identity, as both the Swan Mother, and Eneh, the Deer Mother, was as the Milky Way's Great Rift personified as a creatrix, representations of whom were carved in ivory, stone, and bas-relief by the Gravettian peoples between 30,000 and 19,000 BC. Significantly, their greatest concentration of settlement sites were in what is today the Czech Republic, Austria, and Hungary, exactly where the stellar-based creation myths of the Hungarian peoples later had their inception (Magyar, 1991).

The Shining Island

It was from the island in the Milky Way's Great Rift that the tündér fairies are said to have descended the *White Road,* the Milky Way, to reach the Earth. Their landing place was an earthly island located between two tributaries of the River Danube. Known as *Csallóköz,* the "Shining Island" (Tomory, 2009b), it is Europe's largest river island, bordering the countries of Slovakia and Hungary. Here Tündér Ilona brought forth the ancestors of the Hungarian peoples, making Csallóköz the terrestrial homeland both of the fairies and the Magyar peoples.

Csallóköz was clearly an earthly representation of the Milky Way's Great Rift and Cygnus constellation, an association that perhaps goes back to the Upper Paleolithic age. Indeed, it was on the banks of the Danube in Hungary, sometime around 25,000 years ago that, having broken away from the existing Gravettian culture, the Solutreans emerged onto the European scene for the first time (Wright, 1939: 13-14, 51; Collins, 2014: 180-1). After passing through Germany, the Solutreans settled eventually in central France, southern England, and northern and eastern Spain. Their own interest in Cygnus seems

confirmed with the creation of the shaft scene panel at Lascaux, ca. 16,500-16,000 B.C.

Was it an early human population of the Upper Paleolithic age connected in some manner with the Gravettians who carried a knowledge of the role played by Cygnus and the Milky Way's Great Rift in reaching the sky world to the American continent, perhaps via Central and Eastern Asia? Some of the main settlement sites of the Eastern Gravettians were on Russia's Don River, at a place named Kostenki, and there is evidence to link the evolution of their advanced stone tool technologies with those present at sites in the Altai Mountains of southern-central Siberia attributed to anatomically modern humans *and* Neanderthals over 30,000 years ago (for instance, see Zwyns, 2012).

This is important, for belief in a Mother of Life is not confined to Europe. She is found also in Central and Eastern Asia associated, like the Hungarian Ilona, with both the deer (Jacobsen, 1993) and the swan. Indeed, the Buryat-Mongols recognise a Swan Mother as their creatrix. Under the name *Manzan Gormo,* the Buryat's ancestral mother is said to have created the Milky Way with her breast milk (Coulter & Turner, 2012: 308).

In her form as *Umai Enye,* the wife of the sky-god Tengri, the Swan Mother is venerated from Kyrgyzstan in the west right across to Siberia's Lake Baikal in the east. Her name is Turkic and comes from two words—*umai*, "womb" or "uterus," and *enye* or *ana,* "mother," the very same root behind the Hungarian Ilona and Eneh. This shows how they are all very obviously variations of the same universal Mother of Life, who in her celestial form was associated both with cosmic creation and the birth of the first human beings. What is more, there is clearly a connection between this universal creatrix and the Cygnus constellation through her form as the swan.

Birds on a Pole

Various Siberian tribes revered the swan as the seat and vehicle of the soul, and believed that swans (and other birds) could assume the spirit of those who had previously incarnated in human form (Wilmore, 1974: 203). More significantly, the shamans of the Reindeer Tungus tribes of Manchuria and Siberia would erect tall poles on the top of which were affixed carved images of swans in flight. Next to the poles they would erect altars, and during ecstatic trance ceremonies, in which they would attain altered states of consciousness, the shamans believed their souls departed the body and climbed the sky pole to reach the upper world (Armstrong, 1959: 14, 49).

There seems little question that the sky pole in the ceremonies of the Reindeer Tungus shamans represents the *axis mundi,* the axis of the Earth, seen to link the terrestrial world with the cosmic axis, while the swan itself is quite obviously the guardian of the cosmic axis. These ceremonies very likely hark back to an age when the Cygnus stars occupied the position of Pole Star, ca. 16,500-13,000 B.C. The reindeer shamans seem to have preserved this tradition even though precession has caused the celestial pole to visit at least four other constellations in the intervening time. Very similar motivations were no doubt behind the creation in the Lascaux Caves of the shaft scene with its birdman and bird on a pole around 18,000 years ago.

This very specific cosmic symbolism, present among the indigenous peoples of the Eurasian continent, almost certainly derives from the same root sources as Cygnus and the Milky Way's importance in the rich funerary beliefs and practices of the Native Americans. What is more, a direct line of transmission can be traced between the ancient peoples of Siberia and the first inhabitants of the American continent.

American Origins

In 2013 scientists at the Natural History Museum of Denmark in Copenhagen announced that the nuclear and mitochondrial DNA of a boy who lived in Siberia 24,000 years ago matched that of one third of Native Americans living today (Raghavan et al., 2013; Marshall, 2013). These findings now settle a persisting problem. Although academics have long believed the first Americans came across the Beringia land bridge as early as 15,000 years ago (and arguably much earlier), none of the human DNA

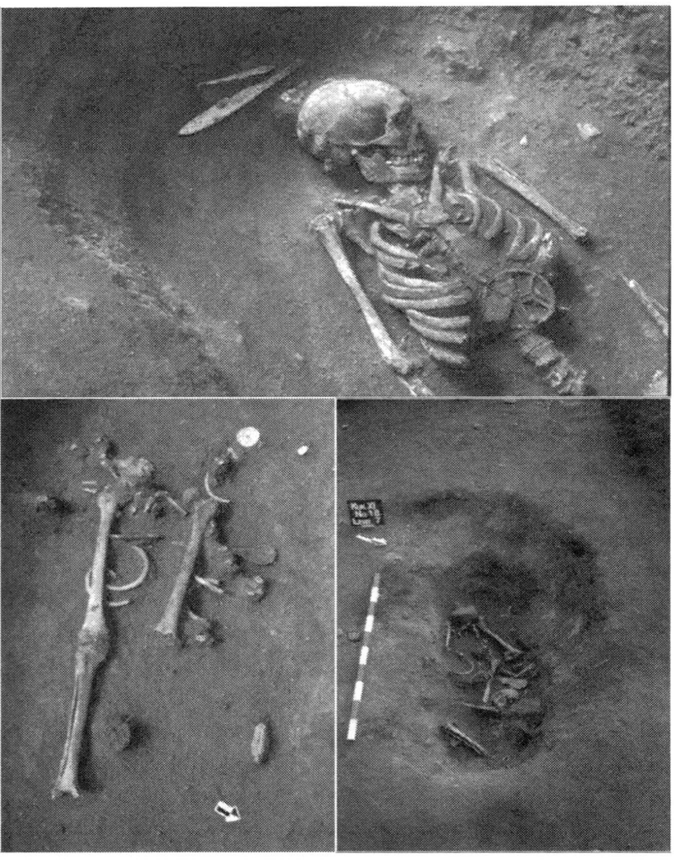

Excavated graves at Baikal. Credit: Dr. Andrzej Weber, University of Alberta, Wikipedia Commons.

found in the Native American population existing today was a match to that of indigenous peoples currently living in northeast Asia. What is more, DNA of European origin present in many Native Americans has allowed some anthropologists and prehistorians to use this as evidence that the first Americans arrived on the continent from Europe (the Solutrean hypothesis). This new DNA evidence from Siberia now confirms that the true place of origin of the Native American peoples was indeed eastern Asia.

All this is important in attempting to determine the origins of the Native American's cosmic geography, for the 24,000-year-old Siberian boy whose DNA offered up these new findings lived close to Lake Baikal, the world's oldest and deepest lake in the southern part of Russian Siberia. At the end of the youth's short life, his remains were interred in a cemetery west of the lake, close to a village on the Angara River called Mal'ta. This extensive cemetery site was where an Upper Paleolithic population known to archaeologists as the Mal'ta-Beret culture came to bury their dead between 24,000 and 15,000 years ago.

Soul Carriers

From the archaeological finds uncovered in the Mal'ta cemetery, it seems clear that this Upper Paleolithic society reached a high level of sophistication, which included the manufacture of delicately carved "Venus" figurines made from mammoth ivory. These depict women either naked or dressed in what appear to be padded fur garments, complete with hoods. Although not full-bodied like those of the Gravettian peoples of Central and Eastern Europe, these slim, erect statues could very well signify something similar. Moreover, their presence in the cemetery, alongside human burials, suggests they represent some kind of primordial mother of creation, their purpose being to emphasize the return of the soul to its place of creation, most likely located among the stars. That the Buryats (the principal indigenous peoples of the Trans-Baikal region) see themselves, even today, as descendents of a divine

swan, identified as the daughter of the sky-god *Esege Malan,* seems relevant here. What is more, there is good evidence that these beliefs have existed in the region since Paleolithic times.

Buried alongside the female figurines in the Mal'ta cemetery were various long, straight pendants, carved from mammoth ivory and clearly representing swans. There is an uncanny likeness between the style of execution of these swans and the female figurines, hinting that if the pendants are not simply lucky charms without real meaning, then their presence among the dead at Mal'ta is a clear indication that the Upper Paleolithic society who manufactured them saw the soul as entering the next world in the form of a swan, or that it was accompanied on its journey by a swan in its role as *psychopomp,* a Greek word meaning "soul carrier" or "soul accompanier."

These are views reflected also in the religious beliefs and practices of the indigenous peoples of Siberia which, as we have seen, feature the swan as a symbol not only of the soul's journey into the next world, but also as a zoomorphic symbol of a Cosmic Mother, a Mother of Life, personified as both the Milky Way's Great Rift and the Cygnus constellation. Very probably these were cosmological beliefs that reached the American continent having been carried by human populations migrating from the Lake Baikal region across the Beringia land bridge somewhere between 15,000 and 20,000 years ago. It was a route that would probably have begun in Southwest Asia and embraced along the way key outposts in Central Asia, such as Lake Balkash in Kazakhstan, the Tien Shan Mountains of Kyrgyzstan, and the Altai Mountains of southern-central Siberia, all of which fall within a humid corridor bordered on both sides by cold desert wastes, ideal for use as a migrational route (Gamble, 2013: 240-1).

There seems little question that our ancestors saw at least some part of our existence, both before and after incarnation, as connected with the cross-like asterism we know today as the Cygnus constellation. They saw also the boundless stream of stars that make up the visible outer rim of our own Milky Way galaxy as a cosmic highway linking the Earth's circular disk

with a sky world inhabited by beings just like us. It is very fitting therefore that NASA should announce this year (2014) that the first Earth-like planet existing in the habitable zone of a solar system has been located orbiting a star in the Cygnus constellation. Christened Kepler-186f, the planet was found using NASA's Kepler Space Telescope (NASA, 2014). In this way, we ourselves in the modern age, are able to perpetuate the long-held view that out there in deep space, somewhere in the Cygnus region and close to the Milky Way's Great Rift, life exists that is little different to our own. It is a belief that in all likelihood goes back to the beginnings of human history some forty to fifty thousand years ago.

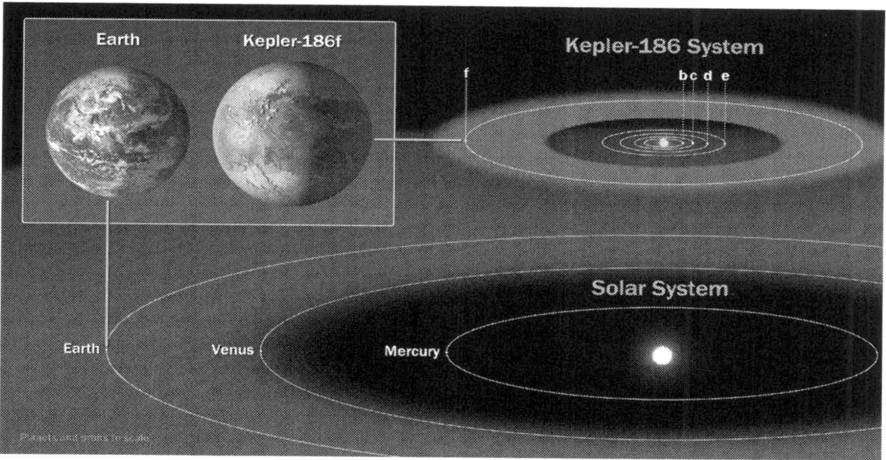

Kepler-186 and the Solar System: "Comparison of the planets in our solar system to Kepler-186, a five-planet star system about 500 light-years from Earth in the constellation Cygnus. The five planets of Kepler-186 orbit an M dwarf, a star that is half the size and mass of the sun. The Kepler-186 system is home to Kepler-186f, the first validated Earth-sized planet orbiting a distant star in the habitable zone—a range of distance from a star where liquid water might pool on the planet's surface. The discovery of Kelper 186f confirms that Earth-sized planets exist in the habitable zones of other stars and signals a significant step toward finding a world similar to Earth." From: NASA, 2014 Press Release.

* * *

All this might be so, but did any of these early human populations contain individuals of extreme height and striking appearance that might be compared, related even, to the "giant" or very large skeletons that have so frequently been found at mound sites throughout the United States? If so, then did these individuals form the ruling elites of the Native American peoples, preserving the starry wisdom of the ancients through until the time of the Adena and Hopewell cultures, and beyond them into the age of the Southeastern Ceremonial Complex? It is these pressing questions that we must address in Part Two of this Afterword.

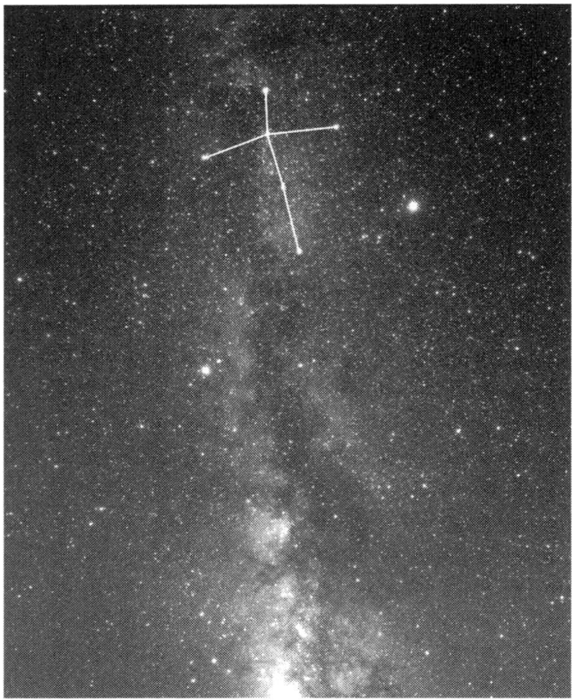

Photo of the Dark Rift and Cygnus. From: NASA.

AFTERWORD—Part II

The Coming of the Giants: Rise of the Human Hybrids

By Andrew Collins

As Greg Little ably demonstrates elsewhere in this book, scholars and academics working on behalf of scientific institutions such as the Smithsonian have on many occasions recorded the discovery at mound sites of skeletal remains where the individual is of exceptional height. They have been found in a great many states, yet by far, the greatest concentration of oversized human skeletons comes from a single region, this being the Kanawha Valley of West Virginia.

Giants or Gigantism?

This last piece of information makes it highly unlikely these tall individuals, who would often appear to have belonged to tribal elites, are simply the result of gigantism, or giantism, a genetic disorder caused by abnormal hormonal activity in childhood, something that results in the excessive growth of the skeletal frame. What was going on in West Virginia clearly indicates the presence of quite regular genetic activity in a population where these physical attributes were, for the most part, *normal* in the first place.

Yet the word "normal" used here might well be a misnomer, for there is no theory in human genetics to account for races of giants, which can only be perpetuated through a gene in the DNA that would mean the recurrence of excess growth in bones in every generation, not just randomly as is the case with gigantism. Nowhere either in Africa or on the Eurasian continent does hard archaeological evidence exist to suggest that entire groups of anatomically modern humans reached over seven feet tall. There is occasional evidence of gigantism, yes. Yet as stated here, this is a genetic disorder, not a recognized feature of normal human genetics.

Blossom Mound's Burial 37

Then we have the apparent elitism afforded the giants of North America. Why should this have been, and how did it come about? The answer to all these mysteries might be determined by examining the appearance in the archaeological record of abnormal human skeletons, such as the one found in 1947 at the Blossom Mound site in the northern San Joaquin Valley of California.

Belonging to a hunter-gatherer from the local Windmiller culture, who lived some 3,750 to 3,950 years ago, the skeletal remains, known as Burial 37, reveal several unusual features (Bartelink et al., 2014; Pastino, 2014). Although only five feet, five inches (170 centimeters) in height, the man's physical appearance marked him as different from other Native Americans. This is shown by the rich array of grave goods buried with him, including forty-eight beads fashioned from shells of the Olivella sea snail, seven ornaments carved from the shell of the abalone mollusk, and an obsidian projectile point. What is more, his body was laid outstretched and face up, his head to the north, whereas the other 176 burials in the same grave mound lay face down, their heads to the west. Some time after interment, Burial 37's skull was removed and placed over his left ankle, which is where excavators found it when the remains were discovered in 1947. All this suggests that the individual, believed to have been in his mid-thirties or forties when he died, had a different journey ahead of him in the spirit world.

Neanderthal Traits

Then we come to the medical condition of the remains, for Burial 37 is believed to have suffered from acromegaly (Bartelink et al., 2014), a rare disorder of the endocrine system related to gigantism. Yet unlike gigantism, where the pituitary gland begins to excrete large amounts of growth hormones during childhood, acromegaly is something that does not occur until adulthood, after the body's long bones are fully formed. A tumor connected with the pituitary gland triggers the release of hormones, which stimulate whatever they can, resulting in abnormalities in the hands, face, and feet. For this individual, it meant a canine in his upper jaw growing upside down and protruding through the bone of his face immediately beneath the nose. Moreover, compared against fourteen other skulls examined from the mass grave, that of Burial 37 was taller and wider. The skull also possessed a heavy brow ridge, while the body had unusually thick arms and legs, traits that are unusual in modern humans but are common in Neanderthal anatomy. In addition to this, he had an elongated chin resulting in a "lantern" jaw, along with a pronounced nose, giving it a beak-like appearance (Bartelink, et al., 2014: Pastino, 2014). On top of this, the bony pocket in the skull that holds the pituitary gland, which is called the *sella turcica* (as it looks like a Turkish saddle), was significantly enlarged.

According to Dr. Eric Bartelink, a physical anthropologist at California State University who led the team that examined Burial 37, all of these strange physiological traits can be put down to acromegaly, which is rarely seen in the archaeological record, and certainly not in burials this old. Having said this, two other cases of acromegaly are known from North America: one in a 600-year-old male burial found in New Mexico, and another in an unsexed 1,100-year-old skull unearthed in Illinois (Pastino, 2014).

As to how, with his "distinctive visage," the man behind Burial 37 might have been perceived by the rest of the Windmiller culture remains unclear, although as Bartelink comments: "I would expect that the person would have been treated differently, but it's hard to say" (Pastino, 2014). This said, there is little question that the individual would have looked striking in appearance, and very much in contrast to other Native Americans of the time.

Strange Sets of Teeth

One of the most significant points about the skull of Burial 37 is the misgrowth of the eye-tooth, or canine, which is upside down and protruding through the bone just beneath the nose. Although this abnormality can be explained as the effects of acromegaly, the presence of unusual or extra teeth in a person is more correctly known in the dental profession as hyperdontism. This can affect any part of the dental arch and result in the growth of any number of so-called supernumerary teeth.

Those readers familiar with stories relating to the discovery of giant skeletons in the United States will be aware of this disorder, as there are various accounts of oversized human skeletons where the skulls have been found to contain a "double row of teeth" in one or both jaws. (For example, see Bancroft, 1882, IV: 694-5, relating to giant skeletons found in caves on San Rosa Island, California, "furnished with double teeth all the way round the jaw," and Weston, 1906: 400, regarding a giant skeleton found in Middleboro, Massachusetts, with "a double row of teeth in each jaw." Many more stories featuring large skeletons with double rows of teeth exist in old newspapers, but their authenticity cannot be verified.

Supernumerary teeth in the skulls of giant skeletons is actually one of the most compelling pieces of evidence for their existence, as it appears far too often in accounts for it not to have some meaning. What it also tells us is that there might be a relationship between endocrine and pituitary disorders and abnormally-sized skeletons in the archaeological record.

Canadian Giants of the Great Lakes

This conclusion seems affirmed in the knowledge that members of the Middle Great Lakes-St. Lawrence culture (hunter-gatherers who occupied sites in the Great Lakes region, across Southern Ontario, Southern Québec and Southwestern New Brunswick between 4000 and 1000 B.C.) were of exceptional height. Men were around six feet tall (180.7 centimeters), while the women reached around five and a half feet (170 centimeters) (Wright, 1995: 257). This was noticeably taller than other indigenous peoples existing in Canada at the time. What is more, the exceptional height of these hunter-gatherers was actually *increasing* as time rolled by. This increase was only by an average of an inch or so per millennium, yet archaeologists and bone specialists who have examined the skeletal evidence of the Middle Great Lakes-St. Lawrence culture have noted this strange fact.

Yet more important by far in connection with this prehistoric hunter-gatherer society—linked with the rise of the mound-building culture of Ohio (Wright, 1995: 257)—is that its exceptionally tall individuals suffered from hyperdontia, the appearance of supernumerary teeth (based on an examination of skeletal remains found at two sites in the Ottawa Valley; see Wright, 1995: 257). This further connection between increased height in Native Americans and hyperdontia cannot be ignored and affords even more weight to the existence in the past of whole groups of individuals of exceptional height, many of them, as stated elsewhere in this work, reaching as much as seven and a half feet tall.

So who were these giants? Were they simply freaks of nature, or a population in their own right?

Genetic Throw Backs

A realistic explanation might lie on another continent altogether. Turkish paleoanthropologist Muzaffer Senyürek of Ankara University made a careful

study of the skeletal remains of the ancient inhabitants of Anatolia and found a high incidence of a dental disorder known as taurodontism (Senyürek, 1949). Like hyperdontia, to which it is related, taurodontism is considered a genetic abnormality that results in the enlargement of teeth out of proportion to the roots of the jaw.

The cause of taurodontism is not properly understood, and is explained, variously, as a genetic mutation, a pituitary malfunction or even an evolutionary throwback (see the Wikipedia entry for taurodontism, for instance). However, we know something else about taurodontism: it is often found in the skulls of Neanderthals, our extinct cousins. They emerged out of Africa as *hominin,* that is, a distinct human species or sub-species, around 200,000 to 300,000 years ago, and quickly spread throughout Europe going as far north as the Arctic region and as far east as the Altai Mountains of southern-central Siberia. Following the appearance in these same territories of anatomically modern humans some 40,000 to 45,000 years ago, the two different types of hominin—*Homo neanderthalensis* and *Homo sapiens*—shared the world, but eventually around 30,000 years ago, the Neanderthals disappear from the archaeological record, either overrun by humans and/or absorbed into the human gene pool.

Rise of the Denisovans

With continuing evidence emerging to the effect that almost every member of the human species outside of Africa has between one and four percent Neanderthal DNA (see, for instance, Yong, 2014), the absorption of the Neanderthal population into that of our own is becoming more and more likely. We mated with our more primitive-looking cousins. That's a fact. Moreover, the discovery of a finger bone and two human molars of a completely unknown human species in the Denisova Cave of the Altai Mountains of southern-central Siberia, and the extraction of its nuclear genome by geneticist Svante Pääbo and his team at Leipzig's Max Planck Institute of Evolutionary Anthropology, suggests that this human type, known

today as the Denisovans, share genetic traits with the Neanderthals (Jacobs, 2012).

Between 300,000 and 40,000 years ago the Densiovans inhabited a vast area of the ancient world that stretched from the Altai Mountains in the west to China and Southeast Asia in the east. In Central Asia they interbred with their cousins, the Neanderthals, *and* with anatomically modern humans. Indeed, current-day human populations, such as the Melanesians (represented by the Pacific islanders of Papua New Guinea) and Aboriginal Australians, all show between four and six percent Denisovan DNA (Jacobs, 2012; Harmon, 2012). Other human populations, such as the Burmans, Malays, Han Chinese, and Polynesians, also have Denisovan DNA but in far smaller quantities (Reich, 2010a & 2010b). Almost no Denisovan DNA has been detected in the populations of Europe and Southwest Asia, which would have been key territories of the Neanderthal populations prior to their disappearance around 30,000 years ago (Reich, 2010b; Jacobs, 2012).

So what has all this to do with giants on the American continent? The answer is that interbreeding between these three different sub-species of the human (*homo*) genus—along with that of a fourth hominin whose existence is known only from the presence of its DNA in a suspected Neanderthal toe

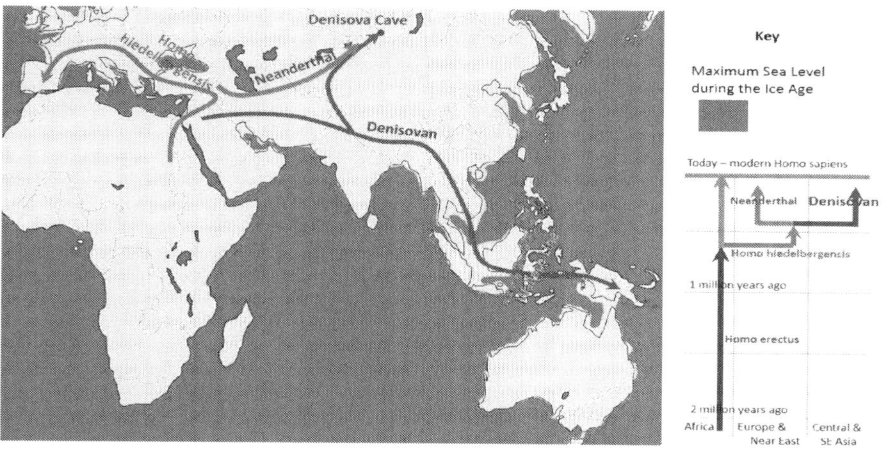

Map showing the proposed spread and evolution of Denisovans.
Credit: John D. Croft, Wikipedia Commons.

bone discovered in the Denisova Cave which also contained *Homo sapiens* and Denisovan DNA (Prüfer, 2013; Sanders, 2013)—is likely to have caused profound changes in modern human DNA. This probably included genetic alterations and mutations, which have resulted in changes both to the body's physiognomy *and* the brain's thinking process (in other words, in the way we perceive and interact with the world around us). This is a study in itself that could take decades to understand.

In addition to this, hybridization (cross breeding) among the four different sub-species of the hominin genus could easily have resulted in genetic mutations leading to various abnormalities. The genetic abnormalities could have emerged as growth disorders. Other mutations might have produced traits that would be interpreted today as evolutionary throw backs. All of the medical disorders cited above—gigantism, acromegaly, hyperdontism, and taurodontism, might easily be connected with hybridization, something that can be seen from the definite Neanderthal traits of Blossom Mound's Burial 37 and the taurodontism present among the earliest peoples of Anatolia. As previously stated, taurodontism was a common trait among the Neanderthal population.

Real Giants Among Us

Neanderthals were in no way giants. Actually, they were smaller in size than the earliest anatomically modern humans (such as Western Europe's Cro-Magnon man or Central Europe's Brünn population—see Collins, 2014), who rarely rose above six feet in height. Denisovans on the other hand *might* have been giants. The size of the two molars recovered from the Denisova Cave are large. The second one found was larger than the first, with a chewing surface twice that of a typical human molar. When the molar was first discovered, Max Planck paleoanthropologist Bence Viola is said to have mistaken it for that of a cave bear. Only when the tooth's DNA was tested was it confirmed to be that of a Denisovan hominin. "It shows you how

weird these guys are," he said. "At least, their teeth are just very strange" (Shreeve, 2013).

Further evidence that Denisovans might have been of exceptional height comes from another genome analysis, this time of a 400,000-year-old femur from a cave known as the Sima de los Huesos ('pit of bones') in northern Spain's Sierra de Atapuerca (Atapuerca Mountains). It belongs to an extinct species of hominin known as *Homo heidelbergensis,* who occupied Africa and much of the Eurasian continent between 800,000 and 200,000 years ago.

Denisovans, Neanderthals, and our own antecedents (*Homo sapiens*) are all thought to have a common ancestor in *Homo heidelbergensis,* although as to when each sub-species split apart and went their own way remains a matter of conjecture and fierce debate. Having said this, anthropologists have always considered that the closest ancestor to *Homo heidelbergensis* was the Neanderthal. Yet an examination of the mitochondrial DNA from the *Homo heidelbergensis* femur found in Spain revealed it to be much closer to that of the Denisovans, who thrived thousands of miles away in the Altai Mountains of Siberia (Callaway, 2013). This was a complete shock to geneticists and prehistorians alike, especially as no hard evidence of Denisovan DNA has so far been found among present-day European populations. Despite this clear link between *Homo heidelbergensis* and the Denisovans anthropologists such as Chris Stringer (head of Human Origins at London's Natural History Museum) still maintain that *Homo heidelbergensis* is more closely related to the Neanderthal populations of Europe and Southwest Asia than what the current mitochondrial evidence implies.

Knowing that the Denisovans are related directly to *Homo heidelbergensis* is significant, for although a reconstruction of twenty-seven complete human limb bones found at cave sites in Spain's Sierra de Atapuerca, including the aforementioned Sima de los Hoesos, has led to the conclusion that the height of *Homo heidelbergensis* in Europe was around five feet,

seven inches (170 centimeters—which is just slightly taller than their cousins the Neanderthals), there is compelling evidence that some of their populations grew *much* taller. Lee R. Burger of the University of Witwatersrand has examined numerous fossil bones belonging to *Homo heidelbergensis* populations that inhabited South Africa between 500,000 and 300,000 years ago and has discovered that these "giants" were routinely over seven feet (2.13 meters) in height (Burger, 2007). This opens the door to the closely related Denisovans being of equal height, and seeing as how their teeth are almost twice the size of our own, this has to be a strong likelihood.

Human Hybrids

It is time now to consider further the giant skeletons with jaws containing double rows of teeth. Those accounts that are *authentic* most likely refer to human or hominin hybrids who carried strong Denisovan-human or Denisovan-Neanderthal-human genetic markers. It is even possible the giants of North America contain DNA belonging to the fourth type of hominin identified from DNA evidence alone, and this type of hominin is now believed to have bred with all three other sub-species—Denisovans, Neanderthals, and archaic humans (Prüfer, 2013; Sanders, 2013)—and may even have survived as a separate population in its own right, entering the North American continent prior to the disappearance of the Beringia land bridge around 10,500 years ago.

As to the identity of this fourth type of hominin, no one will know until its very specific DNA markers can be compared with those of other known hominins, and that could take a while. Species-x, as we shall call them, could be survivors of a *Homo heidelbergenis* population, or they might belong to an even more ancient hominin sub-species known as *Homo erectus* (Waddell, 2013; Timmer, 2013). Although *Homo erectus* entered the scene as much as 1.9 million years ago and stayed around until around 150,000 years ago, it is thought they may have survived in small pockets in Indonesia until around 50,000 years ago and arguably even as late as 27,000 years ago.

It is a conclusion based on anatomical remains of *Homo erectus* recovered from an important hominin settlement site at Ngandong on the Indonesian island of Java (Grün and Thorne, 1997; Rose, 1997).

The final icing on the cake is in the fact that the DNA of the Mixe peoples of Mexico and the Karitiana of Brazil, as well as that of other Native American tribes, contains a small percentage of both Denisovan and Neanderthal DNA (Estes, 2013; Prüfer, 2014). This shows that their ancestors must have come into contact with these populations, or indeed their hybrids, either in Asia or on the American continent somewhere. Although the Mixe and Karitiana tribes are not noted for their extreme height, the fact remains that Denisovan and Neanderthal DNA exists among the Native Americans of today. So there is every chance that human hybrid populations that inhabited the American continent both before and after the drowning of the Beringia land bridge would have preserved at least some of their Denisovan, Neanderthal, and species-x traits across the generations. These would have included not only an increased height (inherited from the Denisovans), but also, like Blossom Mound's Burial 37, prominent brow ridges, thick arms and legs, and other so-called "archaic" features (inherited from Neanderthal, and possibly even from Denisovans and species-x, whomever they turn out to be), as well as skulls with "archaic" features derived from early forms of *homo sapiens*. More important is the fact that these human hybrids would also have been prone to genetic disorders including extreme growth and various other physical abnormalities caused by diseases such as acromegaly, hyperdontism, and taurodontism. Hyperdontism is the most likely cause of the double rows of teeth so often reported in connection with the skulls of giant skeletons, a fact that almost certainly confirms their origin as human hybrids.

Indeed, the authors of this work would encourage anthropologists, archaeologists, and geneticists to cast aside their prejudices and more closely examine reports of giant skeletons in the archaeological record. What is more, the nuclear and mitochondrial DNA of skeletal remains found both on the American continent and elsewhere in the world, which display clear evidence of a genetic disorder of the types described here, should be compared

against the known genetic markers of our hominin cousins. We believe this will prove to be a fruitful exercise which will change the way we perceive the evolution of humankind on this planet.

A Return to the Stars

In conclusion, it seems unlikely that the giants of the American continent are a race, or human sub-species, *separate* to that of anatomically modern humans (*Homo sapiens sapiens*). Almost certainly they are human hybrids that have resulted from interbreeding between three, and possibly even four, different human sub-species. They are the Neanderthals, Denisovans, archaic humans *(Homo sapiens),* and species-x, who were probably either surviving pockets of *Homo heidelbergensis* or, more likely, *Homo erectus,* a very exciting prospect indeed. The coming together of all these different peoples—whose descendents existed in and around the Altai Mountains of southern-central Siberia some 40,000 to 50,000 years ago—no matter how brief or how intimate, changed human evolution in ways we cannot even begin to imagine at this time (and see Collins, 2014, in which the current author explores the impact Neanderthal-human hybrids had on the rise of civilization).

It is too early to say what kind of influence the human hybrids might have had on the cosmological beliefs and practices of America's first peoples. Although the fact they were individuals of extreme height and/or of striking appearance (like Blossom Mound's Burial 37) suggests they would have been classed as special in some way. What is more, if there were whole groups of them, as would appear to have been the case in the Kanawha Valley of West Virginia, chances are they would have become the ruling elites. As such, they would have seen themselves as responsible for the dissemination of their pre-existing belief systems, which probably originally derived from archaic populations that thrived on the Eurasian landmass many thousands of years before the submergence of the Beringia land bridge in around 8500 B.C.

These age-old beliefs might well have included the idea that humankind's own origins and destiny lay among the stars, with a particular emphasis on those stars existing in the constellation of Cygnus, the great sky bird. Here the Milky Way as the Path of Souls forks to highlight the entrance to a world existing beyond our own. Maybe it was for this reason that we came to believe that the giants, the human hybrids, were of the stars themselves simply because they were the ones who provided us with the knowledge of how we as a species could, quite literally, return to the stars. Not in a physical manner, but through the profound journey of the soul.

References

Anderson, D. G. & Mainfort, R. C. (2002) *The Woodland Southeast*. Tuscaloosa: University of Alabama Press.

Armstrong, Edward A. (1959) *The Folklore of Birds*. Boston, MA: Cambridge, UK: Houghton Mifflin/Riverside Press.

Aufderheide, A. C., & Rodriguez-Martin, C. (1998) *The Cambridge Encyclopedia of Human Paleopathology*. NY: Cambridge University Press.

Aujoulat, Norbert (2005) *Lauscaux: Movement, Space and Time*, http://www.american-buddha.com/lascaux.4a.htm. Retrieved April 21, 2014.

Bancroft, Hubert Howe (1882) *The Native Races: IV—Antiquities*. San Francisco, CA: A. L. Bancroft & Company.

Bartelink, E. J., Willits, N. A., & Chelotti, K. L. (2014) A probable case of acromegaly from the Windmiller Culture of prehistoric California. *International Journal of Paleopathology*, 4, 37-46.

Bass, W. M. (1995) *Human Osteology*. Columbia: Missouri Archaeological Society.

Burger, Professor Lee, interview. (2007) "Our Story: Human Ancestor Fossils," The Naked Scientists: Science Interviews, November 25, 2007. http://www.thenakedscientists.com/HTML/content/interviews/interview/833/. Retrieved April 27th, 2014.

Cady, A. C. (1894) *The American continent and its inhabitants before the discovery by Columbus*. Philadelphia: Gebbie & Co.

Callaway, Ewen (2013) "Hominin DNA baffles experts: Analysis of oldest sequence from a human ancestor suggests link to mystery population," *Nature*, December 4, 2013, http://www.nature.com/news/hominin-dna-baffles-experts-1.14294. Retrieved April 27, 2014.

Case, T. S. (1880-1881) *Kansas City Review of Science and Industry—Vol. IV*, Kansas City: Press of Ramsey, Millett, & Hudson.

Childs, H. T. & McNutt, C. H. (2009) Chickasawba. *The Arkansas Archaeologist*, 48, 15-56.

Clark, E. (1966) *Indian Legends from the Northern Rockies*. Norman: University of Oklahoma Press.

Clayton, L. A., Knight, V. J., & Moore, E. C. (1993) *The De Soto Chronicles—Vol. 1 & 2*. Tuscaloosa: University of Alabama Press.

Colavito, J. (2012) How the truth about fossil giants was forgotten. http://www.jasoncolavito.com/1/post/2012/12/how-the-truth-about-fossil-giants-was-forgotten.html

Colavito, J. (2012a) Did cosmic rays from Cygnus create religion? http://www.jasoncolavito.com/1/post/2012/10/did-cosmic-rays-from-cygnus-create-religion.html

Colavito, J. (2014) http://www.jasoncolavito.com/cthulhu-in-world-mythology.html

Colavito, J. (2013a) Is the Smithsonian conspiring to suppress the truth about giants? http://www.jasoncolavito.com/1/post/2013/07/is-the-smithsonian-conspiring-to-suppress-the-truth-about-giants.html

Colavito, J. (2013b) Micah Hanks and the Smithsonian Anti-Giant Conspiracy. http://www.jasoncolavito.com/1/post/2013/08/micah-hanks-and-the-smithsonian-anti-giant-conspiracy.html

Colavito, J. (2013c) Jim Vieira claims my analysis of giants is wrong because I use big words. http://www.jasoncolavito.com/1/post/2013/08/jim-vieira-claims-my-analysis-of-giants-is-wrong-because-i-use-big-words.html

Colavito (2013d) Weird roundup. http://www.jasoncolavito.com/1/post/2013/10/weird-roundup-angels-drive-ufos-ufologist-runs-for-school-board-and-graham-hancock-redates-the-neolithic.html

Collins, A. B. (2009) *Beneath the Pyramids*. Virginia Beach: ARE Press.

Collins, A. B. (1996) *From the Ashes of Angels*. London: Signet.

Collins, A. B. (2014) *Göbekli Tepe: Genesis of the Gods*. Rochester, VT: Bear & Co.

Collins, A. B. (2006) *The Cygnus Mystery*. London: Watkins.

Cordell, L. S., Lightfoot, K., McManamon, F., & Milner, G. (Eds.) (2009) *Archaeology in America: An Encyclopedia*. Westpoint, CT: Greenwood Press.

Cordy-Collins, A. & Merbs, C. F. (2008) Forensic iconography: the case of the Moche giants, 93-112. In: Bourget, S. & Jones, K. (Eds.) *The Art and Archaeology of the Moche*. Austin: University of Texas Press.

Coulter, C. R. and Turner, P. (2012) *Encyclopedia of Ancient Deities*. New York, NY: Routledge.

Cygnus Mystery DVD (2006) Available at Amazon or free: http://www.youtube.com/watch?v=OhgNXbahNrA

Daily Evening Telegraph (September 15, 1870) A giant race, p. 6.

De Bry, Theodor (1591) *Grand Voyages*. Netherlands.

Dewhurst, R. J. (2014) *The Giants Who Ruled America*. Rochester, VT: Bear & Co.

Diamond, D. (May 3, 2012) True or false: Half of all 7-footers are in the NBA? http://www.truthaboutit.net/2012/05/true-or-false-half-of-all-7-footers-are-in-the-nba.html

Dillehay, T. D. (2000) *The Settlement of the Americas*. NY: Basic Books.

Dragoo, D. W. (1958) *Mounds for the Dead*. Pittsburgh: Annals of the Carnegie Museum.

Dunduliene, P. (1988) *Lietuvis liaudies kosmologija*. Vilnius, Lithuania: Moksias.

Encyclopedia Britannica: Schoolcraft (http://www.britannica.com/EBchecked/topic/528158/Henry-Rowe-Schoolcraft)

Estes, R. (2013) "Native Americans, Neanderthal and Denisova Admixture" DNA-Explained—Genetic Genealogy, December 26th, 2013, http://dna-explained.com/2013/12/26/native-americans-neanderthal-and-denisova-admixture/. Retrieved April 27, 2014.

Fletcher, A.C., and La Flesche, F. (1911) *The Omaha Tribe: Bureau of American Ethnology 27th Annual Report. 1905-6*. Washington DC: Smithsonian Institution.

Folsom, F. & Folsom, M. E. (1994) *America's Ancient Treasures*. Albuquerque: University of New Mexico Press.

Fontenrose, J. (1981) *Orion: The Myth of the Hunter and the Huntress*. Berkeley, CA: University of California Press.

Fowke, G. (1910) *Antiquities of Central and Southeastern Missouri*. Washington: Smithsonian Institution, Bureau of American Ethnology, Bulletin 37.

Fowler, D. W. & Wilcox, D. R. (Eds.) (2003) *Philadelphia and the Development of American Archaeology*. Tuscaloosa: University of Alabama Press.

Friou, A. (2008) Creating a new Rosetta Stone. *Hillviews*, Fall/Winter.

Gamble, C. (2013) *Settling the Earth: The Archaeology of Deep Human History*. Cambridge, UK: Cambridge University Press.

Gimbutas, M. (1989) *The Language of the Goddess*. London: Thames and Hudson.

Goebel, T., Waters, M. R., & O'Rourke, D. H. (2008) The late Pleistocene of modern humans in the Americas. *Science*, (319), 1497-1502.

Grün, R., and Thorne, A. (1997) "Dating the Ngandong Humans," *Science* Vol. 276, Number 5318, 1575-76.

Hall, R. L. (1997) *An Archaeology of the Soul*. Urbana: Univ. of Illinois Press.

Hamilton, H. W. (1952) The Spiro Mound. *The Missouri Archaeologist*, 14.

Hammerton, J. A. (1923) *Wonders of the Past*. NY: Putnam.

Harmon, K. (2012) "New DNA Analysis Shows Ancient Humans Interbred with Denisovans," *Scientific American*, August 30, 2012. http://www.scientificamerican.com/article/denisovan-genome/. Retrieved April 28, 2014.

Hartzell, S. T. (March 29, 2000) Life of a promoter, death of a salesman. *St. Petersburg Times*.

History of Bradford County, Pennsylvania (1878) Philadelphia: Everts Co.

History of Winona County (1883) Chicago: H. H. Hill.

Hodge, E. (July, 28, 2011) Gobekli Tepe (*sic*): Fuel for crankery. http://skepticalcubefarm.wordpress.com/2011/07/28/gobekli-tepe-fuel-for-crankery/

Holtorf, C. (2005) Beyond crusades: How (not) to engage with alternative archaeologies. *World Archaeology*, 37 (4), 544-551.

Hudson, C. (1976) *The Southeastern Indians*. Knoxville: University of Tennessee Press.

Jacob, S., et al. (2012) "Ancient genome reveals its secrets," Max-Plank-Gesellschaft, August 30, 2012. http://www.mpg.de/6328259/denisovan_genome1. Retrieved April 28, 2014.

Jacobsen, E. (1993) *The Deer Goddess of Ancient Siberia: A Study in the Ecology of Belief*. Leiden, The Netherlands: E.J. Brill.

Jeter, M. D. (1990) *Edward Palmer's Arkansaw (sic) Mounds*. Tuscaloosa: University of Alabama Press.

Kopper, P. (Ed.) (1986) *The Smithsonian Book of the North American Indians*. Washington, DC: Smithsonian Books.

Lankford, G. E. (2008) *Looking for Lost Lore*. Tuscaloosa: University of Alabama Press.

Lankford, G. E. (2011) *Native American Legends of the Southeast*. Tuscaloosa: University of Alabama Press.

Lankford, G. E. (2007) *Reachable Stars*. Tuscaloosa: University of Alabama Press.

Lankford, G. E., Reilly, F. K. III, & Garber, J. F. (Eds.) (2011) *Visualizing the Sacred*. Austin: University of Texas Press.

Leitch, Y. (2007) *Gwyn, Ancient God of Glastonbury and Key to the Glastonbury Zodiac*. Glastonbury, Somerset: The Temple Publications.

Lepper, B. T. (2013) Scientists disagree on age of Serpent Mound. *The Columbus Dispatch*, November 17, 2013, http://www.dispatch.com/content/stories/science/2013/11/17/1-scientists-disagree-on-age-of-serpent-mound.html

Lepper, B. T. (2005) *Ohio Archaeology*. Wilmington, OH: Orange Frazer Press.

Little, G. L. (1988) Archetypes of Earth: Ancient symbols of North America. *Cocoon*, 1, 2-8.

Little, G. L. (1990) *People of the Web*. Memphis: White Buffalo Books.

Little, G. L. (1997) *Psychopharmacology*. Memphis: ATA.

Little, G. L. (2009) *The Illustrated Encyclopedia of Native American Mounds and Earthworks*. Memphis: Eagle Wing Books, Inc.

Little, G. L. (1987) Tennessee's prehistoric mystery: Unearthing Pinson Mounds. *Fate*, 40 (12), 32-41.

Little, G. L., Van Auken, J., & Little, L. (2002) *Ancient South America*. Memphis: Eagle Wing Books.

Little, G. L., Van Auken, J., & Little, L. (2001) *Mound Builders*. Memphis: Eagle Wing Books.

Magyar, A. (1991) *A Csodaszarvas*. Budapest, Hungary: Magyar Adorján Baráti Kör.

Mainfort, R. C. (2013) *Pinson Mounds*. Fayetteville: University of Arkansas Press.

Mainfort, R. C. & Kwas, M. L. (1991) The Bat Creek Stone: Judeans in Tennessee? *Tennessee Anthropologist*, 16 (1), 1-19.

Mainfort, R. C., & Sullivan, L. P. (Eds.) (1998) *Ancient Earthen Enclosures of the Eastern Woodlands*. Gainesville: University of Florida Press.

May, W. (2009) *This Land*. Colfax, WI: Hayriver Press.

McCulloch, J. H. (1988) The Bat Creek Inscription: Cherokee or Hebrew? *Tennessee Anthropologist*, 13 (2), 79-123.

McMichael, E. V. & Mairs, O. (1969) *Excavation of the Murad Mound, Kanawha County, West Virginia. Report of Archeological Investigations Number 1*. Morgantown, WV: West Virginia Geological and Economic Survey.

Meltzer, D. J. (2009) First Americans: http://www.webcitation.org/5kx7zKJiO

Moore, C. B. (1892) A burial mound in Florida. *The American Naturalist*, 26, 129-143.

Moore, C. B. (1915) Aboriginal sites on Tennessee River. *Journal of the Academy of Natural Sciences of Philadelphia*, 16, 170-428.

Moore, C. B. (1905) Certain aboriginal remains of the Black Warrior River. *Journal of the Academy of Natural Sciences of Philadelphia*, 13, 125-244.

Moore, C. B. (1894) Certain sand mounds of the St. John's River, Florida. *Journal of the Academy of Natural Sciences of Philadelphia, Part I & II* (10).

Moore, C. B. (1907) Moundville revisited. *Journal of the Academy of Natural Sciences of Philadelphia*, 13, 337-405.

Moore, C. B. (1911) Some aboriginal sites on the Mississippi River. *Journal of the Academy of Natural Sciences of Philadelphia*, 14, 365-480.

Moorehead, W. K. (1932) *Etowah Papers*. Yale University. Press.

Murphy, A. (2008) *Island of the Setting Sun: In Search of Ireland's Ancient Astronomers*. Dublin, Ireland: The Liffey Press.

Murray, G. R. & Schmitt, J. D. (2011) Caveman politics: Evolutionary leadership preferences and stature. *Social Science Quarterly*, 92 (5), 1215-1235.

Murray, L. W. (1908) *A History of Old Tioga Point and Early Athens Pennsylvania*. Wilkes-Barre: Reader Press.

NASA (April 17, 2014) Release 14-111. NASA's Kepler Telescope discovers first Earth-sized planet in "Habital zone." http://www.nasa.gov/press/2014/april/nasas-kepler-telescope-discovers-first-earth-size-planet-in-habitable-zone/#.U1G4-hz6erg

National Park Service. Big Bone Lick State Park: http://www.nps.gov/nr/travel/lewisandclark/bbo.htm

Oregon History Project: http://www.ohs.org/education/oregonhistory/historical_records/dspDocument.cfm?doc_ID=95B20FCF-A01E-5813-43C3372FF76325BB

Pacheco, P. J. (Ed.) (1996) *A View From the Core*. Columbus: Ohio Archaeological Council.

Pastino, B. de (2014) "Earliest Evidence of Gigantism-Like Disease Found in 3,800-Year-Old California Skeleton," *Western Digs*, March 24, 2014, http://westerndigs.org/earliest-evidence-of-gigantism-like-disease-found-in-3800-year-old-california-skeleton/. Retrieved April 24, 2014.

Pauketat, T. (2010) *Cahokia*. NY: Penguin/Viking.

Phillips, P. & Brown, J. A. (1978) *Pre-Columbian Shell Engravings from Craig Mound at Spiro, Oklahoma*. Cambridge: Peabody Museum Press.

Pickard, B. (2011) The snake's tale: How old is Serpent Mound? Ohio Historical Society Archaeological Blog, May 3, 2011, (http://apps.ohiohistory.org/ohioarchaeology/the-snakes-tale-how-old-is-serpent-mound/)

Pinelas County. (2005) *The Weedon Island Story*. Tarpon Springs, FL: Pinellas Co.

Popular Archaeology (August 28, 2013) Scientists discover earliest human presence in Bolivian Amazon.

Powell, J. W. (1887) *Fifth Annual Report of the Bureau of Ethnology*. Washington: U. S. Government Printing Office.

Powell, J. W. (1900) *Nineteenth Annual Report of the Bureau of American Ethnology*. Washington: U. S. Government Printing Office.

Powell, J. W. (1892) *Ninth Annual Report of the Bureau of Ethnology*. Washington: U. S. Government Printing Office.

Powell, J. W. (1884) *Third Annual Report of the Bureau of Ethnology*. Washington: U. S. Government Printing Office.

Powell, J. W. (1894) *Twelfth Annual Report of the Bureau of Ethnology*. Washington: U. S. Government Printing Office.

Prüfer, K., et al. (2014) "The complete genome sequence of a Neanderthal from the Altai Mountains," *Nature* 505 (January 2, 2014) 43–49.

Raghaven, M., et al. (2013) "Upper Palaeolithic Siberian genome reveals dual ancestry of Native Americans," Nature (November 20, 2013), doi:10.1038/nature12736.

Randall, E. O. (1905) *The Serpent Mound*. Columbus: Ohio Historical Society.

Rappenglück, M. A. (1999) *Eine Himmelskarte aus der Eiszeit?* Frankfurt am Main, Germany: Peter Lang.

Reich, D., et al. (2010a), "Genetic history of an archaic hominin group from Denisova Cave in Siberia," *Nature* 368: 7327 (December 22, 2010), 1053-1060.

Reich, D., et al. (2012) Reconstructing Native American population history. *Nature*, 488, 370-374.

Reich, D., et al. (2010b), "Supplementary Information: Genetic history of an archaic hominin group from Denisova Cave in Siberia," December 22, 2010. http://genetics.med.harvard.edu/reich/Reich_Lab/Publications_files/2010_Nature_Denisova_Genome_Supplementary-1.pdf.

Reilly, F. K. III, & Garber, J. F. (2007) *Ancient Objects and Sacred Realms*. Austin: University of Texas Press.

Rhees, W. J. (1901) *The Smithsonian Institution: Documents Relative to its Origin and History, 1835-1899*. Washington, DC: U.S. Government Printing Office.

Rhys, J. (1901) *Celtic Folklore: Welsh and Manx,* 2 vols. Oxford: Oxford University Press.

Rogner, M. (2012) Stretch the truth. http://bloguin.com/runthefloor/2012-articles/stretch-the-truth-exaggerated-heights-of-college-basketball-players.html

Róheim, G. (1954) *Hungarian and Vogul Mythology: Monographs of the American Ethnological Society 23*. Locust Valley, NY: J. J. Augustin.

Romain, W. (2000) *Mysteries of the Hopewell*. Akron: University of Akron Press.

Romain, W. (2005) *Newark Earthwork Design Iteration II*.

Romain, W. et al. (2013) Serpent Mound project results—2013. Paper presented at the Midwest Archaeological Conference, Columbus, Ohio, October 2013.

Rose, M. (1997) "Homo Erectus Survival", Archaeology: Archive 50:2 (March/April 1997), http://archive.archaeology.org/9703/newsbriefs/h.erectus.html. Retrieved April 27, 2014.

Sanders, R. (2013) "Neanderthal genome shows evidence of early human interbreeding, inbreeding," UC Berkeley News Center, December 18th, 2013. http://newscenter.berkeley.edu/2013/12/18/neanderthal-genome-shows-evidence-of-early-human-interbreeding-inbreeding/.

Schoolcraft, H. R. (1854) *Information Respecting the History, Conditions and Prospects of the Indian Tribes of the United States*. Philadelphia: Lippincott.

Schoolcraft, H. R. (1847) *Notes on the Iroquois*. Albany, NY: Pease Co.

Schoolcraft, H. R. (1856) *The Indian Fairy Book*. New York: Mason Bro.

Schoolcraft, H. R. & Drake, F. S. (1884) *The Indian Tribes of the United States*. Philadelphia: Lippincott.

Senyürek, Muzaffer Süleyman (1949) "The occurrence of taurodontism in the ancient inhabitants of Anatolia: a preliminary report," *Turk Tarih Kurumu Belleten* 13, 215-27.

Sharpe, K. (2014) Hardening brittle bones. *Archaeology*, 67 (3), 12.

Shreeve, J. (2013) "The Case of the Missing Ancestor: DNA from a cave in Russia adds a mysterious new member to the human family," *National Geographic*, July 2013, http://ngm.nationalgeographic.com/2013/07/125-missing-human-ancestor/shreeve-text. Retrieved April 27th, 2014.

Skull Base Institute (2013) Acromegaly & Gigantism. http://www.skullbaseinstitute.com/pituitary-gland-tumor-surgery/acromegaly-gigantism-endoscopic-surgery.htm

Smithsonian (2010) History of the Smithsonian. http://newsdesk.si.edu/about/history

Smithsonian (1924) *Report of the Secretary of the Smithsonian Institute*. Washington: Gov. Printing Office.

Spalinger, A.J. (Ed.) (1994) *Revolutions in Time: Studies in Ancient Egyptian Calendrics*. San Antonio, TX: Van Siclen Press.

Squier, E. G. & Davis, E. H. (1848) *Ancient Monuments of the Mississippi Valley*. Washington: Smithsonian Institution.

Stanford, D. J., and Bradley, B. A. (2012) *Across Atlantic Ice: The Origins of America's Clovis Culture*. Berkeley: University of California Press.

Straizys, V. & Klimka, L. (1997) "The Cosmology of the Ancient Balts," *Journal for the History of Astronomy* 28: Archaeoastronomy Supplement 22, S57-S81.

Stromberg, J. (March 14, 2014) Ancient migration patterns to North America are hidden in languages spoken today. *Smithsonian Magazine*: http://www.smithsonianmag.com/science-nature/ancient-migration-patterns-north-america-are-hidden-languages-spoken-today-180950053/?no-ist

Sullivan, W. (1996) The Secrets of the Incas. New York, NY: Three Rivers Press.

"Taurodontism:" Wikipedia, http://en.wikipedia.org/wiki/Taurodontism. Retrieved April 27, 2014.

Thom, A. (1967) *Megalithic Sites in Britain*. Oxford: Oxford University Press.

Thom, A., Thom, A. S., and Foord, T. R. (1976) "Avebury (1): A New Assessment of the Geometry and Metrology of the Ring," *Journal for the History of Astronomy* 7, 183-92.

Thomas, C. (May 23, 1884) A mound of the Kanawha Valley. *Science*, 619.

Throop, A. J. (1928) *Mound Builders of Illinois*. East St. Louis: Call Printing Co.

Thruston, G. P. (1809) *Antiquities of Tennessee*. Cincinnati: Robert Clarke & Co.

Timmer, J. (2013) "Pre-modern humans may have picked up genes from *Homo erectus*," *Arstechnica*, December 18, 2013. http://arstechnica.com/science/2013/12/pre-modern-humans-may-have-picked-up-genes-from-homo-erectus/. Retrieved April 29, 2014.

Tomory, Z. (2009a) "Magyar Creation: Part I," http://tomoryzsuzsa.weebly.com/magyar-creation.html

Tomory, Z. (2009b) "Magyar Creation Part II: The Ancient Pannon Sea And The Holy Places Of Our Fairy Ancestors, http://tomoryzsuzsa.weebly.com/magyar-creation-part-ii.html

Townsend, R. F. & Sharp, R. V. (Eds.) (2004) *Hero, Hawk, and Open Hand*. Chicago: Art Institute of Chicago.

University of South Florida (2011) *Tidal Forces: An Exhibition of Pre-Columbian Pottery and Lithics*. University of South Florida, March 28, 2011.

Urton, G. (1981) *At the Crossroads of the Earth and the Sky: An Andean Cosmology*. Austin, TX: University of Texas Press.

Vaiakknas, J. (Ed.) (2008) *Astronomy and Cosmology in Folk Traditions and Cultural Heritage: Archaeologia Baltica 10*. Klaipda, Lithuania: Klaipda University Press.

Waddell, P. J. (2013) "Happy New Year Home erectus? More evidence for interbreeding with archaics predating the modern human/Neanderthal split," Cornell University Library, arXiv:1312.7749v1, December 30, 2013. http://arxiv.org/abs/1312.7749. Retrieved April 29, 2014.

Wainwright, G. A. (1932) "A Pair of Constellations," *Studies Presented to F. L. Griffith,* 373-83.

Wells, R. A. (1993) "The Mythology of Nut and the Birth of Re," *Studien zur Altägyptischen Kultu,* 19, 305-321.

Wells, R. A. (1994) "Re and the Calendars." In Anthony J. Spalinger, 1-37.

Weston, T. (1906) *History of the Town of Middleboro Massachusetts*. Boston, MA, and New York, NY: Houghton, Mifflin, and Company.

Wilmore, S. B. (1974) *Swans of the World*. London: David & Charles.

Windham, B. (February 12, 2006) The mystery of the rattlesnake disk. *Tuscaloosa News*, 1b, 6b.

Wright, J. V. (1995) *A History of the Native People of Canada: 10,000-1,000 BC*. Gatineau, Quebec: Canadian Museum of Civilization.

Wright, W. B. (1939) *Tools and the Man*. London: G. Bell & Sons.

Yong, E. (2014) "Surprise! 20 Percent of Neanderthal Genome Lives On in Modern Humans, Scientists Find," National Geographic, January 29, 2014, http://news.nationalgeographic.com/news/2014/01/140129-neanderthal-genes-genetics-migration-africa-eurasian-science/ Retrieved April 29, 2014.

Zwyns, N., et al. (2012) "Burin-core technology and laminar reduction sequences in the initial Upper Paleolithic from Kara-Bom (Gorny- Altai, Siberia)," *Quaternary International* 259 (2012), 33-47. https://www.academia.edu/1877984/Zwyns_N._et_al._2012_Burin-core-technology_and_laminar_reduction_sequence_in_the initial_Upper_Paleolithic_from_Kara-Bom_Gorny-Altai_Siberia_._Quaternary_International._259_33-47. Retrieved April 28, 2014.

Index

16158140R00148

Printed in Poland
by Amazon Fulfillment
Poland Sp. z o.o., Wrocław